LANGUAGE AND RELATIONSHIP IN WORDSWORTH'S WRITING

Studies in Eighteenth- and Nineteenth-Century Literature

General Editors

Andrew Sanders, Reader in English, Birkbeck College London
David Nokes, Reader in English, King's College London

Published titles

Forms of Speech in Victorian Fiction Raymond Chapman
Henry Fielding: Authorship and Authority Ian A. Bell
Language and Relationship in Wordsworth's Writing: Elective Affinities
Michael Baron

LANGUAGE AND RELATIONSHIP IN WORDSWORTH'S WRITING

Michael Baron

LONDON AND NEW YORK

Longman Group UK Limited,
Longman House, Burnt Mill,
Harlow, Essex CM20 2JE, England
and Associated Companies throughout the world

*Published in the United States of America
by Longman Publishing, New York*

© Longman Group UK Limited 1995

First published 1995

ISBN 0 582 06195 4 CSD
ISBN 0 582 06194 6 PPR

British Library Cataloguing-in-Publication Data

A catalogue record for this book is
available from the British Library

Library of Congress Cataloging-in-Publication Data

Baron, Michael, 1947–
    Language and relationship in Wordsworth's writing
 / Michael Baron.
      p. cm. -- (Studies in eighteenth- and nineteenth-century
literature)
    Includes bibliographical references and index.
    ISBN 0–582–06195–4. -- ISBN 0–582–06194–6 (pbk.)
    1. Wordsworth, William, 1770–1850--Political and social views.
2. Literature and society--England--History--19th century.
3. Language and culture--England--History--19th century.
4. Wordsworth, William, 1770–1850--Language. 5. Interpersonal
relations in literature. I. Title. II. Series.
PR5892.S58B37 1995
821'.7--dc20
                                               94-20478
                                                 CIP

Set by 7.00 in 10/12 Goudy Oldstyle
Produced by Longman Singapore Publishers (Pte) Ltd
Printed in Singapore

This book is dedicated to

Robina Barson

Contents

Acknowledgements

It is a pleasure to remember the moment when Dr Val Vallis and Professor Barbara Hardy first encouraged me to follow my inclination and begin a serious study of Wordsworth, and to record their enthusiastic and loyal but nevertheless pointed help over the years. A draft of this book benefited immeasurably from Barbara Hardy's reading. Collaboration with Michael Slater on another academic project, an edition of some of the novels of Peacock, was a most valuable means of focusing Wordsworth's writing through a non-Wordsworthian perspective. I am grateful to Jonathan Bate and Alan G. Hill for their attention to the final draft and for helpful suggestions, to Robina Barson and Antonia and Nicholas Parsons for broad and probing conversations, and to Ian Graham, secretary of the Cumbrian Dialect Society. In writing these chapters I have also had in mind stimulating discussions with students at Birkbeck College and elsewhere. I thank other friends and colleagues at Birkbeck for their help and forbearance, and I am grateful to Diana Godden for help in word-processing early drafts. General and specific debts to others who have written about Wordsworth are acknowledged in notes and the bibliography. Versions of parts of Chapters 1 and 3 first appeared in *English*.

Abbreviations

BL	S.T. Coleridge, *Biographia Literaria*, ed. James Engell and W. Jackson Bate (Princeton, N.J., Princeton UP, 1983)
Brett and Jones	*Lyrical Ballads*, ed. R.L. Brett and A.R. Jones (London, Methuen, 1963; rev. 1968)
Child	F.J. Child, *The English and Scottish Popular Ballads* (5 vols, Boston and London, Houghton Mifflin, 1898)
Gill	*William Wordsworth*, ed. Stephen Gill (Oxford, OUP, 1984)
Gill, *Wordsworth*	Stephen Gill, *William Wordsworth: a Life* (Oxford, Clarendon, 1989)
Home at Grasmere	Wordsworth, *Home at Grasmere*, ed. Beth Darlington (Ithaca, Cornell UP, 1977)
Letters	*Letters of William and Dorothy Wordsworth*, ed. E. de Selincourt (Oxford, Clarendon); *The Early Years, 1787–1805*, rev. by Chester L. Shaver (1967) [here, *Letters*, I]; *The Middle Years, 1806–1811*, rev. by Mary Moorman (1969) [here, *Letters*, II]; *The Middle Years, 1812–1820*, rev. by Mary Moorman and Alan G. Hill (1970) [here, *Letters*, III]; *The Later Years, 1821–1853*, rev. by Alan G. Hill (four volumes, 1978–88) [here, *Letters*, IV–VII]
Moorman, I, II	Mary Moorman, *William Wordsworth, A Biography, The Early Years, 1770–1803* (Oxford, Clarendon, 1957); *The Later Years, 1803–1850* (Oxford, Clarendon, 1965)
The Prelude	William Wordsworth, *The Prelude or Growth of a Poet's Mind*, ed. E. de Selincourt; 2nd edn. rev. by H. Darbishire (Oxford, Clarendon, 1959)

Prose Works   *The Prose Works of William Wordsworth*, ed.
W.J.B Owen and J.W. Smyser (3 vols, Oxford,
Clarendon, 1974)

PW   *The Poetical Works of William Wordsworth*, ed. E.
de Selincourt and Helen Darbishire (5 vols,
Oxford, Clarendon, 1940–9; rev. edn., 1952–9)

Note on texts

Wordsworth's poems often exist in a number of versions, sometimes in many. His habits of revision before and after publication make problems for editors and readers and have given rise to strenuous critical debates about the ethics, aesthetics and politics of choosing one version of a poem (or arrangement of poems) rather than another. The problems are acute in the case of *The Prelude* and the *membra disjecta* of his planned epic, 'The Recluse'. Some of the issues are discussed in *Romantic Revisions*, edited by Robert Brinkley and Keith Hanley (Cambridge, CUP, 1992), which includes Stephen Gill's important article, 'Wordsworth's Poems: The Question of Text'. Readers should also consult studies of individual texts such as Kenneth R. Johnston's *Wordsworth and 'The Recluse'* (New Haven, Yale UP, 1984). Definitive texts and transcripts of unpublished versions can be found in the multi-volume Cornell Wordsworth, General Editor Stephen Parrish.

I have chosen editions pragmatically, with a view to ease of reference, reliability, availability and the clarity with which editors acknowledge their sources and procedures. Where possible I refer to Stephen Gill's edition, *William Wordsworth* (Oxford, OUP, 1984) in the Oxford Authors series because it presents texts in their earliest published form and is reliable and easily available. For *The Prelude* I use the 1805 text from *The Prelude 1799, 1805, 1850*, edited by Jonathan Wordsworth, M.H. Abrams and Stephen Gill (New York and London, Norton, 1979), but I also refer to the editorial notes and critical apparatus of de Selincourt's edition, revised by Helen Darbishire (Oxford, Clarendon, 1959). Otherwise reference is to the five volumes of the *The Poetical Works of William Wordsworth*, ed. E. de Selincourt, revised edition (Oxford, Clarendon Press, 1952–9). I would draw attention to Michael Mason's edition of *Lyrical Ballads* (London, Longman, 1992), the most rewarding single edition of that volume, and to *Wordsworth's Poems of 1807*, edited by Alun R. Jones

(London, Macmillan, 1987). Prose texts are quoted from *The Prose Works of William Wordsworth*, edited by W.J.B. Owen and Jane Worthington Smyser (three volumes, Oxford, Clarendon Press, 1974).

Introduction

Wordsworth has been made and remade as a cultural icon by generations of readers. Demonised by Francis Jeffrey as one of the 'Lake School' of poets, he was elevated by Coleridge, who expected Wordsworth might produce 'the FIRST GENUINE PHILOSOPHIC POEM';[1] Keats contributed when, working with difficulty at his own poetic identity, he distinguished a kind of aesthetic solemnity as 'the wordsworthian or egotistical sublime'.[2] For Matthew Arnold Wordsworth was the poet who had 'no style' because Nature took the pen and wrote for him (provided he was not writing philosophy, as he did in *The Prelude*, which Arnold disliked).[3] He was also the archetypal poet who outlived his brilliance and became boring, as James Stephens's relatively early parody reminds us: 'Two voices are there . . . One is of the deep . . . and one is of an old half-witted sheep, and Wordsworth, both are thine.' Politically he could be seen as a turncoat and lamented, as in Shelley's poem ('Deserting these, thou leavest me to grieve, / Thus having been, that thou shouldst cease to be'),[4] or reviled, as in Browning's 'The Lost Leader' (if indeed Browning meant Wordsworth). These are iconic responses no less than Arnold's potent praise. In the early twentieth century he came to stand for an English (specifically English) bad habit of allowing the moral consciousness to interfere with aesthetics (Yeats[5] and Pound thought so, both antagonists of the 'English') or, more broadly, for a loosely conceived Victorianism. On the other hand he has been celebrated as the focus of a specifically British and anti-Modernist tradition continued by Hardy, Edward Thomas and (in Donald Davie's argument) Philip Larkin.[6] Both this view and Yeats's implicit charge of insularity seem to be borne out by the fact that Wordsworth has never been widely or even significantly known in continental Europe.

Recent academic conceptions of Wordsworth in Britain and North America are perhaps another matter, yet even here he has had an iconic power, either as a poet of the radical instability of language or as a writer largely responsible for making (unconsciously) a 'Romantic Ideology' in which hard economic facts are systematically ignored in favour of an aesthetic, idealised image of rural life.[7] In a competing view Wordsworth has been seen as part of a tradition of ecological writing in which economics plays a role but is not the only significant aspect of our relation to our environment.[8]

Despite these clustering agreements, it is a striking fact that many of his individual poems provoke as diverse responses among individual readers now as they did nearly two hundred years ago. It is equally striking that many of his poems that contemporaries admired are now regarded as unworthy of comment or even of reading. I have an impression (so broad that it is difficult to prove) that though his reputation remains high, the 'canon' of poems thought and written about is smaller than it was a century ago. How can a poet be so revered *and* so controversial *and* so largely neglected? It is hard to think of a comparable case.

A traditional and partial answer is that Wordsworth did not always write well, and that we have to discount the bad poetry in order to let the 'great' poetry shine with its proper lustre. That raises more questions than it answers, especially questions of value. They cannot all be answered in this book, and I have not tried to offer a systematic revision of our habits of reading Wordsworth, nor pretended that my own views are above partiality or fashion. In fact I raise the question of value in order to explain my arbitrariness of choice. This book is not a tour through the familiar canon of Wordsworth's poems, nor is it about a coherently 'neglected Wordsworth'. It mixes familiar and unfamiliar texts, and its chief claim is that they are all interesting, if from different points of view.

There is nevertheless an intellectual centre of my arguments and choice of texts, and it is to recover early contextualisations of Wordsworth's poems. Scott, Burns and Chatterton remain important for readers of Wordsworth, and so does Southey. These were major writers of the period, and they all make useful comparisons in the following chapters. But I also consider Robert Anderson, Josiah Relph, Thomas Sanderson, William Hamilton, and Thomas Bewick, all of whom had local and sometimes national reputations as artists (poets, engravers) and are now, with the exception of Bewick, largely unknown. This has something to do, I argue, with the geopolitics of culture; texts 'survive', become part of the canon, because they are published in the (or *a*) metropolis (Edinburgh, the 'Athens of the North', competed with London for cultural dominance). I put 'survive' in quotation marks because in fact some regional literary reputations made in Wordsworth's lifetime are *still* current, but *only* regionally: I think particularly of his exact contemporary and fellow Cumbrian, Robert Anderson, still reprinted, still read and still revered. The sense in which Anderson provides a *context* for Wordsworth is perhaps remote, but unfamiliar comparisons can sharpen our evaluative consciousness.

Such comparisons also raise questions about who *read* different poets and why, questions that necessarily (in my view) involve thinking about the status of different publishing centres, the power of the reviewers, and, more important but more abstract, the kind of relation that existed, or that the poet *thought* or *hoped* existed, between himself and the reading public. These actualities find their place in the following chapters, but there is a broader context as well. Much Romantic and post-Romantic writing is suffused with a longing for two opposing impossibilities: one, to make the author *present* on the page, and the other, to make the text anonymous and the author absent, not a source of authority. In Schiller's terms the *sentimental* poet envies the *naïv*, but if the *naïv* poet is known and a contemporary (Goethe was Schiller's great example) he embodies a paradox: he is 'natural' (that is, anonymous) yet also a cultural hero, a sage. His artistic success is measured by his ubiquity and (paradoxically) his absence.

That is a way of looking at a central paradox in Wordsworth's writing: it is often very assertive, having 'palpable designs' on us (as Keats put it), but also most accommodating, urgent but tentative in its concern to be understood. It shows an extraordinary fear of being misunderstood, an 'anxiety of anticipation and repetition' as Coleridge said in *Biographia Literaria* but at the same time an immense confidence in its own constructions. The deep origin of this book is a fascination with these oppositions or paradoxes, especially the way they create relationships between writer and readers, whether actual or imagined. I explore the idea of Wordsworth's poetry (and to some extent Romantic poetry generally) as a series of communal, collaborative acts shared by the poet and other poets, domestic circles, language communities, and readers generally. Imagining communities and theorising about readers are distinct activities, but at different times and in different ways writers have sought to connect them.

Wordsworth's writing seems to me a distinctive and powerful attempt to do so.

In the following chapters, I shall be discussing various texts from a number of viewpoints with a variety of focus and approach, and with a perhaps inevitable arbitrariness of selection and emphasis. But behind it all is a preoccupation with the ways Wordsworth creates relationships, both among the figures in his poems and, more prominently, between reader and writer. I shall explore parallels between human relationships *in* the poems and those reader–writer relationships which are at the centre of his critical and polemical writing in the Preface to *Lyrical Ballads*, in the *Essays upon Epitaphs* and in the 1815 'Preface'. His achievement as a poet of relationship, as distinct from solitude on the one hand and a general notion of 'humankind' on the other, has an emotional and intellectual complexity that needs further exploration: amical, familial and domestic relations, no less than the more transcendental relations we often think of as primary in Romantic poetry (self and other; man and nature; man and God), reflect deeply on the way language itself creates relationship.

Growing out of this general preoccupation there are divergent paths in each of the chapters, and it may be as well to provide a map at the outset. The first chapter pursues the simple and possibly naive question whether Wordsworth's slippery phrase 'the real language of men' / 'a selection of the language really used by men' should be read as a formulation of one *kind* of language only, or as indicating linguistic variety or differences. Like many of his contemporaries Wordsworth had a deep interest in the nature of language in general, but I want to shift the emphasis to the topic of language *variation*, not only as it relates to theories of poetic diction and decorum but also as it reflects differences in *register*, a concept more directly applicable to oral than to written language. How far and in what form was language difference (I do not speak of 'différance') reflected in critical discourse and judgement, and how did it impinge upon a writer with a provincial background and a Cambridge education, an early fascination with London and Paris and a contrasting but deep, perhaps overwhelming, longing for an impossible linguistic simplicity and singleness?

The main manifestation of this longing is his use of the idea of oral communication as a model for the relationship of poet and reader, as if there were an immediacy, a truth, a transparency in oral language that is unavailable in writing. 'A man speaking to men': the metaphor in the Preface to *Lyrical Ballads* is not casual but crucial. But in *what* language? Might Wordsworth have written in the language of rural speech, that is, dialect? What would the choice have involved? Such questions lead to the political implications of linguistic choice, which at the end of the eighteenth century point to the poems of Burns, his cultural status and the power of reviewers in Edinburgh.

It has to do also with consciousness of dialect before dialectology became a separate discourse, and more broadly with ideas of regional and central culture. The term 'regional' has sometimes been attacked (by Tom Paulin, for example, in the introduction to his *Faber Book of Vernacular Verse*) precisely because it seems to imply 'secondary', 'lesser' or 'minor', but I use it here in preference to the more historically accurate term 'provincial' because the latter now has strong pejorative implications. (In fact, changes in the meaning of 'provincial' form part of my discussion.) These terms have shifting meanings, and we must use them carefully. There is a strong temptation to roll them up in the currently fashionable term 'marginal', but that is merely to trade one slippery metaphor for another, even less determinate one, and my instinct is that the discourse of 'text' and 'margin' is the more malleable – politically usable – for its generality.

Still, in origin the metaphor of marginality is about longstanding textual practices, and this does lead us back to Wordsworth. One of the challenges he and his contemporaries offered their readers lay precisely in their integration of non-'textual' material with the text: Coleridge's marginal glosses to 'The Ancient Mariner', Wordsworth's use of narrators who explicitly direct and redirect the reader's attention, the cult of the *annotated* fragment. Even so, we must not politicise the metaphor too easily. Wordsworth's sense of what is marginal in national political terms need not directly reflect the relation of centre and margin in printed texts (or vice-versa), and we muddy both issues if we treat them as one.

There is another aspect of language difference in the theory of genre, a topic that much occupied Wordsworth in 1815 when he arranged his first collected edition in categories *not* sanctioned by classical genre theory. If generic classifications are a way of describing the social perceptions of different kinds of writing, they are also related to the question of centrality and marginality, though not necessarily in obvious ways. Poets of the late eighteenth century who wrote in dialect were allowed praise for their pastoral poems because pastoral was an unambitious genre. Reviewers tended to represent their subject matter and language as if they were equally remote, as if peculiar language went with peculiar customs and could excite only a kind of antiquarian interest. Comparisons with Theocritus were common, and it may be that same presuppositions lay behind the use of the word 'Doric' to describe non-'standard' English in poetry. But many of Wordsworth's poems in *Lyrical Ballads* were both explicitly regional in setting and subject matter (though seldom in language) and philosophic in ambition, and that took the poems out of an easily patronised category.[9]

The first chapter is mainly devoted to these matters and to a few further issues that arise from them, especially Wordsworth's fictions of communication and non-communication, as I would like to put it, in the 'Matthew poems' and others. The second chapter follows the first in examining poems that thematise relationship in the form of imagined communities. The 'Poems on the Naming of Places' (1800) are discussed as a group of poems about linguistic boundaries. They create and explore lines of demarcation between private and public utterance by imagining communities in which private perceptions (acts of naming) have a shared validity, and questioning to what extent such a community is a workable model for writer–reader relations. Much of Wordsworth's later poetry (the travel sequences and the poems on local legends, some of which will be discussed below) are shown to be diverse attempts to explore imaginative acts in terms of specific communities. Other texts that explore boundaries (including and excluding) are 'The Brothers' and 'Michael', and 'Goody Blake and Harry Gill' and 'The Last of the Flock': the latter are discussed in an overtly political context (deriving from Southey's early radical poems and their parodies in *The Anti-Jacobin*), in which the narrator addresses a sectionalised audience and develops a politics of invitation and exclusion.

'Power', the subject of the third chapter, is explored not primarily as a political concept but as an aesthetic one with two slightly different but deeply related meanings: first, as part of the discourse of the sublime (Wordsworth's own fragmentary essay on the sublime and the beautiful is discussed), and, secondly, in terms of reader–writer relations, the 'co-operating powers' he writes about in the 'Essay, Supplementary to the Preface'. This is understood in conjunction with De Quincey's definition of 'literature of power', an idea he acknowledged to be Wordsworth's. Both discourses have, of course, social and political implications, especially as they impinge upon the notion of 'taste'. De Quincey's distinction between power and knowledge is explored in relation to Wordsworth's attitude to contemporary historiography, especially the work of Niebuhr, and to his writing about education in *The Prelude*. Much of this discussion involves close examination of the syntactic structures of Wordsworth's blank verse, which are often puzzling or ambiguous as to the relation of subject and object and as to whether phrases are appositional or additive. The power relations embedded in language seem circular or mutual rather than having a single source and direction. Wordsworth seems more interested in representing process and relationship than in defining terms. In this respect his writing recalls J.G. Herder's, whose concept of power (*Kraft*) can be usefully compared.

The fourth chapter is a limited attempt to deal with sexuality, gender and family relations in some of Wordsworth's poems. There has been an increasing awareness that the familial and the domestic are important topics in Romantic texts, not just in their Victorian successors. *In certain ways* Wordsworth's writing is very family-oriented. The image of the family circle was early associated with Wordsworth, meaning (partly) that as a writer he could count on sympathetic readers in the group of people – women, chiefly – who surrounded him, who were his amanuenses and first readers. Coleridge's poems about Sara Hutchinson strongly support this notion of an intellectual and emotional community in powerfully expressing envy of imagined social and sexual security, a fantasy of spousehood and sisterhood combined.

The chapter moves on to a discussion of images of paternity in Wordsworth's texts, which reveal curious emphases and omissions: lack of interest in lineage (with the important exceptions of 'Vaudracour and Julia', *The Borderers* and 'Michael'), and a general swaying of the balance towards father–daughter relations rather than father–son. (Coleridge's poems to or about Hartley make a strong contrast.) Father–son relations seem to cut across the tendency among male Romantic writers to write as if they were authors of themselves. Their discourse can erase their own parentage and, in the case of Wordsworth, seems to exclude also his replacement by a son. Father–daughter relations pose different threats (crudely, the need to renegotiate domestic authority in another generation) and provide a distinctly different, gendered, framework for the concept of the 'child of nature', the opposition between nature and society, and the figuration of Romantic 'solitude'. These matters arise in an examination of Wordsworth's textual and actual treatment of his sister Dorothy and his daughter Dora, both in her childhood and much later when her prospective marriage and authorship gave rise to troubled and troubling poems.

Much of the fifth chapter is an attempt to recuperate *The White Doe of Rylstone*, Wordsworth's only extended attempt to write a romance, and there are two chief emphases. The first is his competitive attitude to Scott's popular successes with verse romances. The poem densely alludes to Scott's narratives and challenges his readers to rise to the demands of a narrative in which transformations are not merely romantic mysteries. The second and chief emphasis develops from this, the relation of metaphor and metamorphosis. The poem is a critique of metaphorical 'translation', the substitution of one object for another, on the grounds that the mind may be dazzled by the image (the 'vehicle' in Richards's term) and forget the significance, the 'tenor'. Against this static concept of metaphor the poem sets up a temporal concept, an idea of change through time which can be likened to metamorphosis: the figural meaning of an object (the doe, for example) undergoes changes as the narrative creates different states of mind in the perceiver. This process, which is at the centre of the poem, is contrasted with other acts of inter-pretation or figuration, where the temporal element is missing (Norton's response to the banner; preliminary misreadings of the doe in Canto I). Wordsworth uses the temporal dimension of narrative to question acts of interpretation implicit in metaphor and to explore the psychology of superstition and response to religious symbols (part of his anti-Catholicism). Language is shaped by individual perception but also by a sense of communal validity or invalidity. Superstition, for example, is not simply dismissed but considered as an example of communal interpretation or metaphor. The chapter ends with a discussion of the way Wordsworth imports a temporal dimension into visual art in a number of short poems about paintings.

The final chapter is about Wordsworth 'collaborating' in an extended sense in texts where his engagements with other writers through allusion and quotation create a controlling context. The discussion touches on the politics of allusion before moving to an extensive consideration of the 'Yarrow' poems, and then returns to the particular case of Wordsworth's aesthetic companionship with his patron Beaumont. The three poems about the Yarrow are densely allusive, referring to anonymous ballads as well as to works by Nicol Burne, William Hamilton, John Logan and Scott, and function as palimpsests or re-textualisations. Wordsworth's poetry of place is about the imaginative use of place, and acknowledges prior uses, to which his own is an addition. One thing that emerges from this investigation is Wordsworth's interest in the conditions under which poetry becomes anonymous or functions as if it were so – becomes communal rather than the imaginative property of the author (Burne and Hamilton had become one-poem-poets). Another aspect is that in these and a large number of other (generally late) poems about local legend, Wordsworth writes not with the visual emphasis of the picturesque tourist but as a 'reader' of an already textualised place or scene. The picturesque guide-book gives way to the collection of local legends. Scott dominates many of these poems, to whom Wordsworth ascribes (in 'Yarrow Revisited') a complex role; reading, disseminating and retelling local legends – 'reading' landscape in terms of story and vice-versa. In this and other late poems there is a quite different view of Scott from that of the young balladist and the author of *The White Doe*: Scott as Orpheus, also as a reincarnation of Tom the Rhymer; the poet of Northern as opposed to classical legend, the true and contemporary example of a writer who 'collaborated' with the people in allying his art to the communal art of legends. This certainly represents a change in Wordsworth's attitude to Scott, but we should not see it simply in terms of two personalities; rather as a restatement of a central Romantic paradox: the poet becomes famous (and deserves fame) precisely as he writes himself out of his texts and they become common property.

Such a map emphasises breadth and selectivity, and possibly arbitrariness. Because of its breadth, the book impinges upon a number of kinds of writing that are differently theorised, and these frameworks are taken up and acknowledged as appropriate. It would have been impossible (had I wanted it) to write from a single theoretically 'pure' approach. It was written from the conviction that looking sharply at a number of distinct issues might lead to a clearer sense of how particular texts function than a single overview could.

Notes and references

1.   S.T. Coleridge, *Biographia Literaria*, ch. 22 (*BL*, II, p. 156).

2. Keats, letter to R. Woodhouse 27.10.1818 (*Letters of John Keats*, ed. R. Gittings [Oxford, OUP, 1977], p. 157).

3. Matthew Arnold, 'Wordsworth' (1879), reprinted in *Essays in Criticism, Second Series* (1888); ed. G.K. Chesterton (London, Dent, new edn 1964), p. 307.

4. Shelley, 'To Wordsworth'; *Poems and Prose*, ed. Donald H. Reiman and Sharon B. Powers (New York and London, Norton, 1977), p. 88.

5. W.B. Yeats, 'Journal', 9.3.1909; *Memoirs*, ed. D. Donoghue (London, Macmillan, 1972), pp. 179–80.

6. Donald Davie, *Thomas Hardy and British Poetry* (London, Routledge and Kegan Paul, 1973).

7. 'The Romantic Ideology', is J.J. McGann's phrase: see *The Romantic Ideology: A Critical Investigation* (Chicago, Chicago UP, 1983). See also Marjorie Levinson, *Wordsworth's Great Period Poems* (Cambridge, CUP, 1986) and, for a partial account of constructions of Wordsworth over the years, Antony Easthope, *Wordsworth Then and Now* (Harvester, 1993).

8. See Jonathan Bate, *Romantic Ecology; Wordsworth and the Environmental Tradition* (London, Routledge, 1991).

9. The politicised pastoral of Wyatt, Spenser and Marvell appears to have been out of fashion.

CHAPTER 1
Poetry, language and difference

Poetry and languages

So much of Wordsworth's writing about poetry, in verse and in prose, is concerned with the nature of language, and so many of his best-known poems have elements of dialogue or represented speech, elements that can seem to be merely incidental to the poem as a whole but are still somehow at its heart. Dialogue in 'Resolution and Independence', the poem that Coleridge thought had all Wordsworth's strengths and weaknesses, peters out into metaphor ('his voice to me was like a stream / Scarce heard') but remains a formative part of the experience of the poem – if it did not, Lewis Carroll's parody in the poem of the White Knight (' "What is it that you do," I cried, / And thumped him on the head') would not work. The nature of language is a central Romantic field of speculation, especially as it relates to what humans have in common. Often 'humans' turns out to mean members of the same nation, race or even social class, but these differences are usually ignored or disguised in theoretical discussion. But in more pragmatic discussions of *spoken* language such as guides to pronunciation, which abounded in the late eighteenth century, language *difference* is the point at issue: difference that reflects region or education (and therefore financial status and gender). Wordsworth's writing explores both spoken and written language, and I shall argue that we should read it in the light of contemporary thinking about language, whether theoretical or pragmatic. Doing so helps us to understand, I think, the very powerful oddities of poems like 'Resolution and Independence': why is it that *speech* matters in a poem that Wordsworth himself used in the 1815 'Preface' to illustrate the workings of a purely *visual* imagination?

> Choice word, and measured phrase; above the reach
> Of ordinary men; a stately speech!
> Such as grave Livers do in Scotland use

This detail is typical of 'Resolution and Independence' in that it seems merely accidental but can be shown to raise important issues. Language makes relationship by making distinctions, not just between the objects and ideas referred to, but between language users as well. Recent surveys of contemporary usage have been much occupied by the question of how it differs among speakers of the same 'language' (English, French, or whatever else it might be), and educational writers concern themselves with the questions of how much it can be allowed to differ while remaining the same 'language', and of how spoken language relates to a written standard.[1] These questions need not be politically motivated, but they are easily absorbed into political frameworks, and that is one reason why we should be as clear as we can be about the implications of language differences in earlier periods.

Are these questions relevant to readers of Wordsworth? What differences can be perceived, and what do they signify? Wordsworth is best known for his claim that poetic language should be modelled on the (spoken) language of men in 'low and rustic life'. In these lines from 'Resolution and Independence' (a 'literary' title if ever there was one: the Wordsworths privately referred to the poem as 'the Leech-gatherer') he has trouble placing the leech-gatherer's language. The lines register a certain surprised admiration, as if appearance and language conflict. A simple reading suggests that the Leech-gatherer is a cut above the average rustic, but Wordsworth is more specific than that. The man's language is said to share qualities of diction and syntax with the language of Scots people of a certain kind, though it is not itself Scottish. What does the comparison mean? What did it mean to Wordsworth's first readers? Is the Leech-gatherer's language to be thought of as typical of Cumbrian rustics, or is it strange because it is idiosyncratic? If the former, then the narrator's surprise is hard to explain unless he is imagined as unfamiliar with Cumbrian language. Either way the reader is called on to perform acts of recognition involving language difference, even though the topic is submerged because Wordsworth makes no attempt to represent language variation orthographically.[2]

Had Wordsworth used a phonetic representation of variant language – as Burns had done, and as some of Wordsworth's Cumbrian contemporaries did – he would have raised questions that, I suppose, he did not want to raise. Probably his sense of vocation, his ambition to be a great *national*[3] poet like Spenser or Milton, prevented it because it was natural to assume, then as now, that a national poet must write in a national language. There was a well-developed sense of what was correct, even though the now familiar concept of 'standard English' had not been established; and the arbiters of taste were metropolitan professionals. These matters would have greatly complicated the question of how poetic language can be like spoken language, the central topic of the Preface to *Lyrical Ballads*. For Wordsworth considers that topic in general terms, without taking into account the fact that spoken language *varies* in a way that written language does not. Written language is subject to codes of taste and decorum, and these are the subject of Wordsworth's critical consideration, both explicit and implicit, but he writes of spoken language as if it were without variation, either historical or geographical, except in terms of a general distinction between town and country, the potentially national and the distinctly local. But, brought up in Cumberland and educated there and in Cambridge, he can hardly have been unaware of the differences. It was on his journey from Hawkshead to Cambridge, he tells us in *The Prelude*, that he first found language shocking, when he heard a woman curse.[4] It is usually assumed that Wordsworth's variable and malleable phrase 'the very language of men' / 'a selection of the language really spoken by men'[5] points to a single *kind* of language. There is no doubt that he goes to some lengths in the Preface to define a standard, which critics from Coleridge onwards have found problematic or illusory,[6] but I want to argue that this need not rule out of bounds the question whether the metaphor of speech for writing doesn't suggest a diversity of models rather than a single one. Such an enquiry does not replace previous arguments, but it might supplement them by looking at a familiar topic from an unfamiliar angle. One general reason for doing this is that Wordsworth's prose is at least as cogent, if not more so, in defining what he did not like as what he did; and the particularity of his adverse criticism gives us access to a range of contemporary ideas about language (among other things) that cannot be summed up in a single formula. Scorn, even rage, is not the preserve only of the older Wordsworth (the author of, say, the sonnet on 'Illustrated Books and Newspapers' – 'Avaunt this vile abuse of pictured page!'); on the contrary, there is evidence that he was a satirist *manqué*, more in Junius's vein than Pope's, in spite of a deep-seated fear of inflicting personal harm. That much is clear from the 'Letter to the Bishop of Llandaff', 'The Convention of Cintra', even the earlier fragmentary essay on morals; not to mention the 'Essay, Supplementary to the Preface' and the 'Letter to a Friend of Burns', where he finally attacked Jeffrey after eight years of provocation. How could individual differences in speech be seen and recognised as regional or class differences? To what extent do arguments that literary language should be like spoken language take these differences into account? Answers to those questions are partly matters of history, partly of the way we choose to read the poems. Wordsworth was not the first nor the last poet who made prominent use of speech idioms. Chaucer thematised dialectal variation in 'The Reeve's Tale' and the obliquities of spoken syntax in 'The Wife of Bath's Prologue', and the analogy between poetry and speech has become something of a critical commonplace since Eliot pronounced that all poetic revolutions move poetic language closer to common speech and found the process occurring with Dryden as well as with Wordsworth.[7] Like Wordsworth, Eliot writes of 'common speech' as if it were an unproblematic term, although his poetic practice, in *The Waste Land* and elsewhere, certainly includes an awareness of dialect and sociolect. Eliot's theorising ignores differences that must have been matters of personal experience to a provincial American who strove to become both metropolitan and English, whereas his poetry arguably does not. I suggest that Wordsworth's case has similarities, and that the sense of language differences in his poems should lead us to read the Preface in an open-ended way. The argument that poetry should be somehow like speech is both complex in itself – oblique and possibly contradictory because dialectology did not exist as a science in the late eighteenth century – and probably awkwardly related to his poetic practice.

In what sense were these distinctions available to Wordsworth and his readers in the first decade of the nineteenth century? They are explicit in some theoretical discussions, in the example of other poets who *chose* to write in dialect, and they are strongly implicit in the critical practice of reviewers. Joseph Priestley had begun to explore the relation between spoken and written language in terms of diversity and standardisation, noting that spoken language is more diverse than written.[8] In *A Course of Lectures on the Theory of Language, and Universal Grammar* (1762) he noted that the 'use of letters [tended] . . . to fix the modes of it [i.e. language]' (p. 135); that in a politically unified nation like the Roman empire (unlike the warring Greek states) there is a natural tendency to imitate the language of established power and that 'by this means Dialects, though used in conversation, would hardly ever be introduced into writing; and the written language would be capable of being reduced very nearly to a perfect uniformity' (p. 137). Here Priestley is writing specifically about dialects but his subject is language variation, change and uniformity in general. The argument as a whole implies a progression from separate languages and states to uniformity and centralised power, a process he also observed among the ancient Hebrew tribes. There may also be a suggestion that uniformity is equated with maturity, for Priestley certainly implies written language is the language of political sophistication.

Such an argument could obviously be used for nationalistic purposes, as it was by Johann Herder and others during the next four decades. Herder wrote that a nation could not exist without a distinct language and tradition of poetry; and the upshot of his researches and those of his followers was to find – in fact to *create* by putting into print – a body of poetry which would express the spirit of the German nation. It has to be remembered that the 'German nation' was a political project at the time, not an actuality, and that his theory was a powerful political tool for those whose interest it was to unite the German states against potential and then actual French aggression. Yet Herder acknowledged that any theory of language that presupposed an origin in speech[9] must come to terms with the fact that spoken language varies enormously more than written language does: *national* variations coexist with regional variations:

> What explains all the peculiarities, all of the idiosyncracies of orthography if not the awkward difficulty of writing as one speaks? What living language can be learned from its tones in bookish letters? And hence what dead language can be called to life? The more alive a language – the less one has thought of reducing it to letters, the more spontaneously it rises to the full unsorted sounds of nature – the less, too, it is writeable, the less writeable in twenty letters; and for outsiders, indeed, often quite unpronounceable.[10]

Herder's idea of the 'full unsorted sounds of nature' reveals an assumption that spoken language is not only historically prior to written language but somehow a *natural* occurrence, whereas written language is a synthetic, socially contructed imitation. But at the same time he appears to want to *naturalise* social constructions, like a national language and the nation state. Spoken language is a model for written language in its naturalness, but its diversity has somehow to be subsumed under a single identity.

Herder is of more than passing interest because his concept of 'power' as the primary mode of action of the human mind – reason is a subdivision of power – has something in common with Wordsworth's discussion of power in Book V of *The Prelude* and the 'Essay, Supplementary to the Preface', to which I shall return later. For the moment it is worth noting that similar *political* thinking occurs in Wordsworth's more nationalistic poems, such as the sonnet 'It is not to be thought of that the Flood / Of British freedom':

> We must be free or die, who speak the tongue
> That Shakespeare spake.

Well aware of language change, Wordsworth knew 'we' did not speak the language Shakespeare spoke, but the nationalistic attitude, at a time when French invasion was feared, is bolstered by an assertion of linguistic unity and permanence. 'Spake' is not unparalleled in Wordsworth's poetry, but as a slight archaism it makes a gesture towards bridging historical change and division. Shortly before this he wrote 'Resolution and Independence',[11] a poem which looks very hard at regional difference, personal change, and the validity of different kinds of language in expressing as well as overcoming them. A choice of attitudes was available, and it is important that Wordsworth considered them at such a time, for the poem has implications beyond that framework of personal history in which it and the contemporary stanzas of the 'Immortality Ode' are often considered.

To return to an earlier point: a choice of language was also available. Wordsworth could have chosen to write in Cumbrian dialect. The obvious reason for not doing so is that he would not have been widely read. But some contemporaries did choose to write in dialect, and we can study the historical implications of the choice by looking at their work.

In 1794 a 24-year-old Cumbrian visited Vauxhall Gardens and was 'disgusted' at the inauthenticity, as he judged it, of some 'songs, written in a mock pastoral Scottish style'. Appealing to a fellow countryman, who apparently agreed with him, he reckoned he was capable of producing something better. He wrote four poems, one of them about a certain 'Lucy Gray', founded on a tale told by 'a

Northumbrian rustic'. In the same year the poems were set to music by James Hook (father of the playwright Theodore Hook) and 'loudly encored' when sung at Vauxhall. His first volume, *Poems on Various Subjects* (a title much favoured by labouring and artisan poets in the eighteenth century)[12] appeared in 1798, followed by a dialect volume, *Cumberland Ballads* in 1805. Around 1806 he visited Burns's grave and wrote 'an effusion' on the subject. His *Poetical Works* appeared by subscription in 1820, by which time he could describe himself as 'a poor Bard, now in the decline of life'. Wordsworth and Southey were among the subscribers.[13]

Robert Anderson (not to be confused with Dr Robert Anderson, the anthologist, editor of *The Works of the British Poets* [1792–95]) haunts the mind because his story has many points of contact with Wordsworth's, although, as a whole, it is utterly different. He was apprenticed to a pattern-drawer at the age of thirteen, and though his *Cumberland Ballads* proved 'somewhat popular', he could neither make a living out of poetry nor improve his position socially. The 'paltry curacy' Wordsworth rejected with scorn would have well suited his contemporary, if he had had the education. Leaving aside individual abilities, education is the real difference between the two. Anderson's is a story of direct confrontation between a rural tradition of ballad singing and its metropolitan imitation, and this reminds us that Wordsworth's is not: what Cambridge provided was a 'midway residence' (*The Prelude*, III, 554) between the country and the city, where he could safely experience the 'shapes of spurious fame and short-lived praise' (*ibid.*, 627) without investing his life in them, and where the power relations between actor and spectator, leader and led, were seen for the absorbing but fragile things they were.

When Wordsworth left Cambridge he presented himself to his potential readers as a new writer qualified for their attention by his university career. His first published volumes, *An Evening Walk* and *Descriptive Sketches*, appeared in London, not in Edinburgh, Carlisle or Bristol – all of them publishing centres. Replete with topographical and literary footnotes, the volumes give every indication that he presented himself as a young intellectual making the most of his credentials: 'By W. Wordsworth, B.A., of St. John's, Cambridge'. But his publisher Joseph Johnson was associated with radical non-conformists and is now best known for editions of writers like Mary Wollstonecraft and Thomas Paine:[14] people excluded from a university education on the ground of religion or sex. The association may have shocked those who expected more of Wordsworth academically, the uncles who paid for his education, who had earlier thought, as he had, in terms of his becoming part of the academic establishment, perhaps through a study of oriental languages, or at least of his taking orders.[15] But he had been a semi-detached student, spending some of his time on Italian literature, a non-examinable subject; and his account of the Cambridge years in Book III of *The Prelude* wavers uneasily between outright alienation ('I was not of that hour, / Nor of that place') and 'playful' participation. Cambridge was less a fixed 'midway residence' than a *shifting* measure of displacement, a site where potential communities formed and dissolved repeatedly. That is why there is a deep division in the account of his return to Hawkshead in the following Book: a narrative of recognition and refreshment, but also of discovery that to write about people is to be other than they are.

In striking contrast his next volume, *Lyrical Ballads*, was published anonymously by a small publisher in Bristol. That fact should be seen alongside a major change in poetic style, from descriptions addressed to the picturesque tourist to more consciously 'experimental' language,[16] and a corresponding change of subject from composed landscapes and sentimental vignettes to a more morally engaged presentation of rural life. Part of the linguistic change is a move towards the use of more dialectal forms in *Lyrical Ballads*, especially in the 1800 edition, often with explanatory footnotes that gloss names and terms but do not, as the footnotes to *Descriptive Sketches* did, give prose equivalents for poetic descriptions.

If Wordsworth had read Anderson's volume of 1805 or the dialect poems printed in Carlisle newspapers from 1806 he would have come across poems that programmatically juxtaposed the local and the national and mixed verse and prose in ways that add a solid factuality to the discussions of the Preface to *Lyrical Ballads*. Anderson's 'Nichol the Newsmonger' (written and published between 1801 and 1803) thematises dialectal oral communication; it is imagined reportage in a village where local events (illnesses, weddings, pregnancies, cock-fights, the meanness of the local publican) are juxtaposed with national. Anderson was praised by his friend Thomas Sanderson for presenting a very accurate picture of Cumberland customs;[17] in this poem the custom was that of narrating news. It is a report on reporting, implicitly contrasting rural and metropolitan reporting, the former characterised *chiefly* by the habit of mixing local and national, with only a very general sense of ranking the events in any hierarchy of importance. Certainly it begins with matters of national importance, 'Bonnyprat' and the slave trade, together with such acute generalisations as

> America's nobbut sae sae;
> An Englan nit queyte as she mud be –

but thereafter any sense of hierarchy disappears as the local and the trivial increasingly dominate, with only a few matters of national importance thrown in:

> The clogger he's bowt a new wig
> Dawston singers come here agean Sunday
> Lord Nelson's ta'en three Spanish fleets
> An the Dancin Schuill oppens on Monday.

The news of Nelson seems both exaggerated and outdated. There is an attempt to sum up perhaps, when, after reporting the theft of some washing, Nichol remarks that

> Nowt's seafe out o' duirs now-a-days
> Frev a millstone, e'en down to a sickle –

which perhaps bears indirectly on the international affairs mentioned in the poem and reminds us that local conditions are indeed affected by war, though the narrator does not explictly say so. In fact the arbitrariness of his report and the triviality of much of it bring home to us the actualities of rural life at that particular time (there seems to be a reference to the Peace of Amiens) – more strongly perhaps than a direct complaint could; I'm thinking of poems like Southey's lament for his 'weary way-wanderer', parodied in the *Anti-Jacobin's* 'Needy knife-grinder'.

But there's a more immediate bearing on Wordsworth's poetic practice of mixing the 'trivial' with the profound, the habit Coleridge identified as 'accidentality',[18] the

> insertion of accidental circumstances . . . which might be necessary to establish the probability of a statement in real life, where nothing is taken for granted by the hearer, but appear superfluous in poetry, where the reader is willing to believe for his own sake.

Coleridge then duly invokes Aristotle's characterisation of poetry, 'the noblest and most philosophical form of writing'. Characteristically Coleridge (who in the same chapter challenged Wordsworth with the remark that there is 'not a single poet of humble life among [the shepherds] of the *English* lakes and mountains') is presupposing certain limits to the 'poetic' which would be challenged by poems such as 'Nichol the Newsmonger' and *may be* challenged by Wordsworth's similar practice. One can of course imagine what Coleridge might have made of Anderson, but one doesn't have to agree.

I don't want to make too much of this, especially in view of the fact that 'Nichol the Newsmonger' represents an extreme among Anderson's poems in this respect (precisely *because* it is a report of reportage) and may be to some extent a caricature; but it is interesting, at least, that the 'accidentality' Coleridge finds in Wordsworth has a parallel in poetry that has as great a claim as any to represent 'the real language of men'.

Another of Anderson's poems, 'Croglin Watty', is a mixture of a different kind, a mixture of prose and verse; this again could have some bearing on the implications of Wordsworth's views. It differs from, say, *The Beggar's Opera* in that the diction of the verse is in no sense different from that in the prose, both consisting partly of dialogue. It is an archetypal narrative of a village boy (from Croglin) being fleeced in town (Carlisle). There is as far as I can tell no attempt to distingush village and town dwellers by their speech, only by their more rapacious social customs – again with reference to poverty and squalor, both physical and moral.

The upshot is that there are parallels with some of Wordsworth's views and practices in these dialect poems, written just after 1800 in the county neighbouring his native county. Wordsworth's relation to the Cumberland poets is obliquely evident in 'The Two Thieves', a poem easily dismissed as uncharacteristic, a half-hearted attempt at humour like others of his poems in anapests ('Written in Germany', 'The Childless Father'). There *is* humour in it, but of a particular kind: the consciously indulgent acceptance of petty crime as a mere oddity. Old Dan's habit of theft, bordering on kleptomania, is presented chiefly as a spectacle for the neighbours, a piece of fun they rather look forward to than disapprove of, and that view is shared by the narrator. The poem's moral sentiment works only in the confines of such a limited perspective; it could not be generalised (envisaged in a larger community where people did not know each other) without appearing irresponsible. In this way it is an *essentially* local poem.[19] Its cultural connections also lead to this conclusion. It begins with an extended reference to Thomas Bewick, praising his vignettes as a more appropriate medium than language for the subject:

> O now that the genius of Bewick were mine,
> And the skill which he learned on the banks of the Tyne,
> Then the Muses might deal with me just as they chose,
> For I'd take my last leave both of verse and of prose.
>
> What feats would I work with my magical hand!
> Book-learning and books should be banished the land[.]

The collocation of 'the Muses' with 'Book-learning' suggests a general deprecation of the verbal as against the visual, and at times Wordsworth imitates Bewick's art either by freezing narratives into emblematic moments or by emphasising that Dan and his grandson are a visual spectacle to the neighbourhood, an object of amiable instruction like common prints on 'ale-house' walls. But there are further contrasts, more explicit in a rejected manuscript draft of the opening:

> Oh! now that the boxwood and graver were mine,
> Of the Poet who lives on the banks of the Tyne!
> Who has plied his rude tools with more fortunate toil
> Than Reynolds e'er brought to his canvas and oil.

'Boxwood and graver'; 'canvas and oil': technical particularities emphasise the contrast between low and high art, between a popular book illustrator and the late president of the Royal Academy. There is also a contrast between local and national art: it suits Wordsworth's purpose in the poem to associate Bewick with his specific (northern) origin, although he had a national reputation by 1800. Doubtless Wordsworth came to think the comparison with Reynolds an embarrassing hyperbole, but the sense of the contrasts survive in the printed edition.

Bewick was nationally known, but (leaving aside his illustrations of natural history) much of his earlier work was done for popular and sometimes distinctly regional literature, and it is no doubt this work Wordsworth has in mind.[20] 'Regional' and 'popular' are not synonyms, in spite of metropolitan prejudice like that of Jeffrey, but it seems to me part of Wordsworth's purpose in this poem to attempt to blur the distinction, to become truly bucolic – ironically reinforcing that very prejudice. At all events, in invoking Bewick's name in this poem Wordsworth surely alludes to the rural vignettes Bewick contributed to volumes like *Select Fables* (1784), *Robin Hood* (1795), successive editions of Gay's *Fables* (1779 and later), and, more interestingly, a relatively lavish subscription volume of the *Poems* of Josiah Relph (1798), many of which were written in Cumberland dialect. Wordsworth possibly owned copies of the last three of these volumes.[21]

The Relph edition is particularly interesting. Relph was acquiring something of a posthumous reputation in the 1790s, chiefly through the efforts of Jonathan Boucher, who contributed a life of Relph to the 1798 volume and a eulogium in Thomas Hutchinson's *History of the County of Cumberland* (1794–5) and was almost certainly the author of a letter in praise of Relph in the *Gentleman's Magazine* in 1791.[22] Relph's most celebrated poem, 'The Harvest', is an icon of language choice: Robin injures his hand with a sickle while harvesting because he is distracted by the presence of Betty, and in despair at her stand-offishness resolves to sell his flute in order to buy a book of etiquette. Social aspirations compromise the pastoral idiom. Relph's poems were reprinted in 1798 at the instigation of Thomas Sanderson, another Cumberland poet, who was also responsible for the publication of Robert Anderson's 1805 volume. Wordsworth was certainly aware, late in his life, of Sanderson's literary efforts.[23]

These figures suggest that if Wordsworth needed examples of writers who had chosen dialect, they were not lacking. What can we make of his choice? It can be fitted into a large historical pattern, which I had better acknowledge although it is not my chief concern. Timothy Brennan has recently argued that 'the issue of common speech' in the Preface to *Lyrical Ballads* 'was associated with peasant virtue' as against 'cosmopolitan upper classes, intellectuals and others likely to be influenced by foreign ideas':[24] that is, it was one of the chief strategies of early nineteenth-century nationalist thinking to find an essential, defining example of national qualities in 'low and rustic life'. As a retrospective generalisation that has some force (though it is overdetermined, in my view, by post-colonial – post-national – antagonism to the later nineteenth century): Wordsworth's thinking about unity and diversity did change radically in the twenty years after the Preface. We could add a complementary generalisation that mid- and late-eighteenth-century thinking about language shows

a movement from unity to diversity in terms of the proliferation of the
reading public and its pressure on earlier assumptions of cultural unity:
pressures resisted in different ways by Reynolds and Burke after the
beginning of the French Revolution.[25] That view places Wordsworth
at the point of a historical reversal: and it would be easy (too easy, I
think) to give a history of Wordsworth's work that enacted it in
miniature.

Wordsworth seems to have aimed intuitively at the 'language of
low and rustic life', but *'freed from provincialisms'*, as Coleridge put it in
his analysis of 'The Sailor's Mother',[26] apparently conceiving his task
as conveying the *sense* of class and regional differences without straying
beyond an acceptable range (however defined) of diction and syntax.
'Provincialisms', in Coleridge's use, clearly has both class and regional
significance in a largely unexamined combination;[27] and some such
complexity of assumptions lies behind those attacks on the simplicity
of Wordsworth's language that turn into disgusted and sometimes
patently snobbish attacks on his subject matter (Jeffrey's review of the
1807 *Poems in Two Volumes*, for example). We may deduce from this
simply that Wordsworth's ideal, if it was as I've described, was illusory,
but, more positively, we should ask how Wordsworth worked with and
against these unexplained assumptions about socially and
geographically differentiated language.

Dominant (that is, nationally important) voices conceptualised
regional or class differences as divisive or trivial. 'Locality' is Joshua
Reynolds's term for what opposes the 'civic ideal of art': it names a
failure to achieve universality.[28] But at the same time it is a logical
extension of insistence on the actual. Poetry which to any extent
values the regional or local but has limited means of conceptualising
them will need to make gestures of invitation or explanation to a
readership perceived to be central rather than local: centralised by the
dominance of metropolitan critical and cultural values. If at the same
time the poet writes, as Wordsworth did, of the universality of human
nature ('we have all of us one human heart'), there is a conflict: the
poetry emphasises both difference and similarity between subject and
readership, and gestures of invitation are likely to be complicated by
more tenacious kinds of address and will vary from poem to poem.
The politics of invitation, if I can call it that, involve making
assumptions about readership that in Wordsworth's case are every bit
as complex as arguments about the language of poetry – and of course
the subjects are related.

I shall take up that topic in the next chapter. Here I want to emphasise that imagining Wordsworth was conscious of the reality of language difference and language choice at the time should make us reconsider the shape of his career. From 1793 to 1798, the years between his first books and his most famous, his career is often described as a retreat from political radicalism: a turning inwards to listen to the 'still sad music of humanity'. That view is reasonable: it is supported by the texts of 'Adventures on Salisbury Plain' and its variants, mostly unpublished in his lifetime, and probably also by 'The Borderers'. But it is not the whole story: we must recognise that during the war with France a growing emphasis on the regional or local had potentially *two* political directions: one, towards the idea we now associate especially with Burke, namely that it is essentially conservative, the local community being seen as a microcosm – or in rhetorical terms a metonym – of a supposed national community; the other towards decentralisation, resisting the centripetal pull towards London values, whether political or aesthetic. At a time of enormous increase in the power and reach of central government (including the first imposition of income tax), emphasising regional culture could be a willed, positive act. But both directions are evident in the successive editions of *Lyrical Ballads*: as claims for the power of poetry in the Advertisement and Prefaces become more universalising, the diction of the poems comes to include more regionalisms, footnoted so that we do not miss them. 'Resolution and Independence', a kind of retrospective Lyrical Ballad, thematises these matters as well as any of Wordsworth's poems.

> I thought of Chatterton, the marvellous Boy,
> The sleepless Soul that perish'd in its pride;
> Of Him who walk'd in glory and in joy
> Behind his plough, upon the mountain-side[.]

Chatterton and Burns are poets whose careers involved a crucial choice between languages. Chatterton grew up in a fantasy world of 'Rowley' and his fifteenth-century companions and could never quite convert it, as the Brontës did theirs, into a world more nearly resembling his own. The language of the Rowley poems shows he had a facility for verbal mimicry (though in my view very little understanding of early syntax), which he turned to account in journalism, but he persisted in thinking the 'An Excelente Balade of Charitie' should be published as a genuine poem and was disappointed when it was refused. Perhaps that is why some critics and editors are still sentimental about it, in spite of its fake archaism and its lack of the attractive robustness of many of his non-archaic poems. Wordsworth had read Chaucer (Chatterton probably had not) and must have seen through the fraud easily, but paid Chatterton the compliment of imitating his stanza as well as thematising his despondency. I speculate that he did so not only to add his contribution to the already abundant literature on Chatterton (Coleridge's 'Monody on the Death of Thomas Chatterton' was praised by reviewers on its publication in 1796),[29] but because Chatterton, an uneducated provincial, had dared to try to force his language on the metropolitan reviewers: in a different way Wordsworth had done the same with *Lyrical Ballads*.

Burns had a more serious choice of languages, one which his critics were not reluctant to generalise and politicise. We follow Francis Jeffrey and others in dividing Burns's poetry into two kinds, English and Scots. What did the distinction mean? Priestley wrote of Scots as a 'sister-language', something more distinct than a dialect, and yet not entirely independent. In 1809 Jeffrey, magisterially defining Burns's station on Parnassus,[30] tells us, not surprisingly, that

> Scotch is not to be considered a provincial dialect, the vehicle only of rustic vulgarity and rude local humour. It is the language of a whole country – long an independent kingdom, and still separate in laws, character and manners. . . . It is an ignorant, as well as an illiberal prejudice, which would seek to confound it with the barbarous dialects of Yorkshire or Devonshire.

(Why not Westmoreland or Cumberland?) Further, Burns

> wrote in Scotch, because the writings which he most aspired to imitate were composed in that language.

Jeffrey is making a political point: Scots had its own culture and its own literary tradition, whereas 'provincial dialects' apparently did not. The argument was made vociferously during the late eighteenth century, because Scots culture was seen to be sufficiently related to English to make the difference worth insisting on, yet distinctive enough to offer a powerful alternative tradition.[31] Even from Priestley's earlier and less engaged point of view the Scottish language had this special position.

Jeffrey's partisanship hardly needs proving, but it is noticeable that it is more vehement when his argument about nationality becomes compromised by attitudes to social (class) distinctions. Burns lacks 'the delicacy . . . of a gentleman' (p. 181). When a man not born into the nobility says this of another, he means 'he is my moral inferior'. Jeffrey accuses Burns of 'a vile prostitution of language' when he 'rave[s] about friendship and philanthropy in a tavern, while his wife's heart is breaking at a cheerless fire, and his children pining in solitary poverty' (p. 183), an accusation that reveals not only moral distaste but an attitude to language as authoritarian as Humpty Dumpty's. He continues in words which recall the *Lyrical Ballads* Preface:

> contempt for . . . prudence, decency and regularity; and his admiration of thoughtlessness, oddity and vehement sensibility; – his belief, in short, in the dispensing power of genius and social feeling, in all matters of morality and common sense. This is the very slang of the worst German plays, and the lowest of our town-made novels . . . (p. 182)[32]

'Slang': the word attributes coarse feeling to coarse language and identifies both with the sensational novels popular with a metropolitan clique. It is a strategy *Blackwoods* used against Keats, again assuming that rural language *may* be pure but metropolitan language *is* vicious.[33]

There are deep ambivalences about the city and the country. The city is the centre of literary tradition, the meeting place of writers, reviewers and publishers, but it is also full of readers and writers of debased taste who do not adhere to the standards of literary tradition. Jeffrey does not explicitly extend his criticism to the spoken language of the city, but the argument could be so extended (as it was by Keats's *Blackwoods* reviewer) because it is fundamentally *about* standards of purity and taste. The country is equally ambiguous: a place of 'provincial dialect, . . . rustic vulgarity and rude local humour', but also free from the debased taste for 'town-made novels'. The opposition between country and city is subordinate to an insistence on aesthetic and moral standards, and each can be used as a term of abuse.

Wordsworth's criticism of 'sickly and stupid German tragedies' such as Kotzebue's (one of whose plays was favoured by the metropolitan Crawfords in Jane Austen's *Mansfield Park*) and of the need of 'gross and violent stimulants' is reminiscent of Jeffrey's remarks. So is his stigmatisation of the metropolitan. 'Gaudy and inane', the phrase Wordsworth applies in the Preface to fashionable literature, might as easily apply to fashionable (metropolitan) dress, and the taste for 'sickly' literature is implicitly criticised in a cancelled revision of 'Louisa', a poem that explicitly contrasts rural vigour with social refinement:

> Though, by a sickly taste betrayed,
> Some might dispraise the lovely maid,
> Why should I fear to say
> That, nymph-like, she is fleet and strong . . .[34]

Later in the nineteenth century there was a more explicit opposition between stagnating or degenerating metropolitan language and the invigorated language of imperial frontiers.[35] That is congruous with the sense of centre and periphery in Wordsworth's critical and poetical practice, though of course in a different context.

But there are important differences between Wordsworth and Jeffrey. Jeffrey manages to argue against *both* 'town-made novels' and 'rustic vulgarity and rude local humour'. He is able to do so by dissociating 'Scotch' from either, as if it existed in a classless literary traditon. Of course it is the purpose of his argument to establish just that and to show where Burns deviated from it by mistakenly choosing English models. Wordsworth had no opportunity of using a dialect with the cultural status of Scots, and a comparison with Burns can only be oblique. Nevertheless Burns's reception by the leading Scots critic of Wordsworth's time does throw into question matters of decorum and the figuring of the central and the provincial. It shows some of the strategies critics used to construct a unitary tradition. Jeffrey politicises the question of taste. Modern readings of Burns tend to suggest the English verse is more socially conventional than the Scottish, more decorous. The different judgements arise, I think, not from our having a more catholic taste (I doubt if that could be proved as a *general* proposition) but from the usual critical trick of selecting the evidence. Wordsworth thought 'Tam O'Shanter' Burns's best poem; Jeffrey rejected it in favour of the patronising sentimentality (and more nearly 'standard' language) of 'The Cotter's Saturday Night' (p. 195).[36] Perhaps there is wilful obscurity here, because Jeffrey told his southern readers they were incapable of understanding Burns's broader Scots poems (p. 186).

If there is some sense of language difference in 'Resolution and Independence', there is also a movement towards unifying, aestheticising and moralising the experience of the narrator. This is a conflict we ought not to argue away. Coleridge's sense of tonal discord in the poem is accurate,[37] but the matter-of-factness he objected to needs reinterpreting in terms of specific social circumstance. The conflict is between the socially specific and the indistinct, figured as the universal. The ability of language to reflect difference is as important as its ability to transcend it.

The poem is peculiarly conscious of sound, as the first stanza shows, and that puts a particular but oblique emphasis on the description of the Leech-gatherer's speech: 'measured phrase'. This is also a useful description of the syntactic shape of the stanzas: stanzas never run on and the lines are regularly end-stopped, often at the expense of syntactic inversions. It is unusual in Wordsworth.

> There was a roaring in the wind all night;
> The rain came heavily and fell in floods;
> But now the sun is rising calm and bright;
> The birds are singing in the distant woods;
> Over his own sweet voice the Stock-dove broods;
> The Jay makes answer as the Magpie chatters;
> And all the air is filled with pleasant noise of waters.

The endstopping might mean that singing, brooding, chattering, making answer – all similar because they are all sounds – are discrete activities not yet unified in the imaginative mind of the narrator. But there are other unusual qualities of the poem: archaic diction occasionally, but more often a simplicity of diction evident in the proportion of monosyllables. It's tempting to say that there is a discrepancy between the elaborate stanza form and the simplicity of diction, thinking of the one as 'literary' and the other as unliterary or ordinary. But that needs refining. It is well known that the stanza form is identical to Chatterton's in 'An Excelente Balade of Charitie', and Chatterton is thematically important. But it can also be thought of as either a Chaucerian rhyme royal with an alexandrine for the last line or a curtailed Spenserian stanza. The latter makes the more interesting comparison, because it had been used by James Beattie in 'The Minstrel', one of Wordsworth's favourite poems and like 'Resolution and Independence' a meditation on poetic vocation. Beattie thought the Spenserian stanza ideally adapted to variety of effect, proposing to be 'droll or pathetic, descriptive or sentimental, tender or satirical, as the humour strikes me'.[38] Burns made rare[39] use of it in 'The Cotter's Saturday Night', the dedicatory stanza of which reflects elaborately on 'the *lowly train* in life's sequestered scene' and has the avowed purpose of dealing with 'lowly' life in a literary way. (The epigraph is from Gray: 'Let not Ambition mock their useful toil . . .'.) The choice of stanza seems to measure the distance between poetic tradition and the subject of the poem, though at the same time Burns writes of the poem as a 'simple Scottish lay'. That seems odd (what is simple about it?), but less so when Burns pinpoints the social distinction between his addressee (his friend Robert Aiken) and the 'cotter' by imagining the one as the other –

> The native feelings strong, the guileless ways,
> What A**** in a *Cottage* would have been;
> Ah! tho' his worth unknown, far happier there I ween!

– and in the last two stanzas links the virtues of the cottager with those of a literary man and a patriot. In this poem simplicity is projected as a guarantee of genuineness and an essential part of the Scottish character: it is a token of national unity, or, more particularly, of Scottish identity as challengingly different from the dominant English culture. That is how Jeffrey read it. Submerging class differences in the interest of national distinctiveness, it brings together literary ambition and celebration of the 'unliterary'.

Behind Burns's and Beattie's use of the Spenserian stanza lies a more famous poem by another Scot: Thomson's 'Castle of Indolence' (to which Lyttleton had favourably compared Beattie's poem).[40] In the 'Advertisement' Thomson commented that 'the manner of Spenser' necessitated 'obsolete words, and simplicity of diction in some of the lines which borders on the ludicrous'.[41] For Thomson, then, there is a congruity, not a discrepancy, between the elaborate stanza and archaism on the one hand and simplicity of diction on the other. In all these poems there is a special consciousness of literary means and ends, expressed as a relationship between difference and directness or simplicity, a peculiar awareness that language both unites (across classes or regions or historical periods) and distinguishes: all in Spenserian and semi-Spenserian poems.

Language difference, configuring strangeness or foreignness, plays an important part in many of the travel poems of Wordsworth's middle and later years, as well as in earlier poems like 'To a Highland Girl', 'The Solitary Reaper' and 'Stepping Westward', all gathered in 1807 as 'Poems Written During a Tour in Scotland'. It is still usual to say that Wordsworth's poems about figures who do not speak 'standard' English – the term is anachronistic, but I shall make use of it – aestheticise them by incorporating their otherness into a unified text of literary English. Donna Landry, in a fascinating study of 'labouring-class women's poetry' in the late eighteenth century, one of many recent discussions of marginalised writers, makes the passing comment that Wordsworth's 'peasants' lack the 'concretely particularized' presence of those in Janet Little's poems. Those of Little's poems she quotes certainly support her view (and readers of Dorothy Wordsworth also note a greater concreteness of description than in the corresponding poems of her brother), but it is not therefore true that Wordsworth 'typically' produced a 'seamless poetic discourse'.[42] Wordsworth's explorations of otherness include con- sciousness of language difference, usually accompanied by otherness of geographical setting and, sometimes, custom. There are constant irruptions of other language in the travel poems. This is not a peripheral matter in Wordsworth's work as a whole. Travel poems of one sort or another make up a large percentage of his poetry, and it is worth noting that for many years his best-selling book was the *Guide to the Lakes*, a book strongly aware of the differences between natives and (metropolitan) picturesque tourists, ending with a devout but complicated wish to restrict tourism in the *national* interest. Travel books formed a large proportion of what was auctioned of Wordsworth's library in 1850.[43] The sense of regional difference abounds in his writing, and language difference is part of it.

Landry's remark endorses a predominant critical view which, following Hartman, finds that Wordsworth typically encounters otherness, is surprised by it, and then converts the strange into the 'universal'.[44] Wordsworth's poetry of *metaphorical* 'voices' – torrent or cuckoo ('a voice, a mystery') – are read as recollected or constructed moments of epiphany in which the mind meets startling evidence of its own powers. His poetry of *human* voices is often read that way too (as Hartman reads 'The Solitary Reaper'), where surface meaning dissolves and voice becomes a phenomenon of pure sound which the mind is free to reinterpret on a grander scale. It is natural that we should welcome imaginative grandeur in the poems and look hard for it,[45] but it is also important to examine the voices of Wordsworth's human figures in a more analytical way, for many of them are concerned with specific linguistic differences between the figures in the poems and between narrator and addressee (including the implied reader): they are concerned, that is, with determinable social relations. We could choose, with Hartman, Jonathan Wordsworth and others, to regard these facts as mere 'background' to visionary moments, the mass of detail, patiently set out, from which vision erupts:[46] a structure that has been seen as characteristic of Wordsworth's 'spots of time' and (one is tempted to add *therefore*) of his poetry in general. Valuable as it may be, this kind of reading is fraught with difficulties, the chief of them being that it suggests no intelligent way of dealing with Wordsworth's unmistakable 'matter-of-factness', or to put it more strongly, his programmatic attention to 'trivial', non-visionary, detail. We lose much, too, by lumping together the figures in the poems as 'Wordsworthian solitaries'.

Recent deconstruction of the Romantic universal into the politically central and stable has reinforced the notion that the 'major' poets of the age (all male) somehow existed in a uniform culture. We have not forgotten that in Wordsworth's time there was 'the Lake School', 'the Satanic School' and 'the Cockney School', but we forget to reinterpret these terms and see their continuing relevance. Both the Lake School and the Cockney School are defined by language use. In both cases history judges the early critics to have been wrong (Keats's archaisms and neologisms were in no sense Cockney; Wordsworth's and Southey's simplicities did not usually reflect the language of the Lake District), but there is a truth in their remarks that needs recovering. For the most antagonistic criticism of Wordsworth, especially that of the 1807 collection *Poems in Two Volumes*, focused on the human figures in the poems, on Wordsworth's attempts to convey their mental processes in a fit language.

A crucial quality of 'The Solitary Reaper' is its *lack* of matter-of-factness, which is, negatively, a matter of language. The language in which the girl sings is *entirely* unknown to the narrator and therefore more easily invested with spiritual, universal significance. There is a moment when the narrator questions the actuality of her song – 'Will no one tell me what she sings?' – but he doesn't stay for an answer, which would inhibit imaginative flights to the 'Arabian sands'. Association with the cuckoo and the nightingale reinforces the girl's solitude: more accurately they *create* meanings for her solitariness, which is, in the first place, a matter of mere surprise. People do not usually reap alone. That oddity (which Dorothy comments on in her 'Recollections' of their Scottish tour in 1803)[47] is converted into strangeness by her singing and to mystery by the unintelligibility of the song.

It is well known that the germ of the poem was a passage from a guide book, echoed in the last two lines:

> Passed by a Female who was reaping alone: she sung in Erse as she bended over her sickle; the sweetest human Voice I ever heard; her strains were tenderly melancholy and felt delicious, long after they were heard no more.[48]

So, in a curious way, the poem *is* a record of an encounter with another language, but the encounter is incomplete because it does not represent the specific otherness of the speaker, only a general otherness: the language of tourism, the literariness that makes otherness familiar. But there are less well-known poems where the encounter is more explicit and vibrates on more nerves, and I would argue that they are more typical of Wordsworth. One of them is 'To a Highland Girl', an obvious companion-piece to 'The Solitary Reaper'.

'To a Highland Girl' presents a conflict between difference and universality that is by no means 'resolved' at the end. It begins with a viewpoint from which the girl, a figure in a landscape, is thought of as the spirit of the place:

> And these grey rocks; that household lawn;
> Those trees, a veil just half withdrawn;
> This fall of water that doth make
> A murmur near the silent lake;
> This little bay, a quiet road
> That holds in shelter thy Abode –
> In truth together do ye seem
> Like something fashioned in a dream

It ends with a memory that magnifies, spiritualises and fixes her for the future:

> For I, methinks, till I grow old,
> As fair before me shall behold,
> As I do now, the cabin small,

The lake, the bay, the waterfall;
And Thee, the Spirit of them all!

But there are other responses, no less interesting. The initial view-point is that of a tourist, a picturesque framing leading to a glimpse of essential beauty. It is replaced in the second stanza by a philosophical and political idealisation of a peasant girl uncorrupted by metropolitan sexual customs, a 'random seed' 'ripening in perfect innocence':

Remote from men, Thou dost not need
The embarrassed look of shy distress,
And maidenly shamefacedness[.]

Philosophy is clearly compounded with desire, a fact more explicit in the third stanza when the narrator acknowledges that he 'would have / Some claim upon thee if [he] could'. He names his desire as the wish to be elder brother or father, but in an unrestrained verbal gesture is content to be 'anything to thee!'. It needs to be said that sexual desire, usually configured as possessive, directive, protective (that is, patriarchal), but sometimes also as companionable, is much more common in Wordsworth's poetry than is usually acknowledged.[49] This passage makes the climax of the poem because it is the sharpest focus on the *presence* of the highland girl: the last stanza retreats into absence in a new focus on memory. We must notice that Wordsworth's poetry doesn't only *re-represent*, though re-representation in memory may seem its chief force: it represents in more immediate ways that are not just preludes to memory.

What has this to do with language? A crucial passage in the second stanza measures the girl's strangeness by the degree to which she shares the narrator's language.

Thou wear'st upon thy forehead clear
The freedom of a Mountaineer:
A face with gladness overspread!
Soft smiles, by human kindness bred!
And seemliness complete, that sways
Thy courtesies, about thee plays;
With no restraint, but such as springs
From quick and eager visitings
Of thoughts that lie beyond the reach
Of thy few words of English speech;

A bondage sweetly brooked, a strife
That gives thy gestures grace and life!
So have I, not unmoved in mind,
Seen birds of tempest-loving kind –
Thus beating up against the wind.

The 'freedom of a Mountaineer' – the philosophical idealisation – is replaced by a 'restraint' which derives ambiguously either from the guessed customs of her own language or from her unfamiliarity with English. Whichever way we read the passage, it is clear that language difference is the site of sexual attraction: the narrator's ignorance of the girl's language and customs allows him to invent an unrestrained life for her and a restriction for himself in case her freedom should threaten. Retreating from the possibility of entering the girl's life, he translates her into a bird 'of tempest-loving kind' – a being designed to cope with opposition naturally, but also wild, unsocialised. It's in this framework of difference and contained desire that he is then able to indulge the fantasy of having 'Some claim upon thee'.[50] Though Wordsworth doesn't use the word 'wild' in this poem, the image of wildness figured in her approaches to and retreats from the narrator's language is reminiscent of the winning but elusive behaviour – including speech – of the children in poems where 'child' rhymes with 'wild'.[51] Language difference is part of the configuration of a childhood/adulthood barrier as well as of sexual and social differences generally: the 'perception of similitude in dissimilitude', Wordsworth wrote in the Preface to Lyrical Ballads, is the source of 'the direction of the sexual appetite' and 'the life of our ordinary conversation'.[52]

This is more than a picturesque or a universalising view of the girl: and the narrator's designs upon her are not all transcendental. And that is the point. There are many ways of figuring differentness, from the desire to stand back and patronise it by calling it universal to the desire to be *of* it by making yourself part of the scene.

I am not suggesting 'To a Highland Girl' is a *better* poem than 'The Solitary Reaper' for these or any other reasons. I put them together to show what is lost when we take one of them as typical and dismiss the complexities of the other; to say something about the *range* of Wordsworth's response to language differences. 'Stepping Westward' presents a direct response to spoken language as a sign both of human presence and, more particularly, of the casual familiarity of well-meaning strangers – a set of particular social circumstances. Like 'The

Solitary Reaper' it ends by discovering a transcendent significance in a trivial event: Wordsworth turns a casual remark into a statement of metaphysical direction, a destiny:

> '*What you are stepping westward?*' – '*Yea.*'
> 'Twould be a wildish destiny,
> If we, who thus together roam
> In a strange Land, and far from home
> Were in this place the guests of Chance . . .
>
> And stepping westward seemed to be
> A kind of *heavenly* destiny.
> The echo of the voice enwrought
> A human sweetness with the thought
> Of travelling through the world that lay
> Before me in my endless way

But the language has a specific register: 'wildish', 'a kind of *heavenly*', 'endless': the progression is not simply from the local to the metaphysical, crossing boundaries into foreign parts, but from colloquialism of diction ('wildish', 'a kind of *heavenly*')[53] to a fully metaphorical expression of metaphysical transcendence of boundaries ('my endless way').

There is a broad contrast between place, which is strange, and voice, which is familiar. *What* is said is familiar (a greeting masquerading as a question, as many greetings do) and so also is its social register. Place, on the other hand, is progressively generalised as 'travelling through the world', reminiscent of the allegory of *The Pilgrim's Progress*. But this opposition needs refining. The greeting is not so much familiar as familiarising, and it has its own kind of strangeness. Unexpected, it is a passport to the unknown (it 'seemed to give me spiritual right / To travel through that region bright'), received first with mild surprise, then with simple pleasure ('I liked the greeting'), as if the speaker is surprised at not being more surprised. This combination of unexpectedness and familiarity is socially interpreted in the headnote Wordsworth regularly printed with the poem, specifying that the women were 'well dressed' and met in 'one of the loneliest parts of that solitary region', not peasants, but women who could address tourists with an easy familiarity and venture on or inspire polite slang.

There is a moment when the phrase 'stepping westward' becomes naturalised in the poem as part of its generalising reflections –

> And stepping westward seem'd to be
> A kind of *heavenly* destiny [–]

but that is followed by a converse movement from abstract qualities to social distinctions:

> The voice was soft, and she who spake
> Was walking by her native Lake:
> The salutation had to me
> The very sound of courtesy[,]

There is a complex relation between the familiar and the strange. The fascinating thing about this poem, compared with 'The Solitary Reaper', is that speech – socially determinable idiom – here stands for the familiar while in the other poem it is a measure of difference.

As a footnote to what I've said above, it is worth noting that in another poem in the group, 'Glen Almain', where language difference – written language this time – forms an important subtext: visiting the supposed site of Ossian's grave, the narrator finds the place tamely inexpressive of the bard and goes on to celebrate Ossian's absence rather than his continued presence:

> A convent, even a hermit's cell,
> Would break the silence of this Dell:
> It is not quiet, it is not ease;
> But something deeper far than these:
> The separation that is here
> Is of the grave . . .

Instead of resurrecting Ossian the poem reburies him in a deeper silence, sceptical of local attempts to commemorate him. It is impossible not to associate the feelings in this poem with Wordsworth's scorn for the *literary* memorial of Ossian in MacPherson's 'translations', which he regarded (wrongly perhaps) as entirely fraudulent, and which he asserted had had no literary influence whatever – a remarkably insular comment, in view of the immense importance of the texts to German writing.[54] Wordsworth imagines a more appropriate place for Ossian's tomb 'Where sights were rough, and sounds were wild, / And everything unreconciled': a place *not* textually unified, but beyond the reach of words.[55]

Dialogues with the dead: conversation and cultural bequest

The idea of a poet *speaking* to others is also a focus for imagining the posterity of poems. All kinds of metaphors are available to poets when they write about the survival of their work: gifts, offerings, monuments, epitaphs; sculptures, songs, dances, pictures; acts of instruction, of pleasing, of seduction, of retaliation; progeny. If anything general can be said about Wordsworth's metaphors for poetry, it is that he avoids a number of common possibilities. There is nothing comparable to Yeats's 'I have no child, I have nothing but a book', nor Jonson's outrageous, paternalist, inversion of the figure when he describes his dead son as 'Ben Jonson his best piece of poetry'. Nor do we find Dylan Thomas's 'sculpted verse' (in spite of Wordsworth's fascination with monumental epitaphs), nor Eliot's vase or dance; nor will Wordsworth's love live ever young in verse, nor will his book fly to his lady. His poetry is song, talk, a breeze, a stream, a voice, a power, occasionally an inscription, though less often than is sometimes thought, and then only a localised inscription, a 'voice' of a particular place. As parts of a structured *oeuvre* the poems are 'cells and oratories' of a cathedral.[56]

What Wordsworth's common metaphors share is reference to aural rather than visual or tactile experience, above all the aural experience of language, actual or metaphorical. Much has been written about his metaphoric languages ('the speaking face of nature'), but there remains much to be said about his actual languages, especially when they contrast with each other in particular poems. Cultural transmission is often imagined as a battle-ground where different kinds of voice compete, especially in poems about the posterity of experience – as if competing *synchronic* voices might stand for an imagined dialogue with posterity. Wordsworth became notorious for asserting that posterity would judge him more truly (and value him more highly) than his contemporaries, but this essentially Romantic attitude (most tragically symbolised in the figure of Friedrich Hölderlin, Wordsworth's exact contemporary) dismisses the complex communicative strategies of his poems about cultural transmission and bequest.

Speaking to the dead

Think you, 'mid all this mighty sum
Of things forever speaking,
That nothing of itself will come,
But we must still be seeking?

'Expostulation and Reply' does not itemise the things that speak, but they are clearly aspects of 'mother earth' (as 'William's' antagonist puts it, in a highly structured phrase that Wordsworth never uses elsewhere). These, rather than books, are his reading matter. Is this merely the familiar nature *versus* books theme which some critics think a tiresome Wordsworthianism? I don't think so. Though nature is sometimes metaphorically a book in Wordsworth's work, it more often speaks or has 'a speaking face' (a curious double metaphor, in which the appearance of nature is likened to a face which 'speaks' – communicates – through its appearance). Here books are specifically associated with sight only ('that light bequeathed / To beings else forlorn and blind'), while 'things forever speaking' address, metaphorically, the eye, the ear and the sense of touch. The poem is anti-text (always, of course, a paradox in a text), but it is also against over-reliance on sight. The metaphor of speaking and, implicitly, of hearing argues for diversity of experience. It is developed in a nice play on the word 'conversing' in the last stanza, where the word suggests not only spoken conversation but the older sense of 'consorting or having dealings with . . . intercourse, society, intimacy'.[57]

Appropriate to the broad, dialectical way in which the poem works, both Matthew's and William's positions are robustly stated, and each – not just William's, as is sometimes implied – has its ironies. If books are 'that light bequeathed / To beings else forlorn and blind', then sight is impossible without them, which makes one ask how the first book came to be written (Matthew doesn't sound like a revelationist). Again, Matthew describes William as looking around 'mother earth'

As if you were her first-born birth,
And none had lived before you[;]

ironically suggesting Adam, with whom we traditionally associate speaking, naming, *originating* meaning, when in fact William claims only to be *hearing*. Taunting William with the image of Adam,

Matthew reveals the framework of his own ideas: rational and utilitarian of course, but also wedded to a literary culture which regards books as an indispensable bequest of previous generations. Without books there is no light. That image contrasts strongly with images of cultural bequest elsewhere in Wordsworth: in 'A Poet's Epitaph', for example, which raises more issues than those in the companion-piece, 'The Tables Turned'.

At first sight 'A Poet's Epitaph' is an odd version of the *siste viator* genre: a message from the dead claiming the attention of the living. Rather than appealing to the traveller as 'man' in general, as epitaphs usually do, it questions his allegiances in particular figures. It is curious, too, because most of the imagined figures are warned off. Epitaphs generally *invite* the attention of the inattentive passer-by or even a series of distinct passers-by (as Burns's 'A Bard's Epitaph' does); in Wordsworth's time they invite, more precisely, moral reflection from a traveller imagined to be motivated by antiquarian curiosity or a search for the picturesque. This poem does the opposite, sending away a host of figures in satiric portraits, reserving for the 'Moralist' its most baleful expressions:

> – A Moralist perchance appears;
> Led, Heaven knows how! to this poor sod:
> And He has neither eyes nor ears;
> Himself his world, and his own God;

> One to whose smooth-rubbed soul can cling
> No form nor feeling great or small,
> A reasoning, self-sufficing thing,
> An intellectual All in All!

> Shut close the door! press down the latch:
> Sleep in thy intellectual crust,
> Nor lose ten tickings of thy watch,
> Near this unprofitable dust.

As elsewhere, Wordsworth criticises moralising by figuring it as a calculating process; yet the poem moralises strongly in its own way, defined by the particular fiction it adopts. In spite of the title, it is the *visitor* 'clad in homely russet brown', not the poet, who is characterised by his feelings, intuitions and 'music'. If we assume that 'this grave' is a poet's – it is only implied in the title – then the poem works by imagining a live poet meeting a dead one.

The moral imperative in the poem is appropriate to the fiction:

> And you must love him, ere to you
> He will seem worthy of your love.

The idea that moral and social judgement must come *after* affectionate knowledge – a lesson for the 'Moralist' – is conveyed through the fiction of strangers ('Who is he? . . .') meeting, strangers predisposed to sympathy. That predisposition is isolated at the moment of meeting. The living and the dead meet *as if* they were alive. The fiction also develops the implications of the first and subsequent stanzas.

> Art thou a Statesman, in the van
> Of public business trained and bred,
> – First learn to love one living man;
> *Then* may'st thou think upon the dead.

The 'Statesman' (later revised to 'Statist', perhaps to avoid the Cumbrian meaning of 'statesman' Wordsworth defined in his letter to Charles Fox), meaning politicians and others, academics included, trained to think in political terms, is warned not to appropriate the dead, as part of history, as exemplary figures, illustrations, sacred names or damned, as something other than individual persons: as if death were the end of the story and cue for a sermon or an explanation. So the poem evaluates through a determinate fiction the common assumption that the dead are public property, as living individuals are not. The tradition of generalising over gravestones is invoked (Gray springs to mind, but so does Wordsworth's own 'Lines left upon a Seat, in a Yew-Tree') but also examined, particularised and found wanting.[58]

That is the side of the poem that criticises conventions (far more interesting than is usually claimed: Lamb set a fashion for regarding the early stanzas as mere 'vulgar satire').[59] The constructive side is an idea of communication between the dead and the living which can replace the text-based idea of bequest of 'Matthew' in 'Expostulation and Reply'.

General reflection on politicians' and moralists' use of the dead includes specific reflection on a poet's posterity. Dead poets are known by works *or* reputations. In the terms this poem offers, works are equated with intrinsic worth, and reputation with 'public business' (fame) and utilitarian calculations of value: 'Nor lose ten tickings of thy watch.' The meeting of individuals, as opposed to moralising or speaking politically, becomes the model for a reader–writer relationship. What does it mean?

In part, it means addressing the public, the reading public, as if it were a collection of individuals. Wordsworth's later fictions of communication take into account the knowledge that serious poetry readers were mostly addressed as a class – the class that read the new organs of opinion, the *Edinburgh* and the *Quarterly*. For the moment, though, he made use of an association, common in his poetry of 1799–1802, between individuals meeting and the domestic milieu.

> – Come hither in thy hour of strength,
> Come, weak as is a breaking wave!
> Here stretch thy body at full length;
> Or build thy house upon this grave. –

(Only the 1800 edition, the first published, has the dash at the end,[60] dividing the last stanza completely to indicate either a resolved point of view – an *envoi* – or, on the contrary, an invitation to the reader to complete the poem himself or herself.) The stranger is welcomed in gestures that imply intimacy and rest, or, alternatively, intimacy and work: building upon a grave is a startling image of the conjunction of the living and the dead, though it would not startle the girl in 'We are Seven', and suggests, to revert to the topic of readership, that reading is work, sympathetic and constructive work. The Moralist has his own house, inviolate with its door and latch, and his own shell, his 'intellectual crust'. 'Building upon', on the other hand, is an image of trust in another and in the future ('Upon this rock I will build my church'). Yet rest and building, weakness and strength, are not contradictory.

Conversation and cultural bequest (ii): 'Matthew'

Not only dead poets make cultural bequests through imagined conversation. 'Matthew' in the poem of that name (originally 'If Nature, for a favourite Child') is contemplated in death and remembered in life through oddly connected images. After an unsurprisingly solemn opening (the poem is an epitaph) images of his past vitality and conviviality contrast strongly with his present silence:

> Poor Matthew, all his frolics o'er,
> Is silent as a standing pool,
> Far from the chimney's merry roar,
> And murmur of the village school.

But at the heart of remembered life lies another silence and profundity that picks up and modifies the pool image:

> Yet sometimes when the secret cup
> Of still and serious thought went round
> It seemed as if he drank it up,
> He felt with spirit so profound.

Matthew's profundity in life is remembered as part of a convivial experience, a social ritual verging on the sacramental, which modifies the pool image, changing it from an idea of apartness to one of known (and loved) depth. The initial contrasts remain, of course, (interior/exterior; silence/sound), but this final image refocuses silence as part of conviviality and conversation, not their opposite.[61]

Like 'A slumber did my spirit seal', 'If Nature, for a favourite Child' juxtaposes images of life and death that contrast but are also startlingly similar ('She seem'd a thing that could not feel'; 'No motion has she now, no force; / She neither hears nor sees'). And as the 'Lucy' poem has been read ironically, so can this one be: Wordsworth, the argument goes, can imaginatively encompass other humans only in images that suggest death.[62] But we can look at it the other way: the poems bring death into life, as 'We are Seven' does, in this case with the purpose of imagining the transmission of human values (in texts or not, as the case may be) from the dead to the living, in images of convivial conversation and silences.

'Matthew' and 'Lucy' are counterparts, Wordsworth's two chief fictional figures of late 1798 and early 1799, and should be considered together. During his visit to Germany, which increasingly came to be represented as a period of exile (see, for example 'Written in Germany'), Wordsworth imagined a lover and a teacher and learned from both. Lucy, whose death Wordsworth feared in 'Strange fits of passion' and for whom he competed with 'Nature' in 'Three years she grew', is a figure easily and regularly elided into a projection of 'Wordsworth's' own solitude, but there are reasons why we should look further into the way these poems invoke and suppress dialogue. One of the sources of Lucy's mystery is that she is silent. Considering the poems as working through the fiction of a changed relationship, we can say that 'A slumber did my spirit seal' derives much of its power from the fact that the beloved is absent and the narrator's mourning is not answered, even with remembered words. Roland Barthes observed that the lover-as-supplicant will tolerate any response except none at all: without dialogue there is no acknowledgement that the speaker exists.[63] In this poem there is a bewilderment generated by the complete unknownness of the object, which forces the narrator to reflect on the fallibility of language at the best of times – that is, when Lucy was alive. Lucy's silence makes a silence in the speaker, because there is so little to attach feeling to, only 'rocks, and stones, and trees': a collection of objects, and she is another. Hartman described the second stanza as 'tonally unreadable':[64] there is no tone of voice rendering a particular emotion, because the narrator is speaking *to* no one, neither to Lucy nor, formally, to any 'extra-textual' addressee. The poem exists in solitude, lacking the double consciousness – private *and* public – of epitaphs, which make private things public.

Lucy's silence is even more striking in poems in which she is more visually present: 'Three years she grew' and 'Strange fits of passion'. Formally 'Three years' consists almost entirely of speech, but speech of a peculiar order: the speech of 'Nature'. The speaking voice is disembodied, inhuman and not located in time and place. 'Nature' begins to speak when Lucy is three years old, and by the end of the poem Lucy is dead, but it is not clear how the two acts are related, nor do we know what time has elapsed between Nature's speech and the present moment of the poem. An abrupt transition to the voice of the narrator in the last stanza provides no certain narrative information:

> Thus Nature spake – The work was done –
> How soon my Lucy's race was run!
> She died . . .

'The work was done' suggests Nature's plan was carried out, but how does this relate to her death? What connection is there between the acts (separated here by logically opaque dashes): done; run; died? Each verb suggests ending or closure, but the narrative remains unenclosed by causal or even sequential clarity.

Narrative disorientation, I would argue, is only one aspect, though perhaps the most immediate, of the narrator's being literally at a loss for words. Nature's voice, predicting Lucy's life, has become a *fiat* enclosing it, not part of a dialogue. Uneasiness arises from the uncanny fiction of the poem, a *personal* relation between Nature and Lucy which excludes the narrator. Wordsworth does not elsewhere personify nature in this way: a dominant figure; benevolent and protective, but physically and morally prescriptive and possessive:

> And vital feelings of delight
> Shall rear her form to stately height,
> Her virgin bosom swell,
> Such thoughts to Lucy I will give
> While she and I together live
> Here in this happy dell.

It is hard to resist the idea of sensual appreciation here, but equally hard to say so without risking reductiveness. These are, at least, the words of a lover who is in some sense the narrator's competitor for Lucy's companionship. What matters in the poem is that Nature's version or vision of Lucy is the only one we have. The narrator's counterclaim—

> How soon *my* Lucy's race was run!

— is pathetically insubstantial in comparison: he simply has no opportunity to put his case, to give an alternative version of Lucy which would enshrine his recollections.

Hartman's readings of these poems[65] emphasise solitary voices that are embodiments of the speaker's own 'nature-buried past', and that they often represent the 'spirit of poetry'. These have been influential readings, and rightly so, but I am suggesting we look at the poems as texts that *define* solitude by the absence, truncation or opacity of dialogue. No one would dispute that voice, sound and speech are predominant themes in Wordsworth's poetry and that they are invested with a range of meanings. I question in what ways it is appropriate to consider them as expressions of solitude or individuality, for two reasons. Wordsworth's own discussion of speech as a model for poetry takes into account the fact that speech implies an auditor, and that corresponds with commonsense views about all kinds of writing *except* poetry (you can 'write for yourself', as many authors claim to do, but to talk aloud to yourself is popularly taken as a sign of madness, though we talk to ourselves silently all the time).

Furthermore, there are arguments against the supposition that 'the monologic utterance . . . [is] the ultimate reality and the point of departure for all thinking about language'. I paraphrase and quote Volosinov's criticism of what he takes to be a central assumption of Romanticism, and follow his view that consciousness exists only in the realm of the sign (in languages of various kinds) and therefore already includes the social. 'The *word is oriented towards an addressee* . . . There can be no such thing as an abstract addressee, a man unto himself, so to speak. With such a person we would indeed have no language in common, literally and figuratively.'[66] Volosinov's theory interestingly turns some common Romantic assumptions on their heads: that consciousness is individual *before* it is social, and that language accommodates itself to our inner world. Both these views, he argues, are diametrically opposite to experience: language *is* social before it is solitary, and our inner world accommodates itself to the potentialities of language.[67] It is easy to find late-Romantic arguments that the solitary precedes the social – Eliot's 'overheard' voice;[68] Yeats's early conviction that 'things are wise before they become foolish, and secret before they cry out in the market-place'[69] – so easy to see why an early twentieth-century Marxist should attack that view. I suspect that since Wordsworth never had the European following of Byron or Scott or Shelley, earlier theorists of Romanticism did not take him into account. That is speculation, but there is a useful congruency between the social aspect of Wordsworth's preoccupations with language and more recent anti-monologic theories.

Wordsworth in any case provides his own contrasts. 'The Matthew Poems' is a phrase as prevalent in discussions of Wordsworth as 'the Lucy poems', yet the former have never had quite the prominence of the latter. One reason for looking at them here is that they are overt dialogues of various kinds and contrast, with deep similarities, with the explicit solitudes and implicit dialogues of the other group. They are concerned with cultural transmission through a pupil–teacher relationship, or that between father and son or friend and friend. All start with the assumption that dialogue is possible, explore various kinds of dialogue, and reflect on them in ways which do not always contradict the sad conclusion – the sense of loss – of the Lucy poems.

Cultural bequest, to return to the term I used above, is prominent in 'The Fountain'; it leads into the heart of the dialogue that makes up the poem. This is the only poem to which Wordsworth attached the subtitle 'a conversation'. We are apt to generalise from Coleridge's subtitle to 'The Nightingale' and think of 'conversation poems' as blank verse meditations which are not in fact conversations: they would be better called monodramas, except that that word had already been used by Southey in 1797 for poems in which historical figures – Sappho, Lucretia, and others less well known – address the reader. 'The Fountain' is a real conversation, but a failed one, in which the narrator invites intimacy with 'Matthew' but is refused. And it is poetry or song that the narrator imagines as the meeting-place of minds, where a shared act of reciting or singing will spark off renewed intimacy.

> Now, Matthew, let us try to match
> The water's pleasant tune
> With some old Border-song, or catch
> That suits a summer's noon.
>
> Of the Church-clock and the chimes
> Sing here beneath the shade,
> That half-mad thing of witty rhymes
> Which you last April made!

It is an invitation to assert the continuity of past and present, in terms of historical or cultural time, and of personal time ('last April'), to match the continuity of nature in the figure of the fountain. Matthew picks up the metaphor and turns it on its head, reading into it differences between humankind and nature: distance, self-division and grief. His reading denies, too, the narrator's claim to fix him in a phrase as a 'grey-hair'd Man of glee'. The phrase implies conviviality – a *reputation* for wit – as does, in a different way, the fact that his rhymes are sung about the church clock, a focus of communal consciousness, and both these acts of interpretation are undermined by Matthew's morose, egocentric rejection of the 'many' who love him as not loving him enough. The narrator's two claims – that Matthew partakes of continuity and communal life – come together in his equally egocentric offer to be 'a son to thee' and in the confident 'we' with which the poem opens. After this it is hard to see Matthew's singing his rhymes as a fulfilment of the narrator's offer.

The situation imagined in the poem is that the narrator tries to recreate the moment of composition of the 'rhymes' by insisting he is both companion and successor ('son') to the poet. Repetition, he implies, is the same as invention if the circumstances can be revived.

Matthew denies this, insisting the moment and the individuality are irreplaceable.

The 'Matthew' figure in the poems (including 'Expostulation and Reply') is as Protean as 'Lucy', and it is dangerous to read a lot into the name, but some comparisons and generalisations can be made. The group is augmented by the so-called 'Five Elegies' Stephen Gill published in his recent edition: poems which show Wordsworth experimenting with a balance between grief and celebration.[70] The celebratory qualities of the poems Wordsworth actually published (recollection of life as a pattern against which to measure the silences of death) abound in the unpublished poems too, in images of Matthew (or 'Mathew', as he is sometimes spelled, as in 'Expostulation and Reply') as a teacher whose familiarity with language makes him a focus of communal communication – writing love-letters for the 'ruddy damsels past sixteen' and providing mirth to 'Staid men' who 'quaffed / Such wit as never failed to please'. That patriarchal image surely recalls 'If Nature, for a favourite child'. What the unpublished poems lack is an opportunity for Matthew to deny the interpretive claims the narrator puts upon him. This is a case, not unique, in which Wordsworth was more daring in print than he was in draft.

Of the poems he did chose to publish, Wordsworth regularly (1800, 1805, 1850) printed 'The Fountain' after 'If Nature, for a favourite child' and 'The Two April Mornings' (and sequence was important to him, as I have argued). The last of them imagines the uncomfortable situation when a pupil declares he is the teacher's 'second self', to use a phrase from 'Michael', and the teacher insists on personal differences; when the narrator's companionable familiarity ('That half-mad thing . . . you . . . made') begins to look more like presumption. As an image of cultural transmission achieved by collapsing the distinction between past and present and between reader and friend (or son), the poem searches but finds a negative conclusion. Matthew *does* finally sing his 'witty rhymes', but his has become a solitary voice, contrasting with the narrator's initial invitation to a duet.

It is the fictions that matter, of course, not the conclusions. As a group the poems explore through speech and silence the relationships of friends, of father and son, of teacher and pupil, of the living and the dead, and each becomes a vehicle for reflection on the conditions of poetic communication. The sequence, ending with Matthew's solitary voice and the narrator's silence, suggests a *rite de passage* in which the writer is finally confronted with his own isolation.

Notes and references

1. See, for example, Lars Andersson and Peter Trudgill, *Bad Language* (London, Blackwell, 1990).

2. Nothing in the scrap of direct speech given to the Leech-gatherer suggests specifically dialectal variation, though the first stanza has a specifically northern rhyme ('chatters . . . waters') in the narrator's voice. The same is true of the much longer passages of direct speech in the original manuscript version (J.R. Curtis, ed., *Poems, in Two Volumes, and Other Poems, 1800–1807* [Ithaca, Cornell UP, 1983]). Gene W. Ruoff argues, as part of a larger interpretation, that Wordsworth's 'grave Liver' is a descendent of Burns' 'Unco Guid' (*Wordsworth and Coleridge* [London, Harvester Wheatsheaf, 1989], pp. 131–2).

3. The question 'Shall I ever have a name', inscribed in a notebook of 1798–9, shows how early Wordsworth had such an ambition. It surely suggests nation-wide if not language-wide fame.

4. *The Prelude*, VII, 412ff.

5. The mutations of the phrase are best set out and commented on in *Prose Works*, vol. 1, pp. 173ff.

6. One of the most stimulating recent discussions is Derek Attridge's *Peculiar Language* (London, Methuen, 1988).

7. 'The Music of Poetry' (1942), in *Selected Prose of T.S. Eliot*, ed. F. Kermode (London, Faber, 1975), p. 111.

8. The fact is noted by Tony Crowley in *The Politics of Discourse* (London, Macmillan, 1989), pp. 125ff.

9. As most theories in the eighteenth century did (for example, Condillac's and Rousseau's). See James H. Stam, *Inquiries into the Origin of Language* (New York, Harper and Row, 1976).

10. Herder, *Essay on the Origin of Language* (1772), reprinted in John H. Moran and Alexander Gode (eds) *On the Origin of Language* (Chicago, University of Chicago Press, 1966, repr. 1986), p. 93.

11. The sonnet was published in the *Morning Post* (16.4.1803) just before the resumption of war with France but written during the previous year. 'Resolution and Independence' was written in May–July 1802.

12. On the popularity of such titles, see Morag Shiach, *Discourse on Popular Culture* (Cambridge, Polity, 1989), *passim*.

13. Quotations in this paragraph are from Robert Anderson's preface to his *Poetical Works* (Carlisle, 1820). A list of subscribers is included in the volume.

14. Johnson printed but did not issue Blake's 'The French Revolution'.

15. Moorman, I, pp. 186ff.

16. Advertisement to *Lyrical Ballads*, 1798: 'The majority of the following poems are to be considered as experiments . . . to ascertain how far the language of conversation in the middle and lower classes of society is adapted to the purposes of poetic pleasure' (Gill, p. 591).

17. Thomas Sanderson, *A Companion to the Lakes in Lancashire, Westmoreland and Cumberland* (Carlisle, printed by B. Scott, in the Market-place, 1807), p. 139.

18. *BL*, II, p. 126.

19. Worthsworth later took a moralistic attitude to the poem and unconvincingly projected it on to the boyhood experience the poem recalls (*PW*, IV, p. 447).

20. Bewick's policital radicalism may also be relevant. See *A Memoir of Thomas Bewick Written by Himself* (1862), ed Ian Bain (London, OUP, 1975).

21. The entry 'Relph's Poems' in Wordsworth's MS 'A Library Book . . .' (now in Harvard University library) is interpreted by Chester and Alice Shaver as a reference to the first edition of Relph's poems, *A Miscellany of Poems* (1747), but it may just as well refer to the Bewick volume (Chester L. and Alice C. Shaver, *Wordsworth's Library: A Catalogue* [New York, Garland, 1979], p. 213). The Shavers generally assume references are to first editions unless there is contrary evidence. The entry 'Gay's Fables' may similarly refer to one of Bewick's volumes rather than to the first edition of 1727–38 (Shaver, p. 101).

22 *Gentleman's Magazine* (1791), 520. The letter, signed 'Septentrionalis', is reminiscent of Boucher's biography of Relph (*Poems*, 1798) and notes that Relph's grave is unmarked. We learn from Thomas Sanderson, a fellow Cumbrian, that Boucher subsequently had a stone put on Relph's grave ('Address to Boucher', quoted in an obituary of Boucher in *Gentleman's Magazine* [1804], 593). Boucher, who had been tutor to George Washington's step-son, is best known as the author of *A View of the Causes and Consequences of the American Revolution* (1797).

23. Wordsworth tells an anecdote of Sanderson's death in a letter to Dyce, 20.3.1833 (*Letters*, V, pp. 598–9).

24. Timothy Brennan, 'The National Longing for Form', in Homi Bhabha (ed.), *Nation and Narration* (London, Routledge, 1990), p. 53. The last phrase is quoted by Brennan from Bruce King, *The New English Literatures* (Macmillan, 1980), p. 42.

25. See, for example, John Barrell, *The Political Theory of Painting from Reynolds to Hazlitt* (New Haven and London, Yale UP, 1986). For the specific argument about Reynolds see his 'Sir Joshua Reynolds and the Englishness of English Art', in H. Bhabha (ed.), *Nation and Narration.*

26. *BL*, II, p. 271 (italics added).

27. See below, Chapter 6, for a discussion of Coleridge's use of the word.

28. Barrell, 'Sir Joshua Reynolds and the Englishness of English Art', p. 159.

29. Richard Holmes, *Coleridge, Early Visions* (London, Hodder and Stoughton, 1989), pp. 114–15.

30. Review of R.H. Cromek (ed.), *Reliques of Robert Burns* in *Edinburgh Review*, xiii, Jan. 1809, pp. 249–76; quoted in Donald A. Low (ed.), *Burns: The Critical Heritage* (London, Routledge and Kegan Paul, 1974), pp. 179–80.

31. The doubleness of this attitude is best explored in Robert Crawford's *Devolving English Literature* (Oxford, Clarendon, 1992), Chapters 1 and 2.

32. Both this and the previous quotation appear in part in Wordsworth's 'Letter to a Friend of Robert Burns' (*Prose Works*, III, pp. 126–7).

33. On the politics of this usage of 'slang', see below, Chapter 2.

34. *PW*, II, p. 28.

35. See, for example, Max Müller's *Lectures on the Science of Languages* (1864), p. 49 (quoted by David Trotter, 'Kipling's England', in P. Mallett (ed.), *Kipling Considered* [London, Macmillan, 1989], p. 62).

36. But, as Ruoff argues, Wordsworth's deepest poetic source in Burns may be 'The Vision'. Ruoff, *Wordsworth and Coleridge*, pp. 165ff.

37. *BL*, ch. 22.

38. Letter to Blacklock, 22.9.1796. Quoted in Dyce's 'Memoir of Beattie' prefixed to *The Poetical Works of James Beattie* (Aldine edition [1866]), p. xix.

39. As far as I am aware Burns used this stanza only once elsewhere, in the early 'Stanzas on the Same Occasion [i.e. the prospect of death]'. Burns, *Poems and Songs*, ed. James Kinsley (Oxford, OUP, 1969).

40. Letter to Beattie, 8.3.1771; quoted by Dyce, p. xxxvii.

41. *The Complete Poetical Works of James Thomson*, ed. J. Logie Robertson (Oxford, OUP, 1908), p. 252.

42. Donna Landry, *The Muses of Resistance. Labouring-class Women's Poetry in Britain, 1739–1796* (Cambridge, CUP, 1990), p. 235.

43. Chester L. Shaver and Alice C. Shaver, *Wordsworth's Library: a Catalogue* (New York and London, Garland, 1979).

44. Hartman writes of Wordsworth's 'summoning of voice out of the silence of a nature-buried past' and of Wordsworth's distrust of such voices despite the fact that they are (in Hartman's view) metonyms of the survival of the spirit of poetry. See *The Fate of Reading* (Chicago, University of Chicago Press, 1975), pp. 184ff.

45. See David Pirie, *William Wordsworth, The Poetry of Grandeur and of Tenderness* (London, Methuen, 1982).

46. Jonathan Wordsworth, *William Wordsworth: The Borders of Vision* (Oxford, OUP, 1982), pp. 314ff.

47. Quoted *PW*, II, p. 444.

48. Thomas Wilkinson, *Tours to the British Mountains* (1824), p. 12; quoted Gill, *Wordsworth*, p. 717. Wordsworth had read the manuscript.

49. See Chapter 4 below for further discussion of sexual feeling in Wordsworth.

50. Donna Landry notes that the habit among Scottish women of washing clothes with their feet was met with fascinated disapproval by (male) English commentators. See *The Muses of Resistance* (Cambridge, CUP, 1990), p. 220.

51. See Chapter 4 below.

52. Gill, pp. 610–11. See also Jean Hagstrum's discussion of physicality and sexuality in Wordsworth's poems in *The Romantic Body* (Knoxville, University of Tennessee Press, 1985), pp. 72ff.

53. 'Wildish' is italicised in editions after 1807. It is recorded in the *OED* as early as the seventeenth century, but I assume it (and 'a kind of') still had in Wordsworth's time a colloquial force similar to Lady Catherine de Burgh's 'a prettyish kind of a little wilderness' (*Pride and Prejudice*, ch. 56).

54. Wordsworth's passage on the Ossianic 'translations' in the 'Essay, Supplementary to the Preface' (1815) is as vehemently scornful as anything he wrote. For recent views on the authenticity of MacPherson's texts, see Morag Shiach, *Discourse on Popular Culture*, ch. 4 and references.

55. See further discussion of the travel poems in Chapter 6 below.

56. Wordsworth's 'Essays upon Epitaphs', especially the first of the three (reprinted in 1814 as a note to *The Excursion*), can tempt us to read his views about epitaphs as views about poetry in general, especially when he

writes about the truth of an epitaph as being 'the joint offspring of the worth of the dead and the affections of the living'. But there are reasons for resisting this generalisation: are readers of poetry pilgrims to the poet's tomb? For a different view see D.D. Devlin, *Wordsworth and the Poetry of Epitaphs* (London, Macmillan, 1980) and Frances Ferguson, *Wordsworth: Language as Counter-Spirit* (New Haven and London, Yale UP, 1977).

57. *OED*, s.v. 'conversation', sense 2 (last entry 1770 [Langhorne]).

58. William H. Galperin reads the poem somewhat as I have, but with an emphasis on a deflected narcissism I find alien to its apparent purposes (*Revision and Authority in Wordsworth: The Interpretation of a Career* [Philadelphia, University of Pennsylvania Press, 1989], pp. 102ff).

59. Letter to Wordsworth, January 1801; quoted in Moorman, I, p. 429.

60. A poem unpublished in Wordsworth's lifetime, 'Remembering how thou didst beguile', shares this feature. See Gill, pp. 144–5.

61. Galperin (*Revision and Authority in Wordsworth's Poetry*, pp. 104ff) has a different argument, about Matthew as a surrogate for the speaker.

62. D. Ferry, *Wordsworth and the Limits of Mortality* (Middletown, Ct, Wesleyan UP, 1959).

63. Roland Barthes, *A Lover's Discourse: Fragments*, trans. R. Howard (Harmonsworth, Penguin, 1990).

64. *Saving the Text* (Baltimore, John Hopkins UP, 1981), pp. 147–8.

65. See Geoffrey Hartman, *Wordsworth's Poetry 1787–1814* (New Haven, Yale UP, 1964), pp. 23–5, 157–62.

66. V.N. Volosinov, *Marxism and the Philosophy of Language* [1929, 1930], trans. L. Matejka and I.R. Titunik (New York, Seminar Press, 1973), p. 85.

67. Volosinov, p. 90.

68. T.S. Eliot, 'The Three Voices of Poetry', *Atlantic Monthly*, 193 (1954), pp. 38–44.

69. W.B. Yeats, 'The Symbolism of Poetry', repr. in *Essays and Introductions* (London, Macmillan, 1961), p. 158.

70. Gill, pp. 142–7.

CHAPTER 2

Community

The word 'community' occurs fairly seldom in Wordsworth's poetry, and when it does it usually suggests 'communion' among all humankind, rather than a socially defined group of individuals. Of the major poems only 'Home at Grasmere' has it in the strongly social sense we are now familiar with, and it is a poem about a very restricted community, a community of two, using *spousal* imagery to project the sense of belonging. Still, the sense of community of various sorts is inescapable to readers of Wordsworth, and they need to be defined and put in a historical context.

I use the word as a chapter heading with some hesitation, on two grounds. The first is that what I have in mind are always *imagined* communities (in Benedict Anderson's phrase),[1] and literature can imagine communities in any number of ways. Wordsworth's ways of constructing communities need to be examined for what they include and what they leave out. The second ground is that I do not intend 'community' to mean the opposite of 'society'. In Britain the two terms have been highly politicised, especially since Margaret Thatcher, a recent Conservative Prime Minister, claimed there was no such thing as society and was instrumental in imposing a 'community charge', known to its opponents by the historical term 'poll-tax'. 'Community' was put forward as a more ostensibly friendly notion than 'society', less close etymologically (and therefore politically) to socialism. It is beyond the scope of this book to explore the ironies of a political programme that insists on local feeling while removing the democratic answerability of local councils: I mention the matter merely to get it out of the way. 'Community', like 'society', will bear different meanings. One good reason for using it in a discussion of Wordsworth is to avoid the polarisation of 'individual' and 'society' that often dominates discussion of Romantic writing, and I hope this can be done without misunderstanding. I do not suggest there is a consistent concept of 'community' in Wordsworth, only that the word can isolate moments of tentative generalisation. Discussing the 'Immortality Ode', J.P. Ward argued many years ago that Wordsworth 'expressed very clearly (though he did not see its significance) what nineteenth-century sociologists later realised analytically, that *community* (as opposed to society) is underpinned by kinship, the family, the blood-tie'.[2] This is a valuable observation, even if one disagrees with it, as I do. Wordsworth's treatment of familial relations shows many ambiguities about the relation of blood and 'community' (of various kinds), and I shall be arguing that there are other bases – other than the biological, that is – for such constructs: this is merely one kind of metaphor for community.[3] More broadly, I think there are competing or overlapping notions of community which call into question the whole notion of marginality in Wordsworth's poems. His 'border figures', to use a phrase of Jonathan Wordsworth's,[4] are not simply people excluded from some stable and monolithic 'society'; they can figure, as the Leech-gatherer does, as signs of different kinds of community. So the distinction is important and needs to be explored.

Wordsworth used the word 'commonalty' in memorable contexts, and this is important because it relates his writing to seventeenth-century republican texts such as Milton's *The Readie and Easie Way to Establish a Free Commonwealth*, where it means the 'common people' as opposed to lords and bishops – as in the House of Commons. Yet Wordsworth doesn't use the word in his series of political sonnets of 1802 ('Milton, thou should'st be living at this hour' and 'It is not to be thought of that the flood / Of British freedom' are the best known): such a use would have been anachronistic and possibly incomprehensible. What seems to have happened – I speculate – is that in using the phrase 'joy in widest commonalty spread' in *The Prelude* he was translating Bentham's utilitarian phrase 'the greatest happiness for the greatest number' into a less quantifiable form.[5] 'Happiness' had been politically defined in material, measurable terms, but 'joy' remained more nebulous. If so, he was *perhaps* consciously reverting to seventeenth-century language, as Coleridge often did, in reaction to the infant science of political economy at the end of the eighteenth century.

These political matters of terminology are important, but I shall not be using them as a rigid framework for discussion of the idea and images of community generally in Wordsworth's poems. The poems embody various kinds of belonging that can be called a sense of community, and though all these kinds have political implications, I shall emphasise in the first place the ways in which this sense is constructed in a number of poems and groups; whether through work and labour relations, through the testing of pastoral conventions, through images of church and churchyard as metonyms for communities, through consideration of the way language reflects or contructs communities and through the generation of local legend. Following the concerns of the previous chapter, it is appropriate to begin with a group of poems, 'Poems on the Naming of Places', that directly treat both language and the sense of community and explore their relationships.

'Poems on the Naming of Places'

This important group of poems, written in late 1799 and 1800,[6] gave a new direction to Wordsworth's work that remained dominant in the decades after. They are programmatically private, domestic, and autobiographical; much more so than any poems he had yet published. A particular anxiety about publishing them is evident in the fact that he gave them a separate title page and advertisement in Lyrical Ballads, 1800. The advertisement repays attention:

> By Persons resident in the country and attached to rural objects, many places will be found unnamed or of unknown names, where little Incidents will have occurred, or feelings been experienced, which have given to such places a private and peculiar interest. From a wish to give some sort of record to such Incidents or renew the gratification of such Feelings, Names have been given to Places by the Author and some of his Friends, and the following Poems written in consequence.

A title page and advertisement, by their very nature, make a special claim for our attention to the poems; but the substance of the advertisement is its modesty. It is in the nature of an author's apology for his works; but humility is complemented by an insistence that the reader will find the poems worthy of his attention if only he reads them in the appropriate frame of mind. The reader is invited to become one of a circle of people who feel the 'private and peculiar interest' of the incident or feeling celebrated. The incident or feeling is celebrated in a word – the name given to the place – and more broadly in words: the poem which recounts the act of naming and the incidents leading up to it. The community presented in the poems, which the reader is invited to join, is one which shares a language, and it is the community which gives validity to the language. Wordsworth approaches the idea that meaning is essentially a social phenomenon, that only shared associations give language its strength and veracity. A corollary of this idea (which was discussed by a number of French philosophers of the eighteenth century)[7] is that meanings derived from a particular community may not be valid outside the community. So the experiment of writing poetry from within a small community is an experiment to find a universal language for 'private and peculiar interests' arising from shared experience. These poems combine a sense of community with radical reflections on the validity of language, and they involve distinct interfaces or barriers between the local and the universal, the private and the public. The advertisement is one of them.

The distinctive quality of the poems, taken as a group, is that they are troubled assertions. Typically the speaker assigns to a particular place the name he associates with it, but he does so in the absence of the person whose name is used, without his or her immediate confirmation. He trusts that his verbalisation of shared experience may be accepted by the sharer, but the sharer is silent. The best known of the poems, 'It was an April morning', may be summarised as an example. A solitary ramble in a wooded dell leads to the sight of a cottage, with the suggestion of future domestic happiness in it. It is implied, though, that Emma (Dorothy) – the person with whom the future is envisaged – never visited the place. The speaker nevertheless names the dell after her and entertains the hope that the local shepherds will adopt the name and thereby give it, and the experience that gave rise to it, a universal, public validity. Tension is generated by the juxtaposition of certainty and immediacy in private experience with future contingency. Wordsworth's walk in the dell is characterised by an intense *presentness* in which landscape and feeling merge entirely:

> The spirit of enjoyment and desire,
> And hopes and wishes, from all living things
> Went circling, like a multitude of sounds

The merging of inner and outer is signalled by a reversed metaphor: it is surely the *sounds* that circled, *like* desires, hopes and wishes. There is further internalising when Wordsworth plays on the ambiguity of a preposition:

> Up the brook
> I roam'd in the confusion of my heart,
> Alive to all things and forgetting all.

The 'roaming' is both inner and outer. The very intensity of present experience leads to a conviction of its permanence:

> . . . like some natural produce of the air
> That could not cease to be.

But when he sees the mountain cottage, conviction turns abruptly into mere hope, with the recognition that the experience has been, after all, private:

> I gaz'd and gaz'd, and to myself I said,
> 'Our thoughts at least are ours; and this wild nook,
> My Emma, I will dedicate to thee.'

And though the spot soon became 'my other home', the bestowing of the name is never validated by Emma's presence. This is the first linguistic barrier in the poem, but there is another. He further hopes that the name might have a wider validity, but it looks a remote possibility:

> And, of the Shepherds who have seen me there,
> To whom I sometimes in our idle talk
> Have told this fancy, two or three, perhaps,
> Years after we are gone and in our graves,
> When they have cause to speak of this wild place,
> May call it by the name of EMMA'S DELL.

The hesitant syntax, full of qualifications, contrasts poignantly with the earlier certainty. The contrast points to the general situation of these poems, which is analogous to that of the poet addressing his silent public: naming, placing, defining human experience without knowing that his formulations will have general acceptance. It is because the poems are intensely private in subject matter – domestic and autobiographical – that Wordsworth's anxiety before the public is acute.

The analogy between addressee and reader is most explicit in the poem Wordsworth addressed to his brother John, 'When, to the attractions of the busy world', in which both William and John figure as poets, and each is the other's reader. The community between them is one in which each responds to a particular place through the other's perception of it. John is a metaphorical poet (a 'silent poet') but a literal reader:

> while Thou,
> Muttering the verses which I muttered first
> Among the mountains, through the midnight watch
> Art pacing thoughtfully the vessel's deck
> In some far region . . .

William, the poet in fact, 'reads' John's perceptions metaphorically: John, with

> a watchful heart
> Still couchant, an inevitable ear,
> And an eye practised like a blind man's touch,

has understood nature in discovering a path through the fir-grove which is the central object and shared place of the poem, and William finds the path only after John has defined it. He is then able to 'love the fir-grove with a perfect love'. It is not accidental that the shared object is a path, because a path, a space where

> to and fro
> My feet might move without concern or care,

is the necessary setting for William's meditation; it is a place where composition can occur. Similarly John meditates and 'mutters' William's verses while abstractedly pacing a ship's deck

> In that habitual restlessness of foot
> That haunts the sailor.

The acts of composition and reading or reciting are brought together as physically similar: there is a shared object, a shared activity, a shared sensibility. Wordsworth's reader is able so to share the spirit of his poetry that he (John, the reader) can make a wordless poem of the kind the poet himself would write; succeeding where the poet failed, understanding nature – in the poet's own habitat – by discovering (not imposing) the path and making it known. Wordsworth's immediate audience in this poem is one person only (unlike some of the other poems, such as the one to Dorothy), though its particular impulse – of gratitude, and wonder at a discovered fellowship – is easily generalisable. What is strikingly successful about the poem is its powerful and moving presentation of a three-way communion, between the two men and nature; a sense of separateness overcome, and of secret things made known. The grove had been secluded and therefore inviting (as a refuge from 'sharp season . . . of continual storm'), but had baffled – excluded – the poet, leaving him unable to prize it as he wished; further, John's life, as evoked in the poem, had been a separate solitude from the poet's ('the solitude / Of the vast sea'), and his discovery of the path is never, in fact, confirmed but only surmised. But Wordsworth's 'pleasant conviction' that it is so brings insight into both nature and human nature. As a symbol of communion the path stimulates Wordsworth's visionary faculty in John's absence. Distance, separation, is overcome; but John, the reader, the other poet, the sharer of perceptions, retains his separateness. The final paragraph of the poem is a joyful celebration of the relationship, bringing together vision, poetry, and the two habitats, the grove and the sea:

And there I sit at evening, when the steep
Of Silver-how, and Grasmere's peaceful lake
And one green island, gleam between the stems
Of the dark firs, a visionary scene!
And while I gaze upon the spectacle
Of clouded splendour, on this dream-like sight
Of solemn loveliness, I think on thee,
My Brother, and on all which thou hast lost.
Nor seldom, if I rightly guess, while Thou,
Muttering the verses which I muttered first
Among the mountains, through the midnight watch
Art pacing thoughtfully the vessel's deck
In some far region, here, while o'er my head
At every impulse of the moving breeze,
The fir-grove murmurs with a sea-like sound,
Alone I tread this path; – for aught I know,

> Timing my steps to thine; and, with a store
> Of undistinguishable sympathies,
> Mingling most earnest wishes for the day
> When we, and others whom we love, shall meet
> A second time, in Grasmere's happy vale.

The syntactical arrangement of the last sentence, a lengthy thematic coda similar to that in 'Tintern Abbey', emphasizes the reciprocity of the relationship. A series of sharp juxtapositions (thou/I, 'Among the mountains,/through the midnight watch', 'In some far region,/here, while o'er my head') is contained within the sinuous but nonetheless powerful overall flow of the sentence, which itself is appropriately symbolised by the breeze, which makes the fir-grove 'murmur with a sea-like sound'.

I have suggested an analogy between the addressee of this poem and Wordsworth's putative readership. Clearly it is an *ideal* readership he is here defining, one that understands the spirit in which he composes and can render back its own imaginative perceptions; one which fulfils Wordsworth's requirement that the reader be 'invigorated and inspirited by his leader, in order that he may exert himself; for he cannot proceed in quiescence, he cannot be carried like a dead weight'; a readership which participates in the communication of poetic 'power'. We can say that the analogy works two ways, because the path is, metaphorically, John's 'poem', and Wordsworth puts himself in the place of the reader. There is a danger in persisting with this metaphor that we devalue the act of verbalising, the art of poetry proper (something Wordsworth never took lightly, as we know from his minute revisions of his own poems and minute criticisms of the poems of others). But the poem invites the metaphor by comparing the meditative habits of a poet and a seafarer. In comparing John's perception with his own, and in calling him a 'silent poet', Wordsworth again approaches the concept he outlines in Book XII of *The Prelude* when he wishes that a poem of his might become 'a power like one of nature's'. But this is an ideal only when he is assured of an ideal reader, and in none of the other poems of the group does he have this assurance. The poem is less tentative than the others because of the nature of its reader.

Of the other poems in the group 'To Joanna' most clearly illustrates Wordsworth's conception of his readership. This is partly because it is an epistolary poem, opening with a light-hearted preamble in which Wordsworth explains to Joanna – and to the reader – why the 'trivial' story the poem recounts deserves to be told:

Amid, the smoke of cities did you pass
Your time of early youth, and there you learn'd,
From years of quiet industry, to love
The living Beings by your own fire-side,
With such a strong devotion, that your heart
Is slow to meet the sympathies of them
Who look upon the hills with tenderness,
And make dear friendships with the hills and groves.
Yet we who are transgressors in this kind,
Dwelling retired in our simplicity
Among the woods and fields, we love you well,
Joanna! and I guess, since you have been
So distant from us now for two long years,
That you will gladly listen to discourse
However trivial, if you thence are taught
That they, with whom you once were happy, talk
Familiarly of you and of old times.

These lines emphasize the difference between Joanna's background and the poet's own, but they also introduce, as a gesture of welcome, a familiar, indeed humorous tone which is characteristic of the poem as a whole. Wordsworth consistently exaggerates the strangeness of his ways (he and his circle are 'transgressors') in order to represent them as wild or outlandish, and Joanna's by contrast as reasonable. The particular complex of feelings here is also at the heart of the poem: a respectful recognition of differences combined with a humorously apologetic acknowledgement of his own singularity, and beyond and despite these, a wish to overcome differences through a familiar mode of address. Certainly the narrative content of the poem is strange. Wordsworth tells how he incurred the disapproval of the local vicar by carving Joanna's name on a rock, 'reviving obsolete idolatry . . . like a Runic priest' (again the exaggeration suggests a lumbering, genial humour); he then relates to the vicar the incident which the carving commemorates: the uncanny echoing of Joanna's laughter by the surrounding hills. The word 'uncanny' in fact points to Joanna's response to the sound, which includes fear; but the point of the incident is that it provokes a different response from Wordsworth himself, and yet another from the vicar, and that these different responses symbolise different relations with the particular place and community evoked in the poem. To Joanna not only the incident, but also the place, the community and Wordsworth's association with them is uncanny, weird, slightly threatening; to the vicar – a solid, unimaginative member of the community (like the 'homely priest of Ennerdale' in 'The Brothers') – the echoed laughter is astonishing and amusing; to Wordsworth's imagination it is a powerful manifestation of the spirit of the place. It is just this spirit of the place, the sense of a community evoked in a series of named objects, that causes Joanna's fears. At her laughter the place, which up to this point was merely a scene to be regarded aesthetically, becomes a living community:

> The rock, like something starting from a sleep,
> Took up the lady's voice, and laugh'd again:
> That ancient Woman seated on Helm-crag
> Was ready with her cavern; Hammar-Scar,
> And the tall Steep of Silver-How sent forth
> A noise of laughter; southern Loughrigg heard,
> And Fairfield answer'd with a mountain tone:
> Helvellyn far into the clear blue sky
> Carried the Lady's voice, – old Skiddaw blew
> His speaking trumpet; – back out of the clouds
> Of Glaramara southward came the voice;
> And Kirkstone toss'd it from his misty head.

The peculiar quality of the passage is that it evokes both strangeness and familiarity, through suggested personifications; it is deeply ambivalent, looking forward to Wordsworth's and Joanna's different responses. To Wordsworth the mountains form part of a community because they have human associations and names; just as Wordsworth's own act of naming, the carving of a name on the 'native rock, / Above the Rotha, by the forest side', is an imprinting of human value on nature, a way of making the object familiar, known. Wordsworth implies that his own inscription is of a piece with those already existing in the place ('*reviving* obsolete idolatry') and draws our attention in a footnote to the fact that they are thought to be 'Runic' but are really Roman: since he is evoking a rural community through named objects, he is concerned with suppositions and beliefs rather than facts. (Footnotes referring to local topography or legend abound in the 1800 volume of *Lyrical Ballads* and are rare in the 1798.)

Familiarity of this kind is of course strange to an outsider: it excludes and threatens. It is left to Wordsworth (the figure in the poem) to make a final act of inclusion:

> And, while we both were listening, to my side
> The fair Joanna drew, as if she wish'd
> To shelter from some object of her fear.

This gesture is a correlative of the overall tone of the poem: Wordsworth builds familiarity out of difference by deprecating his own habits and responses in order to reassure Joanna that hers – her fear of the unfamiliar – are entirely reasonable. It is entirely appropriate that he chose to end the poem with this gesture of protection by reversing the natural sequence of events the poem narrates.

The situation and attitudes of the poem have a clear analogy with those of a poet who assumes, and tries to overcome, differences of association and expectation in his readers. It is in fact one of the rare poems in which Wordsworth's apologia for his own preferences is not handled solemnly; yet it is, of course, a serious poem and a moving one. Wordsworth valued it highly, as having (along with 'Nutting') more imagination than anything else he had written. It seems a strange evaluation perhaps (what of 'Tintern Abbey'?), but we may guess that he felt the poem needed defending as one which cost him the great imaginative effort of bringing together his own response to nature and a strongly contrasting one – one which might have been dismissed as altogether unworthy. That he did not so dismiss it, that the poem is full of tenderness and respect, makes it a very touching gift. Like the poem to John, 'To Joanna' is about affections and imagination overcoming differences; but the differences are preserved because he evokes precisely the individual consciousness of the person addressed, the particularities of their emotional and imaginative life. But his own imaginative processes are specifically those of a poet: his 'reading' of John's silent 'poem', and the 'dreams and visionary impulses' touched off by Joanna's laughter. They are poems in which the generally human is not praised at the expense of the specifically poetic, in which the poetic imagination lodges in human community but is not subdued by it.

It is clear from these poems of 1800 that Wordsworth's imagination was 'humanised' well before 'Peele Castle' was written in 1805, not 'housed in a dream, at distance from the kind' but fully integrated into human community. My argument has been that this integration is not merely a matter of theme and philosophy, but of poetic strategy and poetic validity. For Wordsworth the *primary* aim of poetry is communication, and any meditation on subject matter and style inevitably involves imagining a reader. If this is so, we should regard Wordsworth as a poet whose art consists not in his receptivity to 'dreams and visionary impulses' but in his ability to express the relationship between these impulses and the broader concerns of living – those of his own life and those of humankind in general. In saying this I am identifying humankind in general with Wordsworth's readers. The equation is in some sense illusory, but we cannot neglect it because it is one Wordsworth himself made. It was to be tested more and more radically during the years 1800–20 (when he began to be sure that he had an audience), but he clung to it. In 1815 it drove him to make a distinction between 'the public' (the reading public, misled by reviewers) and 'the people', the mass of humanity which had not been miseducated and which therefore might respond to his concerns.

In thinking of Wordsworth's concern with the general, we should not, however, overlook the particular and local character of these poems: they deal with customs, legends, associations which derive their validity not from truth to fact but from their shared, communal nature. (These poems form a gateway to the mass of itinerary poems Wordsworth wrote in the 1820s and 1830s.) Their poetic success depends on the particularity with which they evoke the qualities of people and places. One of the slighter poems of the group, 'To M.H.', is remarkable for the unobtrusive way in which the qualities of a place suggest the qualities of the person. The place described is above all secluded, a 'slip of lawn' with a pool, which can be reached only after walking 'far among the ancient trees'; but it has also the property of sheltering those who find it:

> nor did sun
> Or wind from any quarter ever come
> But as a blessing to this calm recess,
> This glade of water and this one green field.

The language becomes metaphorical through the word 'blessing', suggesting ministration, purpose, as though the place ('made by Nature for herself') has the power to absorb and transmute all external influences. Its calmness and beneficence prompt a fancy of living there:

it is beautiful,
And if a man should plant his cottage near,
Should sleep beneath the shelter of its trees,
And blend its waters with his daily meal,
He would so love it that in his death-hour
Its image would survive among his thoughts[.]

It is a vision not of man domesticating nature, but of nature domesticating man, and this is the basis of the metaphorical application of the description 'To M.H.'. The transition appears abrupt –

Its image would survive among his thoughts,
And, therefore, my sweet MARY, this still nook,
With all its beeches we have named from You

– but when we cast our eyes back over the poem we notice that all the qualities of the place can be applied to the person; so that, for example, the lines

The travellers know it not, and 'twill remain
Unknown to them, but it is beautiful . . .

suggest a retiring nature whose beauty is likely to be overlooked but is none the less worthy for that; perhaps, indeed, worthier. As in the other poems Wordsworth makes a delicate but firm compliment by attending closely to the person addressed.

I shall conclude with the shortest poem of the group, one which commemorates the naming of a mountain after Wordsworth himself. Since it is hardly ever looked at, I shall quote it in full.

There is an Eminence, – of these our hills
The last that parleys with the setting sun.
We can behold it from our Orchard seat,
And, when at evening we pursue our walk
Along the public way, this Cliff, so high
Above us, and so distant in its height,
Is visible, and often seems to send
Its own deep quiet to restore our hearts.
The meteors make of it a favorite haunt:
The star of Jove, so beautiful and large
In the mid heav'ns, is never half so fair

As when he shines above it. 'Tis in truth
The loneliest place we have among the clouds.
And She who dwells with me, whom I have loved
With such communion, that no place on earth
Can ever be a solitude to me,
Hath said, this lonesome Peak shall bear my Name.

It is a solemn poem, though never pompous or coy, which is
something of an achievement given its subject. It is not in fact, or not
directly, a poem of self-praise, but one which celebrates a place and a
relationship. As an expression of domestic love the last four lines
could hardly be excelled in so short a space. Their success depends
largely on Wordsworth's control of tone, which is evident throughout
the poem: the matter-of-fact statement of remarkable things. The
landscape is familiarised, almost domesticated, by Wordsworth's
simple, unsurprised, unostentatious address. In this way he creates, as
in the other poems, a known, familiar scene whose virtue is precisely
its familiarity. In this sense it is the most private and intimate of the
'Poems on the Naming of Places'. But at the same time the objects
and events are extraordinary; their strikingness remains unsuppressed.
There is an ambivalence throughout the poem because it gives value
to both the ordinary and the extraordinary, the domestic and the
cosmic, private affection and public interest. The 'eminence' has the
distinction of being 'the last that parleys with the setting sun' but it is
also a companion in the orchard. Again, it is a public landmark (line
5) yet it seems to single out Wordsworth and his companion for a
special gift of quietness. It is the haunt of meteors and (occasionally)
of Jupiter: these celestial bodies are drawn into the domestic circle of
the poem (partly by the personifications), but they retain their public
significance (Jupiter shines 'in the mid heavens' as well as over the
peak). The ambivalence is summed up in lines 12–13:

'Tis in truth
The loneliest place we have among the clouds.

It is remarkable that he claims a place 'among the clouds' as his own,
but his tone is utterly unostentatious, as though he were merely
exhibiting a remote corner of his garden. (The phrase 'in truth', I
suggest, is to be paraphrased as 'as a matter of fact', and not as
'strangely enough'; though the fact *is* strange.) With these
ambivalences the poem is both a piece of topographical writing –

showing one of the sights of Cumberland to the literary tourist, the reader – and an evocation of harmonious private life within a community of two. It looks both inward and outward. The naming of the Peak after Wordsworth is no mere self-congratulatory flourish. It makes the poem deeply self-reflective, a meditation on the poetic consciousness itself. As the Peak dominates the scene, so Wordsworth's consciousness dominates the poem in its startling power to evoke and control in measured, precise language. And like the Peak, the poetic consciousness has both a private and a public domain. Wordsworth draws strength from communion with Dorothy but also from a sense of public recognition, or at least of the public availability of his symbol. Wordsworth reflects that the 'eminence' of the poetic calling (the pun is a conscious one, I imagine) consists in the poet's *being* a landmark, a man whose language has a public as well as a private validity. Correspondingly Dorothy's naming of the peak is a double gift: a memorial to their relationship and (it is hoped) the bestowal of a permanent name. (Her gift of the name is matched by his gift of the poem: as though the one caused the other; as though Dorothy herself were responsible for the poem.)

This poem differs from the others in the group because the namer and the person after whom the object is named are both within the community, in which language is validated simply by its being shared. It is not, like the others, overtly a poem of invitation and explanation, and correspondingly the barrier between the known community and the unknown is not symbolised by the presence of a stranger. But it is none the less a poem central to Wordsworth's endeavour at this period because the distinction between the known and the unknown, the certainty of private relations and the uncertainty of public acceptance, is located *within* the poetic consciousness. We cannot speak of the inner as if it were self-sufficient and the outer as something merely added. Of course it is true that writers need readers. For Wordsworth, I have been suggesting, a consciousness of his readers, a need to be understood by using 'a selection of the real language of men' (however obscure or inadequate the concept), occurs at the beginning of the creative process, not at the end.

The discussion above reflects a conflict between two conceptions of language. The first is of language as natural, in the sense that it *belongs* to certain places or objects (as names belong to individual objects and places) as if it grew out of landscape. In some cases the connection is evident though not inevitable, the name being the appearance or profile of a place. ('Long Meg' and 'The Old Man of Skiddaw' are examples. They are to my mind nearly as fanciful as the phrase 'the man in the moon'.) The second is the more modern concept, from the early eighteenth century, of language as a human construct and therefore a matter of division and negotiation. This is the concept behind my discussion of the 'Poems on the Naming of Places'. Still, the idea of natural language had a powerful influence on Romantic writers, and in a sense I am arguing that Wordsworth seems to have *wanted* to believe in it, but experience led him in the opposite direction.

The idea of natural language can be related to the myth of Adam's naming the animals in Eden. It provides a powerful image of original language, language that creates meaning out of pure, unmediated correspondence. Given the late eighteenth-century hypothesis that the essence of language, as of any other human construction, can be found in its origin, it is tempting to think of Romantic acts of naming – Wordsworth's naming of places, Blake's naming of states of the soul[8] – as imitations of Adam. Jonathan Bate argues so in an important essay on the 'Poems on the Naming of Places'.[9] But in my view the story of the tower of Babel is an even more powerful underlying myth for Romantic writers. According to Genesis God recognised that having a single language encouraged humankind to aspire to divine knowledge (the aspiration symbolised by the tower), and his punishment was to make humans unintelligible to one another by giving different groups different languages so that they could never again collaborate in such a project. The story proposes linguistic commonalty as the human ideal and difference as the actuality, the fallen state, a condition of negotiation rather than revelation. Wordsworth's awareness of language difference and his construction of language communites can usefully be seen in this context.

For this reason I disagree with Jonathan Bate's linking the 'Poems on the Naming of Places' directly with 'Home at Grasmere', in spite of their supposed contemporaneity.[10] The force of 'Home at Grasmere' is that the 'beloved vale' the poet finds is sacred to him and his sister, and it abounds with spousal and sacral images. The idea of a private domain or lost garden is certainly part of the 'Poems on the Naming of Places' but, as I've argued, by no means the whole. They strain outward rather than inward as 'Home at Grasmere' does: counterparts rather than companions. Outwards in time as well as space: the poems imagine future communities as well as present ones, and there is inevitably a double source of doubt and, by the same token, trust. In 'Emma's Dell' the narrator trusts that his imagined community will include other kinds of people – 'shepherds', not individuated but classed by an economic relation to place – bridging a gap between aesthetic and economic inhabitation; and that the community will persist. Trust is in both 'horizontal' enlargement of the group, taking in more people, and temporal change. In fact one of the remarkable things about Wordsworth's poems is that they repeatedly confront the idea that posterity begins *now* and explore the future often in the very act of remaking the past. They are full of metaphors of growth (*The Prelude*), maturity ('Tintern Abbey'), profitability and profitable exchange ('Tintern Abbey', 'Immortality Ode', 'Peele Castle'), terms that these days suggest another context altogether,[11] a fact one might want to relate to Wordsworth's querulous probings of fame in his letters (a habit he shared with Keats, though he lacked Keats's winning bashfulness).

The 'Poems on the Naming of Places' are crucially important in Wordsworth's *oeuvre* and in Romantic writing generally. They look forward to his later poems about place and legends but, more broadly, they make Wordsworth seem Victorian in his commitment to the local and domestic. Some readers find it hard not to blame Wordsworth for not being whole-heartedly 'Romantic' like Blake or Shelley, whole-heartedly transcendent. It might be more appropriate to think of him as a proto-Victorian in his concern with the relation between poets and society and in his valuing of the local and the domestic.

Aesthetic and economic values: 'Michael'

Wordsworth commended 'Michael' to the attention of his friend Thomas Poole as 'a picture of a man . . . agitated by two of the most powerful affections of the human heart; the parental affection, and the love of property, *landed* property, including the feelings of inheritance, home, and personal and family independence'.[12] Emphasis on inheritance is rare in Wordsworth's writing,[13] but the concept of 'landed property', linking landscape and economic effort, can easily be seen as a development of the idea of aesthetic ownership implicit in the 'Poems of the Naming of Places'. Wordsworth's comment points to the social and political force of the poem.

Yet the most famous act of praise of 'Michael', Matthew Arnold's in his 1879 introduction to a selection of Wordsworth's poems, used it to formulate an aesthetic criterion of naturalness in poetry, a naturalness which was at the same time the 'expressive[ness]' of Wordsworth's poetry at its most characteristic. The line 'And never lifted up a single stone' exhibited, according to Arnold, a kind of non-style (or perhaps meta-style) in which '[i]t might seem that Nature not only gave him the matter for his poem, but wrote his poem for him'.[14] Such poetry owed nothing to language and everything to nature.

On the face of it there is no necessary conflict between these views, because one is broadly about subject matter and the other about style. But recent readings have shown how the poem joins the two in a dialogue or conflict between aesthetic and social matters. Marjorie Levinson's widely influential discussion in *Wordsworth's Great Period Poems* is professedly materialist, asking questions about the precise economic circumstances of Michael's ownership of his 'landed property' (if Michael paid off his mortgage on the land by producing a surplus income, why can't he pay off his new debt in the same way after Luke leaves?) and arguing that Michael falls into the trap of sacrificing his son by putting a price on his life – doing what Abraham in the biblical narrative was prevented from doing. These problems are left unresolved in the poem because Wordsworth is more interested in poetry than in work: the poem has a framing narrative of how the speaker himself learned the story of Michael and why he is passing it on to others

> for the sake
> Of youthful Poets, who among these hills
> Will be my second self when I am gone.

As Michael hopes (but fails) to pass on his land to his son Luke, Wordsworth hopes (and succeeds) in passing his narrative on to readers, potential poets. There are two parallel stories of inheritance, and, in Levinson's view, the poem values aesthetic inheritance more highly than legal inheritance of landed property.

This parallel is important in providing a way of linking economics and aesthetics, but there is a broader and, I think, more precise context available if we look at different kinds of aestheticisation in the poem. In the first place the action has an inevitability which gives it a kind of tragic form, and we can link this with Wordsworth's comment about the poem to Charles James Fox. Writing of 'small independent *proprietors* of land', he argues that ownership of inherited land immeasurably deepens the 'domestic affections' in a way 'inconceivable by those who have only had an opportunity of observing hired labourers, farmers, or the manufacturing Poor':

> Their little tract of land serves as a kind of permanent rallying point for their domestic affections. . . . It is a fountain fitted to the nature of social men.[15]

Wordsworth goes on to say that this 'class of men is rapidly disappearing'. Two things need attention here, first, that he is writing at a moment of perceived social decline, so that Michael's failure to hold on to both land and family symbolises a general problem that needs a political solution: arresting the drift towards towns and factories and controlling the depression of wages and rise in prices. All these factors are mentioned in the letter to Fox. Wordsworth makes tragedy out of a specific historical moment. This raises the question of how effective a political generalisation can be made out of a very particularised section of society: Michael's way of life is important partly *because* it is uncommon. The second point is that there is a blurring of aesthetic and emotional experience in the quoted passage that complicates any simple opposition between the aesthetic and the economic. The same thing happens much more extensively in the poem itself.

The crucial passage is that in which Michael's feelings for the land and for his son become mutually supportive:

> He with his Father daily went, and they
> Were as companions, why should I relate
> That objects which the Shepherd loved before
> Were dearer now? that from the Boy there came
> Feelings and emanations, things that were
> Light to the sun and music to the wind;
> And that the Old Man's heart seemed born again. (207–13)

'Light to the sun': the phrase reminds us of one of Wordsworth's formulations of imaginative awakening in *The Prelude*: 'an auxiliar light / Came from my mind'. Michael invests Luke with the power to waken his (Michael's) imagination, and so Luke becomes the aesthetic property or agent of his father. In this way Michael's experience and values are so inward-looking that he is left vulnerable to any 'outside' influence, which must inevitably disturb what he has emotionally achieved. He has himself created a hard line between inner and outer in the act of internalising Luke's (imagined) experience. It is *this* inevitability, I think, that makes the poem tragic as well as elegiac: Michael's emotional strengths are also his limitations. It is much more concentrated and self-contained than the 'Poems on the Naming of Places' and its companion-piece 'The Brothers', which I shall consider below, nor does it have a dynamic debate about the barrier that divides within from without, as some of Wordsworth's ballads do. Significantly his house is a *symbol* of work for the surrounding community but not a scene of communal economic relations. Harmonious *spousal* relations within the cottage are symbolised by the two spinning wheels, but *to others* 'The Evening Star' as the cottage is named is 'a Public symbol of the life, / The thrifty Pair had lived': a thing *apart* from their neighbours, a landmark seen from afar, not a centre of communal life.

The other kind of aestheticisation (which Levinson and others draw attention to) is Wordsworth's self-reference as a poet who, as it were, grew into the role of poet by hearing such stories as the one he relates: 'Michael' is a poem to make poets out of economists.

> It was the first,
> The earliest of those tales that spake to me
> Of Shepherds, dwellers in the vallies, men
> Whom I already loved, not verily
> For their own sakes, but for the fields and hills
> Where was their occupation and abode.
> And hence this Tale, while yet I was a boy
> Careless of books, yet having felt the power
> Of Nature, by the gentle agency
> Of natural objects led me on to feel
> For passions that were not my own, and think
> At random and imperfectly indeed
> On man; the heart of man and human life. (21–33)

In these lines Wordsworth's speaker uses Michael for his own aesthetic purposes just as Michael uses Luke for his emotional purpose,

'Not verily / For their own sakes'. This supports the view that the poem is about transforming economic actuality into aesthetic values, but we must also give due weight to the sense of inner and outer as it applies in both these fields. Though Michael's imaginative world is closed, as I have argued, the narrator's is not. There is a prior passage of definition and invitation at the beginning of the poem that has to do with generic distinctions and therefore with implicit assumptions about the reading habits of those who bought and read *Lyrical Ballads*; in short, there is a gesture of invitation and warning to the reader that functions to some extent like the 'Advertisement' to the 'Poems on the Naming of Places'.

> If from the public way you turn your steps
> Up the tumultuous brook of Green-head Gill,
> You will suppose that with an upright path
> Your feet must struggle; in such bold ascent
> The pastoral Mountains front you, face to face. (1–5)

The pedestrian (in both senses) progress here imitates contemporary guide books, though it differs from them in using the second person pronoun. The same mode introduces the object to which the story is attached:

> Nor should I have made mention of this Dell
> But for one object which you might pass by,
> Might see and notice not. Beside the brook
> There is a straggling heap of unhewn stones!
> And to that place a story appertains . . . (14–18)

An exaggeration of prosaic description, yet the lines insist on claiming attention by using 'you' rather than referring to the reader/traveller indirectly. Placed immmediately after the subtitle 'A Pastoral Poem' they juxtapose two kinds of writing, pastoral verse newly interpreted as a vision of unalienated labour, and the fashionable mode of the picturesque, descriptions of nature in prose that attempted to reproduce the framing and structuring devices of painting, an aesthetic discourse based on the experience and knowledge of fairly wealthy connoisseurs. These lines seem, in fact, to *take the place* of the serious construction of *within and without* communities that we find in the 'Poems on the Naming of Places'; or rather, that debate is displaced into a more overtly aesthetic framework at the beginning of 'Michael' that makes it at once more prominent and less effective.

Dialogue and community: 'The Brothers'

'The Brothers' is a companion poem to 'Michael' chronologically and to some extent in subject matter, but its different narrative mode and point of origin are important. A striking aspect of it is that the protagonist, Leonard, discovers as a returning Native, that his story has already been told: his life has been turned into (usurped by) a narrative and a moral. It has become the property of the community. Meeting the Priest, whom he gradually realises to be the author of his supposed story, he experiences a loss of heart, induced perhaps by guilt at abandoning his younger brother, that prevents him from asserting his own story. He conceals his identity from the Priest in 'weakness of heart', as he puts it: fearing, perhaps, the Priest's emotional upheaval as well as his own. For the Priest all along emphasises that an individual's history is inscribed in the landscape and in communal memory; the former becomes a metaphor of the latter. There is a perpetual play on inclusion and exclusion, and Leonard, finding his own history included, finds himself excluded. In a sense he brings the discovery upon himself, yielding to the temptation of overhearing how history reports him –

> 'These Boys I hope
> They lov'd this good old Man—' (237–8)

– and after that he is caught in the paradox of being and not being the subject of the tale, which slips beyond his control when the Priest insists on relating the accepted story of his death. Compliance with that fiction puts Leonard in something of the position of Duke Vincentio in *Measure for Measure*, tempted to seek knowledge of himself *incognito*, as though it were an objective or final truth, divorced of social relations. Leonard's disappointment at finding his brother has died is of a different kind from the Duke's, of course, but he too discovers another version of himself, and the comparison at least serves to underline the fallibility of local tradition. Leonard's dilemma is sharpened by the Priest's comments on his response to the half-true story he hears –

> If you weep, Sir,
> To hear a stranger talking about strangers,
> Heaven bless you when you are among your kindred! (232–4)

– for he earns this commendation under the pretence of *not* being among kindred. His present emotion, like the facts of his life in the past, are meaningfully and therefore painfully supplanted.

The dilemma explored in these emotions, the politics of speaking *for* and *from*, has social, economic and political roots that are not identical with those in 'Michael'. Wordsworth has the Priest define the community of the poem in a remarkably centralised way. First, he sets up an ideal of the family as a working unit in the image of the Priest feeding the wool his wife has carded to their daughter at the spinning-wheel. They are contrasted with Leonard's family, the Ewbanks, an uncle and two orphans, which turns out not to be economically successful. The emotional bonds between them are threatened by legal 'bonds' between Walter and a creditor outside the community. In this case, unlike 'Michael', the creditor is not a kinsman who can call on family as well as financial ties, but kinsmen do play a role in the figure of the uncle, who introduces Leonard to a maritime career. As in 'Michael', someone has to go away to earn money and bring it back into the community. Michael's son Luke is not successful, but Leonard is, and the tragedy in this poem is that money is no longer of any use because the community has reformed in his absence and after the death of James. The point, however, is not that Wordsworth idealises a community which turns out not to be economically viable, as Marjorie Levinson argued in the case of 'Michael',[16] but that the community generates its own history, including economic history (there are winners and losers) which, the 'stranger' finds, excludes him. That is made more explicit in the introductory paragraphs about a graveyard in which there are no inscriptions: a circumstance that one wants to think of as meta- phorically equivalent to a graveyard in which the inscriptions are worn into illegibility. It is probably a symbol of poverty, but it seems more odd, more like Borges's library in which books have no authors' names: it means that facts never become written history, not even in the very coded language of epitaphs, and the *sole* vehicle of history is the spoken word – which, in this poem, means the Priest's. (The poem is a very strong counterpart to Wordsworth's interest in epitaphs in the *Essays Upon Epitaphs*.) The Priest's major functions is to correct Leonard's impressions. He does it more than once, and this reinforces his authority. Reading this poem we might want to reverse Foucault's argument that we remember and celebrate authors in order not to be overcome by an unclassifiable chaos of authority.[17] There are social structures in which one person's *speech*, uncontrolled by the written word, has an unchallengable authority. Speech can force people into silence as effectively as writing can. The Priest is offical recorder of values as well as facts.[18] Such a centralised view of community is as remarkable for what it excludes as for what it includes. Most prominently, it excludes 'Tourists' with pencil and paper, who

> look and scribble, scribble on and look,
> Until a man might travel twelve stout miles,
> Or reap and acre of his neighbour's corn.   (8–10)

Insiders, that is, use the land profitably; outsiders attempt to 'read' it aesthetically or in the case of sentimental moralists ('moping son[s] of Idleness') for moral purposes. The fact that the graveyard has no tombstones or inscriptions literally prevents the stranger from reading about the community.

The Priest's metaphors of relationship ('Brother fountains'; 'fellow tales') link landscape and story, reminding us that it is *his* consciousness that, he assumes, controls both. That guardianship, which in the narrative splits the fellowship of two *actual* brothers, who are more divided in death than Leonard's feelings suggest they need be, is the work of an authoritarian narrator, and I would argue that Wordsworth uses the poem to define the limits of a narrator who consciously identifies so intimately with his community that he excludes the possibility of its being rewritten. (Does he forget, too, that his income and social status derive in part at least from an outside, institutional, benefactor, which protects him from the economic failure of the Ewbanks?) Again, it is a quality of the poem that the Priest is able to suggest a large and thriving community ('If he had one, / The lad had twenty homes') although the only family named declines through no fault of its own and provides the focus for the persistent *elegiac* tone. It is that tone, perhaps, that has encouraged readers to understand Wordsworth's letter to Fox about 'Michael' and 'The Brothers' as a political recommendation of the kind of life it depicts, reinforcing the view that Wordsworth wrote with an essentially conservative purpose. Whatever his conscious purpose, the poem offers a stringent critique of authoritarian narrative using the fiction of insiders and outsiders, tellers and listeners, inscribers and readers.

The communal and the oral (i): the ballad debate

I claimed above that the problematic relation between speaking and writing is particularly evident in those of Wordsworth's poems that are concerned with making and defining communities, and that he grappled with the question directly in 'Poems on the Naming of Places'. But it operates less explicitly in many of the better known ballads, through the use of oral locutions, stylistic features that reproduce or imitate oral narration, often in front of an imagined audience that can be called on to agree or disagree, to acknowledge comprehension or incomprehension, to be, at all events, a community of readers in sympathy with the writer. For writers of the Romantic period there was a convenient paradigm in the communities which were supposed to have given rise to ballads, communities in which, according to Scott, the poet, the 'minstrel', was in a mysterious way the 'voice' of the group. The very term 'border ballads' suggests a uniquely close connection between genre and place, text and audience. I believe this myth of a ballad community *is* a myth, a fiction, but we need to understand its origin.

As it happens the question *how* ballads reflect a community was widely debated in the period 1780–1800 and beyond, much of it concerned with the status, even the existence, of the 'minstrel'. The idea that 'traditional' or 'minstrel' ballads are an essentially popular form of culture that nevertheless expresses the values of a whole society is, as Morag Shiach has shown, largely the invention of Romantic poets and editors, especially Scott.[19] Scott projects 'a model of a coherent and integrated culture, supported by simple, earthy, illiterate peasants, which is suddenly under siege'.[20] Scott's ideal society includes class difference but not 'class antagonism', and one culture served for all. Shiach's argument depends mainly on Scott's 'Introductory Remarks on Popular Poetry', written in 1830 and prefixed to a reissue of the third edition of *Minstrelsy of the Scottish Border*, but related ideas are evident in the largely historical 'Introduction' to the first edition of 1802, where Scott claims the social customs and even the language of the Border inhabitants were peculiar to themselves.[21] In the 1830 'Remarks' Scott insists, against Ritson's strictures, that Percy was right in thinking ballads were recited or sung by 'minstrels' who were composers of their own work as well as performers.[22] Such minstrels are to be distinguished from modern 'reciters' and 'transcribers' who degrade and vulgarise 'the rugged sense and spirit of the antique minstrel' ('Remarks', pp. 11–12). Scott associates the antique minstrelsy with an earlier age, tracing its spirit both to the very springs of language and society and to a state of nature: 'Like the natural free gifts of Flora, these poetical garlands can only be successfully sought for where the land is uncultivated; and civilisation and increase of learning are sure to banish them, as the plough of the agriculturalist bears down the mountain daisy' (pp. 23–4).

Those of Scott's views which he adopted from Percy (many of them reaffirmed in John Pinkerton's *Select Scotish Ballads* [1783]), had already been challenged by Ritson in one or other of his essays, and in spite of Ritson's well-earned reputation for pedantry and abusiveness, the debate isolates the issues (and political oppositions) involved in the concept of the minstrel and has important implications for a study of the relation between 'ancient' ballads and modern poetry. Ritson had denied there was such a thing as a 'minstrel' in Percy's sense and that the border minstrels wrote in a language peculiar to their society and geographical area (noting that, in any case, not all border ballads are extant in the same dialect).[23] He had presented a picture of, on the one hand, balladists singing from printed copies of poems written by others, 'smooth and regular, . . . and generally united to a simple but pleasing melody', and on the other, 'minstrel songs . . . without tune, [which] could not be performed, even by themselves [i.e. the minstrels], without the twang of a harp, or the scrape of a fiddle'.[24] Moreover it is not the case, Ritson had argued, that the older the ballad the better – another view of Percy's that Scott embraced.[25]

This last point is in some ways the nub of the matter. Scott emphasised that the minstrel ballads were originally an oral form of art, transmitted orally and therefore inevitably 'likely to be deteriorated . . . by passing through the mouths of many reciters'. The spread of print in the sixteenth century also contributed to the demise of the ancient minstrel.[26] Ritson wanted nothing to do with the mysteries of oral transmission, finding enough difficulty in the more determinate evidence of textual transmission.

Reading Percy, Ritson and Scott is an odd experience, because Scott more or less ignores Ritson in his 1802 'Introduction', and though he considers Ritson's views in the 1830 'Essay' he dismisses them without adducing the kind of detailed historical evidence Ritson's arguments require. It is as if Scott simply suppresses Ritson in the interest of romanticising the minstrel more fully even than Percy, a symptom of his desire to project a coherent and distinct culture. There is a huge historical gap between 1765, the date of Percy's Essay, and 1830, the date of Scott's, but it is as if nothing had happened in between. In fact the period was filled with scholarship, and the best of it was Ritson's. It is tempting to conclude that Ritson's rational doubts were simply buried under the tide of a fashion for the Scottish in which the English compensated the Scots aesthetically for the powers they had removed politically.[27]

Scott takes the nostalgic view that the ballad culture has passed, and he follows Percy's argument that the minstrel's art reflected a peculiarly intimate connection between poet and society. He laments the spread of print as the sign and moment of the passing of such a culture, and for him the minstrel's art necessarily degenerates with the spread of print. It appears that Scott's mythologising of the minstrel developed in the mean time, partly in his narrative persona in *The Lay of the Last Minstrel*, a figure reminiscent of Goethe's sombre *Harfenspieler*:

> An die Türen will ich schleichen,
> Still und sittsam will ich stehn,
> Fromme Hand wird Nahrung reichen,
> Und ich werde weitergehn.
>
> Jeder wird sich glücklich scheinen,
> Wenn mein Bild vor ihm erscheint;
> Eine Träne wird er weinen,
> Und ich weiss nicht, was er weint.

Goethe's minstrel is a figure whom time has made ambivalent: on the one hand speaking for the soul of the audience, and on the other a houseless vagrant who is careless of the auditor's soul; a figure whose loss of social status points silently to a more convivial, more socially coherent, past. Scott's is ancient, a survivor of an earlier age, and though he is a good deal more domestic in his retirement than Goethe's (he lives in a cottage with a 'little garden hedged with green / The cheerful hearth, and lattice clean'), he is also a quintessentially Romantic figure. But both are quite unlike anything in Wordsworth because Wordsworth was not interested in nostalgia. It is important to recognise what Wordsworth would *not* do with his art.

The communal and the oral (ii): 'The Thorn'

In an essay on 'linguistic utopias', Mary Louise Pratt argues that writers on linguistics usually exclude certain common kinds of language use as irrelevant to their concerns, and notes that this practice is gendered, androcentric. Excluded or devalued verbal practices include gossip, anecdote, repetition for phatic purposes (keeping contact), and talking to things that don't know language (objects, animals, babies).[28] It is striking how frequently Wordsworth and his narrators in Lyrical Ballads spend their time gossiping and talking to objects. Coleridge talks to an uncomprehending infant more than once. This is a sign of informality; is it also a sign, as Pratt would argue, of feminisation? The suggestion is useful, especially when we remember that some contemporary critics thought of Wordsworth's linguistic habits in Lyrical Ballads and Poems in Two Volumes (1807) as puerile. The word 'manly', common in Wordsworth's writing, is opposite to both 'feminine' and 'childish', and it may be that critics who used 'puerile' might just as well have said 'feminine'. It seems clear that Wordsworth cultivates the modes of casual conversation, gossip, talking to oneself or to objects, in order to project a sense of lived language, language not authorised for serious debate, and it is probably true that this is one of the main reasons his poems were criticised as feeble or puerile. Many of the most remarkable poems suggest or envisage a consciousness of community precisely because they are made of language that differs from the rational contact assumed by philosophers, the heavier reviewers and (more recently) academics. Reading Lyrical Ballads, one very quickly notices how poetry can reflect kinds of speech act that are common, but for that reason very complex. Although it would be a severe simplification to think of the poems exclusively in terms of speech acts or kinds of conversation,[29] these matters are unavoidable when they are thematised, as they are in, for example, 'The Thorn'.

'The Thorn' consists of a reported dialogue in which numerous other dialogues are implicit, either actual or possible.

> 'But what's the thorn? and what's the pond?
> And what's the hill of moss to her?
> And what's the creeping breeze that comes
> The little pond to stir?'
> I cannot tell: but some will say
> She hanged her baby on the tree,

Some say she drowned it in the pond,
Which is a little step beyond,
But all and each agree,
The little babe was buried there,
Beneath that hill of moss so fair. (210–20)

'Some say': within the framing conversation between questioner and
narrator, the substance of the narrative about Martha Ray is *gossip*,
and Wordsworth is careful to choose a speaker who is tempera-
mentally susceptible to gossip but at the same time sufficiently
distanced from the gossiping community to be both speaker and
hearer. He has no independent access to the facts of the case (though
he has come across Martha Ray on stormy nights) and is prevented by
his sympathy for her and his experience of the beauty and
particularity of the moss, the thorn and the pond, from joining in the
general condemnation. He excludes himself from the community of
'all and each'. His distance from them is measured by the way he
refuses to give a connected account of what has happened (assuming
it *has* happened), refuses, that is, to invent on his own account when
communal invention is so free.

For it is a harsh piece of imagining that condemns Martha for
hanging her new-born infant on a thorn tree or drowning it in a
pond, especially, we might feel, when we are not told that the gossips
much condemned Stephen Hill for jilting Martha. The community is
retributive, partisan and conventional in its apportioning of blame.
The speaker, however, is not part of it (Wordsworth emphasised this
in his Note to the poem: the narrator is a 'retired sea-captain' in
'some village or country town of which he was not a native'),[30]
distinct from the community of which Martha was a part. To them,
the mound, tree and pond are *evidence*, grounds for suspicion; to him,
they are objects of beauty, wonder and terror – so much so that his
questioner asks in vain for a *narrative* explanation.[31] But, as I implied
above, the narrator's refusal to make a narrative represents not just an
obsession with appearances but a critique of communal story-telling
which, by its communal nature, excludes foreign narratives.

It is important to recognise the differences between the captain's
view and the community's, because that is a central fact of
Wordsworth's remodelling of his source narrative, 'Des Pfarrers
Tochter zu Taubenheim'.[32] The German poem uses Gothic imagery to
anticipate and fulfil disaster. Wordsworth takes liberties with suspense

(when *will* the story be told?), and the captain's description of the
natural objects involved in the story turns towards the beautiful, then
the sublime, rather than suggesting mere narrative props. There is a
philosophical element in his fixation, the connection between
superstition and the sublime, which is quite absent from 'Des Pfarrers
Tochter'.

Interest in the narrator's mental processes has loomed large in
critical commentary on the poem, not least, I suppose, because of
Wordsworth's note; on that basis critics have written about the
layering of narrative consciousness in the poem: how the events are
mediated by two levels of narration ('narrator' and interlocutor/
poet).[33] But the mental life of the community is important, in that it
is at a measured distance from Martha Ray's consciouness (as Mary
Jacobus has shown)[34] and also, as I have argued above, from the
narrator's and the interlocutor's. It is in these gaps between narratives
that superstition lodges, and *that* is one of the main concerns of
Wordsworth's poem: the creation of legend out of unwarranted
certainty and imaginative doubt. 'The Thorn' is a reworking of
Ovidian metamorphosis in which Wordsworth imagines both the
frame of mind that generates legend and that which reports and
evaluates it.

The narrative content of 'The Thorn' may seem so simple that
these imposing comparisons are inappropriate. But we can compare
the poem with less sophisticated contemporary texts such as Southey's
'The Witch'. Its story is not unlike Wordsworth's 'Goody Blake and
Harry Gill', but it is told by the Harry Gill figure in conversation with
his son. He catches Margery stealing twigs and accuses her of witchcraft, citing (to his son) their horse's illness. The local curate tries to
persuade both they are being unchristian, but without success. The
supernatural (witchcraft) is evoked through conversation between the
farmer and his son and reported gossip with others. But Southey's
poem lacks the middle layer between the suspicion of the community
and the liberal sensibility of the curate: it lacks a focus of imagination,
the mode of superstition but *not* suspicion. In fact the comparison
isolates the distinctiveness of Wordsworth's poem: it separates
superstition and suspicion as narrative media.

Community and conversation: 'Goody Blake and Harry Gill'

There are various ways of inviting the outsider into a specific locality: one is to speak solemnly about things that seem merely local and *therefore* accidental (as Reynolds insisted that truth is what is natural, and anything odd is not nature and therefore not true: the genetic concept of the 'sport' that, as gardeners know, might be the ancestor of a dominant strain, is not part of Reynolds's discourse)[35] and by solemnity to invest them with seriousness, centrality. Wordsworth did this less often than those who quote the poem on Wilkinson's spade imply. Another way is to exploit familiar and neighbourly language in poems that are not about capital offences like infanticide, as Wordsworth did in 'Goody Blake and Harry Gill'. This poem has also to do with superstition but in a different perspective, the narrator adopting (but not consistently) a tone capable of moralising and cajoling easily but without embarrassment. The bald narrative of the poem emphasises superstition: a relatively wealthy man catches a poor woman in the act of stealing kindling from his hedge, hears her pray to God that he will never be warm and finds the prayer answered. But in the subtitle of the poem ('A true story') and again in a comment in the Preface to *Lyrical Ballads* Wordsworth insists, following his source, Erasmus Darwin's Zoönomia, that superstition must not be dismissed: he argues in the Preface that it is testimony to the power of suggestion. 'It is a fact' that 'the power of the human imagination is sufficient to produce such changes in our physical nature as might appear almost miraculous.'[36] The poem bears this out, as I read it, but it needs to be added that this power functions in a very particular and fairly well-defined community, and that the idea of community is central to the way it is narrated.

Darwin describes the figure corresponding to Harry as being in a state of 'lunacy' after the curse has operated, and though Wordsworth does not say so explicitly, Harry's perpetual mutter, 'Poor Harry Gill is very cold' (not in Darwin), reminds us of the assumed lunacy of Poor Tom in *Lear*. Yet Wordsworth converts the story into something more than the mere psychological curiosity it is in Darwin's account by invoking responses which vary as the poem proceeds and as the narrator addresses distinguishable groups of people. Point of view in the poem moves into and out of a community of Goody Blake's neighbours. There is no formal dialogue between narrator and a more or less communicative local (as in 'The Thorn') or between strangers ('O, what can ail thee, knight-at-arms') but the poem begins abruptly with a question which, though formally implying the voice of an outsider – someone who wants to know – nevertheless expresses excited familiarity in its repetitions and contractions: 'Oh! what's the matter? what's the matter? / What is't that ails young Harry Gill?' The idea that the narrator adopts the view of the neighbourhood is reinforced by his familiarity with Harry ('young') as well as by the use of narrative tags which look generic but which are in fact specifically directed:

> The neighbours tell, and tell you truly . . .

> As every man who knew her says . . .

> And all who see him say, 'tis plain . . .

Narration by overt report of gossip, but the narrator does not distance himself from his sources: on the contrary he shares it and in doing so adds to the 'fact' of the case, which Wordsworth dwells on in the Preface, a projection of the kind of *communal* sensibility that accepts it as true: a bustling, disturbed neighbourhood, distressed and gratified at the same time by a wonder.

Most of the sympathy is for Goody Blake, but there comes to be a shifting sympathy for Harry Gill as well: at the outset worried curiosity; then, when the cause is told, a certain humour not without the moral satisfaction that accompanies gossip –

> Yet still his jaws and teeth they clatter,
> Like a loose casement in the wind

– then, through the reference to *Lear*, sympathy. The two latter dominate at the end in an awkward though typical combination. Possessiveness and by implication acquisitiveness are satirised in a comic figure, and the moral point might have been made there: 'Now think, ye *farmers* all, I pray, / Of Goody Blake and Harry Gill': an admonition addressed to propertied men (whether landowners or tenants), asking for sympathy for the unpropertied. But the passing echo of Poor Tom expresses sympathy for *Harry* and complicates satire with more neighbourly knowledge. A complex point of view does justice to the ways neighbourly responses and judgements are made –

the narrator 'chatters' as much as Harry's teeth – as well as to the specific directions of satire and moral imperative.

The point of this perhaps over-solemn attention to a poem in part comic is to show that it generates distinct meanings for the terms I have used. Words like 'community', 'communal', 'neighbourly', define different kinds of relationship between speaker and hearer or observer and object. These distinctions have social and political significance of a kind familiar to readers of, say, Tony Harrison's 'The School of Eloquence', reflecting on the question whether and how a writer educated away, as it were, from his origins, speaks *of* or (on the other hand) *for* a politically identifiable group or a locality with specific political experience and needs. (Harrison's sequence also, though in different ways, meditates on differences in spoken language.) It is an over-simplification to say that Wordsworth pretends to be one of the community in order to speak for it: that ignores political divisions *within* the community.

It is interesting that Wordsworth relocates the story, moving it from Warwickshire (in Darwin's account) to Dorsetshire, the first rural area he lived in as an adult, where, as he knew from his own experience,

> coals are dear,
> For they come far by wind and tide.

On the other hand the language, unlike Harrison's, in no sense imitates local dialect. In fact the two non-standard words in the poem – 'auld' and 'canty'[37] – are Scottish, 'canty' being fairly common in Burns (e.g. in 'The Twa Dogs'). Why this is so I can only guess: readers would be familiar with Scottish terms and spellings in Burns and in Percy's *Reliques*, and it may be that Scottishness metonymically stood for regionalism generally – just as, even now, certain dialects are understood immediately as regional or peripheral while others are hardly known outside their locality. At all events, the *meaning* of 'canty' in Burns (pleasant, amiable: often associated with sociable chat) is entirely right for the image of Goody Blake sitting on her doorstep in summer, 'as any linnet gay'.

Like many ballads, 'Goody Blake and Harry Gill' is explicit in its invitations to the reader. Here they have a specific social status: we are asked to imagine ourselves neighbours –

> You would have said, if you had met her

– and to accept trivial faults in a neighbourly way:

> And now and then, it must be said,
> When her old bones were cold and chill,
> She left her fire, or left her bed,
> To seek the hedge of Harry Gill.

These things can usefully be thought of in relation to Wordsworth's comments on the poem in the Preface, which combine attention to ballad metre and an explanation of the psychology of reading. He defends the use of metre by constructing an analogy between the experience of reading and that of writing. In 'successful composition' the subject-emotion is accompanied by pleasure; similarly, the 'music of metrical language' gives a 'complex feeling of delight' that tempers in the reader 'the painful feeling which will always be found intermingled with powerful descriptions of the deeper passions'. This passage can be read as a simple ethic of pain and pleasure or a version of the ancient maxim that a poet teaches through pleasing, but Wordsworth goes on to define different pleasures or sources of pleasure in a number of striking phrases and metaphors: 'the sense of difficulty overcome';

> the perception of similitude in dissimilitude. This principle is the great spring of the activity of our minds, and their chief feeder. From this principle the direction of the sexual appetite, and all the passions connected with it, take their origin; it is the life of our ordinary conversation[.][38]

Each of these formulations implies difference, even a barrier, between material and reader which nevertheless increases pleasure when it is overcome. Following Reynolds, Adam Smith and Coleridge, Wordsworth's editors Owen and Smyser interpret the barrier as that which exists always and everywhere between actuality and artistic representation, the difference between imitation and mere copying (assuming the word 'copy' has any meaning when applied to representation).[39] But metaphors of difference have their own specific values, and one of Wordsworth's compares interestingly with Reynolds. Art, says Reynolds, addresses the imagination. Lacking the authenticity of the 'camera obscura', it repays the spectator's effort of attention with pleasure; pleasure is the pimp for its sister, truth ('lena sororis'). Reynolds's sexual metaphor, quoted from Du Fresnoy,[40] is distinctly different from Wordsworth's, which implies no such intermediary between poem and reader, painting and spectator. Truth itself is the object of desire, yet with a difference, a strangeness, that makes it something other than a mere reflection of the self. The sense of difference need not be merely physical as Owen and Smyser suppose,[41] but rather intellectual and emotional.

What has this image to do with 'the life of our ordinary conversation'? That phrase points to different habits of expression (as well as opinions) that nevertheless coexist in a sufficiently shared framework of understanding. Again the image is typical of Wordsworth: in it he speaks of *mutual* understanding that depends on difference; yet it is not difficult to remember or imagine failed conversations. ('We are Seven' records a failed conversation; and so, in a slightly different way, does 'Alice Fell'). Poems like 'Goody Blake' are or contain acts of invitation with the *personal* focus of conversation, where understanding is subject to modification and correction over the narrative span of the poem. Assumptions and prejudices may be exposed, though not necessarily relinquished, but the risk of misunderstanding remains. Wordsworth's model for poetic communication *is* a risky one, but the perception of difference – in the case of ballads like 'Goody Blake', the perception of a particular kind of community or ethos different from the (supposed) reader's own – is crucial to the whole strategy of *Lyrical Ballads*: Wordsworth *foregrounded* in this collection those differences between the reader's ethos and the subject's that had lent charm to Percy's compilations and to MacPherson's, Chatterton's and (yes) Percy's inventions, the charm of the distant or the exotic, a charm that nevertheless survived and must account for much of the popularity of fantasies like Moore's *Lalla Rookh*. (This is distinct from the question of authenticity, which in the 1780s so moved Ritson in his strictures on Percy, and Johnson and others in their response to MacPherson. That has an ironic echo in Wordsworth's scorn of MacPherson in the 1815 'Essay, Supplementary to the Preface'.)

It is not clear whether the argument in the Preface is gender-oriented. The phrase 'the *direction* of the sexual appetite' is ambiguous: is it personal or general? But experience of conversation is often gendered, of course, as Mary Wollstonecraft argued, by differences in familial and educational practices; and Wordsworth's line of female protagonists whose language is reduced to a cry of pain ('The Thorn', 'The Complaint of the Forsaken Indian Woman', 'The Mad Mother',

'Ruth' and 'The Ruined Cottage') suggests his thinking about conversation as a model for poetic communication may have a gendered element. I shall return to this later when considering Wordsworth's literary uses of Dorothy and other female friends.

Community and politics

What I have said about 'Goody Blake and Harry Gill' has a specific political colouring in relation to its period that is perhaps clearer when we look at more overtly radical poems like 'The Last of the Flock'. Charles Burney wrote of it: 'If the author be a wealthy man, he ought not to have suffered this poor peasant to part with the last of his flock'.[42] We can take this as a naive response, if we want, confusing art with life, but it is more fruitful to recognise it as a response to a poem that baffled expectations of 'art' and ran the risk of being read as *reportage*, so bringing Burney's moral considerations into play. And expectations of art were to some extent politically shaped, since conservative critics commonly responded to Wordsworth, as to Keats, by denying their work was poetry and *therefore* feeling free to attack their ideas and allegiances as if they were unmediated. Burney's remark in fact echoes Canning's response in *The Anti-Jacobin* to some of Southey's radical poems of 1793, an episode that lays bare some of the assumptions underlying criticism of *Lyrical Ballads*.

Canning thought he had fixed on a weak point in 'jacobin' poetry when he asked why Southey did not give money to his 'Weary way-wanderer' rather than just expressing sympathy.[43] That is an argument which, as Blake would say, 'depresses art', depresses its power to multiply sympathy and not just publicly exhibit it (as did some popular works of sensibility), and to focus on particular social circumstances. But Canning was too astute merely to make this reductive point, and he used his indisputable literary skills to make Southey ridiculous. His 'The Friends of Humanity and the Knife-Grinder', which begins

> Needy Knife-grinder! whither are you going?
> Rough is the road, your Wheel is out of order,
> Bleak blows the Blast; – your Hat has got a whole in't,
>   So have your Breeches!

and ends

I give thee Sixpence! I will see thee damned first –
Wretch! whom no sense of wrongs can rouse to vengeance –
Sordid, unfeeling, reprobate, degraded,
        Spiritless outcast!

(*Kicks the Knife-grinder, overturns his Wheel, and exit in a transport
of republican enthusiasm and universal philanthropy.*)[44]

parodies two of Southey's poems, 'The Soldier's Wife. Dactylics' and
'The Widow. Sapphics',[45] the former through its first phrase, the latter
through its stanza form. Canning returned to the attack in the fifth
number with another parody aimed at the same two poems:

         The Soldier's Friend. Dactylics
Come, little Drummer Boy, lay down your knapsack here:
I am the Soldier's Friend – here are some Books for you;
Nice clever Books, by TOM PAINE, the Philanthropist.

Here's Half-a-crown for you – here are some Hand bills too
Go to the Barracks, and give all the Soldiers some.
Tell them the Sailors are all in a Mutiny.
[*Exit Drummer Boy, with handbills, and half-a-crown. Manet
Soldier's Friend.*][46]

The fact that these parodies overlap (drawing attention to each
other), and that the first stanza of 'The Soldier's Wife' was originally
printed with quantity marks over the syllables to illustrate faithfulness
to 'the Laws of Latin Prosody' suggest a strong link between literary
pretention and political difference. By emphasising Southey's use of
classical metres Canning in fact implies he is an upstart who lacks the
gentleman's exclusive *right* to learning. His pretention (the argument
goes) challenges both literary decorum and social organisation. The
same point is made in Gillray's cartoon, 'New Morality', which
appeared in *The Anti-Jacobin* accompanying Canning's poem of the
same name: the most prominent of the texts emerging from a
'Cornucopia of Ignorance' are two entitled 'Southey. Sapphics' and
'Coleridge. Dactylics'. In a similar way *Blackwoods* later sneered at
Keats's poetry as 'Cockney'; and Clare's first volume of poetry was
censored by his patron, Lord Radstock, on the grounds of its 'radical
slang'.[47] Canning's argument is of course radically shaped by his own
presuppositions: Jacobinism is not only dangerous, it is dangerous
ignorance and therefore not appropriate to parliamentary gentlemen.

Southey's poems are in fact a gift to the satirist, because they deliberately and solemnly upset literary decorum. Like Wordsworth's 'Idiot Boy', they experiment with the relation between style and subject and therefore leave themselves open to ridicule from readers and critics for whom appropriateness of subject and style – that is, decorum – is the mark of learning and taste. Southey's poems differ from Wordsworth's, however, in their monotonous solemnity and their self-conscious subtitles. Upsetting decorum is itself a common comic and parodic device (Southey's 'Gooseberry-Pie. A Pindaric Ode' is a pleasant example), but the truth is that his Sapphics and Dactylics come close to parodying themselves. Here is Southey's 'The Soldier's Wife. Dactylics'.

> *The Soldier's Wife. Dactylics*
> Weary way-wanderer, languid and sick at heart,
> Travelling painfully over the rugged road,
> Wild-visaged Wanderer! God help thee wretched one!
>
> Sorely thy little one drags by thee bare-footed,
> Cold is the baby that hangs at thy bending back,
> Meagre and livid and screaming for misery.
>
> *Woe-begone mother, half anger, half agony,
> As over thy shoulder thou lookest to hush thy babe,
> Bleakly the blinding snow beats in thy haggard face.
>
> Ne'er will thy husband return from the war again,
> Cold is thy heart and as frozen as Charity!
> Cold are thy children – Now God be thy comforter!
>
> *Bristol*, 1795.

*This Stanza was written by S.T. Coleridge.

The subject was common, and so was the attitude of unremitting sympathy.[48] Clearly it was Southey's display of learning that singled out this poem and its companion-piece.

It is tempting to dismiss Charles Burney's attack on Wordsworth's 'The Last of the Flock' as *merely* second-hand, but it is also inept. Wordsworth had avoided literary pretension by adopting a simple diction, an octosyllabic metre, and a particularly 'naive', almost Blakean, attitude to the subject,[49] which could invite Burney's naive response. But though the poem clearly reflects a specific social ill (a system of poor-relief with a built-in poverty trap), its scope is broadened by the modes of address and self-expression Wordsworth's farmer adopts. It is a confrontation between the main narrator, an impoverished farmer carrying a lamb on the public highway because he cannot afford a more convenient means of conveyance, and a pedestrian by choice, a traveller whom the farmer instinctively addresses as 'Sir' and feels the need to explain himself to: *himself*, not only his situation. In doing so he acknowledges a temptation to 'wicked deeds' and the beginnings of a persecution mania. Poverty leads to unreasonable guilt feelings, and these are a main focus of the poem. But the farmer's way of speaking reveals a degree of demoralisation he is unaware of: repeated, exaggerated and sudden expressions of despair –

> Upon the mountain they did feed;
> They throve, and we at home did thrive.
> – This lusty lamb of all my store
> Is all that is alive:
> And now I care not if we die,
> And perish all of poverty   (35–40)

– suggest a complicity with his fate, a suggestion reinforced by inconsequent jumps from the past to the present, unsignalled by change of tense:

> Sir! 'twas a precious flock to me,
> As dear as my own children be;
> For daily with my growing store
> I loved my children more and more.
> Alas! it was an evil time;
> God cursed me in my sore distress,
> I prayed, yet every day I thought
> I loved my children less;
> And every week, and every day,
> My flock, it seemed to melt away.   (81–90)

The parallel phrases 'Sir! 'twas' and 'Alas! it was', both in the past tense, show the narrative disrupted by a mental paralysis of self-accusation ('I *thought* / I loved my children less') and a nebulous identification of his two 'flocks', his sheep and his children. Repetitions – 'My flock, it seemed to melt away' and the refrain 'For me it was a woeful day' – adapt a ballad technique to emphasise both an inner condition[50] and the fact that the narrator's compulsion to explain is a *social* necessity: he is having to *parade* his poverty (a condition imposed by the poor laws) 'in the broad high-way' and is acutely aware of loss of status.

It will be said that loss of status is trivial compared with loss of income. That doesn't seem to be the point of view of the farmer, whose self-esteem is tied-up with productivity ('And every year increased my store'), visibly measurable. Production of another kind – his ten children – reverts from a symbol of wealth to a symbol of poverty. It may have been in response to Malthus's deprecation of the fecund poor that Wordsworth changed the number to six in the 1800 and all subsequent editions.[51]

Lacking the developed politics of invitation we find in 'The Thorn', 'Goody Blake', 'The Idiot Boy' and 'Simon Lee', this poem nevertheless invites attention to certain social dynamics which broaden and deepen Wordsworth's attack on a system of parish relief and prevent us from resting in the merely generalised sympathy that provided Canning with so easy a target. That Wordsworth was prepared to take aesthetic risks in *analysing* political sympathy is evident in any reading of 'The Old Cumberland Beggar', a poem which has rightly come to be controversial because it tries to turn utililiarian thinking on its head and comes dangerously close to justifying homelessness on aesthetic grounds.

There is a broader political perspective. Canning's eulogy of 'our feelings, our preferences, and our affections, attaching on particular places, manners and institutions, and even on particular portions of the human race' (*The Anti-Jacobin*, 'Prospectus', November 1797),[52] together with his valuation of 'domestic happiness' and 'reciprocal duties' in the same piece, are typical of that conservative thinking which takes the moral high ground by transferring emotions associated with the familiar and the local to the nation and the constitution. Burke's notion that love of one's country is an extension of loyalty to one's own 'platoon' has a similar force, but in this case the metaphoric strategy is more explicit: we could answer, 'yes, but only if the state is seen as having a pyramidic structure like the army', and deny the premise. Canning's expression is less individual and therefore more opaque: its premises vaguer. What is clear is that Canning enunciates a very common link (still in use: perhaps it is not surprising that the family/state metaphor is so beloved of members of parliament, whose own 'locality' is the institution itself), which had a particular force in the years after Godwin had sought to sever the ties between affection and virtues of all kinds, including justice. It is often argued, therefore, that Wordsworth's interest in the local and the familiar is essentially conservative, part of his reaction to Godwinian progressive rationalism. My argument is that Wordsworth's emphasis on the distinctness of different localities is in fact a way of severing a different link, beloved of traditionalists, between the local and the domestic on the one hand and the nationalistic thinking of the anti-jacobins. That is the political aspect of his rhetoric of difference, 'similitude in dissimilitude'. Of course the patterns of nationalist feeling in Wordsworth's poems vary a great deal, and he does on occasion – especially when invasion seemed imminent in 1802 – use strategies similar to Canning's. But in 1797–8 he was attempting, I believe, to rescue the local and the domestic from their blindly nationalistic associations. If this is true, we should no longer accept a simple narrative of his retreating from radicalism in 1794. To speak of the local, particularly the regional, at that time of war could be itself a radical act.

'Home at Grasmere': utopias and dead-ends

There's a strikingly determinant metaphor of community in Book VI of *The Excursion* beyond those I have discussed: simple topographical contours. The fells surrounding the valley are barriers to include and exclude, not as a matter of human negotiation (and therefore politics), but as simple physical limits. In a way this is the most obvious of all metaphors for human community, and it is deeply implicated in that familiar idea of the country village as a homogeneous community with finite limits, an ideal of manageable human life. It is clear that Wordsworth was drawn to this metaphor, both in the *Guide to the Lakes* and in his fascination with Switzerland as a 'mountain republic'.[53] It figures, too, in the appealing set-piece of description that begins Book VIII of *The Prelude* ('What sounds are those, Helvellyn, which are heard / Up to thy summit?'), where a fair, with its multiple points of interest, is given a summary view as it were from the mountain top, looking down on the valley. The visual perpective is chosen to unify human activity, and typically it is the image of a vale that conveys unity, closedness. Many of the Pastor's stories in Books VI and VII of *The Excursion* acknowledge social and political differences, but the framing metaphor (the vale standing for

community) seems to belie difference. There is a very prominent
tension in the poem between sameness and settledness on the one
hand and idiosyncracy and questing on the other.[54] But in relying
heavily on the former the narratives avoid the questions of
community and difference (problems of language) I discussed in the
'Poems on the Naming of Places'.

So it is in 'Home at Grasmere'. In the aesthetic economy of the
Lake District, mountains afford sublimity, valleys familiarity,
domesticity. But the very simplicity of this model is its frailty. It
depends on homogeneity and cohesion so deep that they erase
political consciousness. 'Home at Grasmere' is the most enclosed
poem Wordsworth ever wrote, certainly the text that most extensively
and intensively moves between domestic and transcendental ideals
and, more distinctively, implies that these are compatible, sometimes
identical. The 'beloved Vale' is the dominant image. Topography
becomes a metaphor of a spousal relationship, itself represented as
enclosed and exclusive.

The poem's dominant strategy is to question, adjust and sometimes
obliterate the division between the familiar and the unfamiliar,
between discovery and recognition. 'Home' is made to signify the
object of both acts, and the poem seems to be a short version of the
grand narrative of paradise lost and regained that M.H. Abrams found
in *The Prelude*.[55] But that narrative tells of the journey of a single
individual, and 'Home at Grasmere' makes its discoveries, recognitions
and appropriations on behalf of the speaker *and* a companion, and the
sense of 'home' is therefore more difficult but more resonant.
Corresponding passages in the two poems make the differences clear.

> Now I am free, enfranchised and at large,
> May fix my habitation where I will.
> What dwelling shall receive me, in what vale
> Shall be my harbour, underneath what grove
> Shall I take up my home, and what sweet stream
> Shall with its murmurs lull me to my rest?
> The earth is all before me – with a heart
> Joyous, nor scared at its own liberty,
> I look about, and should the guide I chuse
> Be nothing better than a wandering cloud
> I cannot miss my way.
>
> (*The Prelude*, I, 9–19)

Echoing the end of *Paradise Lost*, where Adam and Eve, expelled from
Eden, walk 'hand in hand' ('The world was all before them, where to
choose / Their place of rest, and providence their guide . . .'),
Wordsworth's lines both invert Milton's image of loss and redemption
and invoke and erase the domestic companionship of Adam and Eve
in contrast with the speaker's embrace of solitude. This is the first of
many celebrations of liberty *as solitude* in the poem, and it is supple-
mented by the claim that the individual is able to 'chuse' his guide,
whereas Milton's 'providence' is given, not chosen. I have argued
above that the Romantic discourse of solitude is masculine; in this
respect it is the more easily assimilated to an essentially masculine
concept of liberty, and in combining the two this passage leaves little
room for a strong sense of 'home'. Here 'home' is something to 'take
up', not to *find*, and it is secondary to the concept of making one's
way.

Perhaps this is natural in a text concerned with setting out rather
than arriving. But my point is that the notion of arrival, finding,
recognising, which is also a curb on liberty as the passage conceives it,
is inescapable in this series of images.

In contrast 'Home at Grasmere' recognises the problems of identity
and ownership implicit in the word:

> On Nature's invitation do I come,
> By Reason sanctioned. Can the choice mislead
> That made the calmest, fairest spot on earth,
> With all its unappropriated good,
> My own; and not mine only, for with me
> Entrenched – say rather, peacefully embowered –
> Under yon Orchard, in yon humble Cot,
> A younger Orphan of a Home extinct,
> The only daughter of my parent dwells.
>   Aye, think on that, my Heart, and cease to stir;
> Pause upon that, and let the breathing frame
> No longer breathe, but all be satisfied. (71–82)[56]

Here the notion of ownership involves recognising others' claims in
the very act of asserting that the place is as yet 'unappropriated'. In
purely legal terms the assertion is dubious, but it is clear that *aesthetic*
ownership is at least equally emphasised. What does this amount to?
Aesthetic ownership or appropriation contrasts with legal appropriation in that it is *in principle* shared; it refers to standards of taste

that are assumed or argued to be common or at least shareable within a class or region. The issue of aesthetic as against legal ownership is central to much modern ecological and (in a different way) conservationist thinking, but the adoption and fashionability of certain landscapes by writers on the picturesque in the eighteenth century had already brought about this distinction. Jonathan Bate reminds us that Izaak Walton preferred imaginative to legal possession on the grounds that the former is liberty without the responsibility either of ownership or of being answerable to an owner.[57]

These issues impinged as strongly in the Lake District as anywhere else in the kingdom. The picturesque discourse of 'stations' – points of view – is a formalisation of aesthetic ownership: something that Wordsworth attempted to counteract in his own *Guide to the Lakes*.[58] In finding (or inventing?) a piece of Cumbria that could represent freedom Wordsworth had to negotiate not only legal ownership but the complex of ideas involved in aesthetic ownership.

But always with Wordsworth choice is a problem when it involves other people. Grasmere is 'my own; and not mine only' in two ways: first, his land is exclusively his own but what he sees from it is someone else's; secondly, Grasmere belongs to his partner as well as to him, his childhood companion, Dorothy. But he does not give her a *voice* in 'Home at Grasmere'. She is part of himself.

There is a shutting down of options in 'Home at Grasmere', a narrowing into assertion that I think unusual in his work. The phrase 'my own; and not mine only' so presses upon us its potential contradiction ('my own / not mine only' [and subliminally 'not mine own']) that it becomes a crux in a poem full of logical tensions. The sequence 'entrenched . . . embowered . . . Home' diminishes and finally obliterates the idea that freedom from other people, other owners, must be solitary. At first they are 'entrenched', implicitly against the outside world (though they are themselves outsiders for the moment); then embowered in a nuptial setting; then they become the resurrected Home.

This is represented as so entire an accomplishment that it is like death, the heart ceasing to stir, the frame ceasing to breathe. It is a release from anxiety and apparently from the problems of identity explored in *The Prelude*, but these do not evaporate. They are transformed into problems of identification and ownership, the self as defined by the place and the companion. This text pushes into the background the question of choice as an expression of individual freedom and desire (which was so perplexing in the first book of *The Prelude*) for after all the speaker is here on 'Nature's invitation'; but the previous paragraphs lay heavy emphasis on the cost of making a choice to settle in the first place, as if the decision to make a home involved choosing to end all further choice.

Notes and references

1. Benedict Anderson, *Imagined Communities: Reflections on the Origins and Spread of Nationalism* (London, Verso, 1983).

2. J.P. Ward, 'Wordsworth and the Sociological Ideal', *Critical Quarterly*, 16 (1974), p. 343.

3. See below, Chapter 4.

4. Jonathan Wordsworth, *William Wordsworth: The Borders of Vision* (Oxford, OUP, 1982).

5. The phrase occurs in Bentham's *Introduction to the Principles of Morals and Legislation* (1789).

6. In the following discussion I exclude the late poem 'Forth from a jutting ridge' (written 1845), which is included as one of the 'Poems on the Naming of Places' in subsequent editions. I include, however, the poem on John Wordsworth ('When, to the attractions of the busy world'), which was not finished in time to be included in *Lyrical Ballads* (1800) along with all the others. It first joined the group in 1815.

7. H. Aarslef, *The Study of Language in England 1780–1860* (Princeton, N.J., Princeton UP, 1967).

8. Robert Essick, *William Blake and the Language of Adam* (Oxford, Clarendon, 1989).

9. Jonathan Bate, 'Wordsworth and the Naming of Places', *Essays in Criticism*, 39 (1989), pp. 196ff; reprinted in modified form in his *Romantic Ecology: Wordsworth and the Environmental Tradition* (London, Routledge, 1991).

10. The evidence is only contextual. See *Home at Grasmere*, ed. Beth Darlington (Ithaca, Cornell UP, 1977), pp. 9ff. I have argued that this is by no means conclusive in a review of Kenneth R. Johnston's *Wordsworth and 'The Recluse'* (New Haven, Yale UP, 1984) in *English*, 34 (1985), pp. 157–63.

11. See Marjorie Levinson's discussion of 'Michael' in *Wordsworth's Great Period Poems* (Cambridge, CUP, 1986).

12. Letter to Poole, 9.4.1801; quoted in Gill, p. 700.

13. See below, Chapter 4.

14. Matthew Arnold, 'Wordsworth' (1879); *Selected Poems and Prose*, ed. Miriam Allott (London, Dent, 1978), pp. 238–9.

15. Letter to Fox, 14.1.1801 (*Letters*, I, pp. 314–15).

16. Levinson, p. 7.

17. Michel Foucault, 'What is an Author?', reprinted in David Lodge, *Modern Criticism and Theory* (London, Longman, 1988), pp. 197ff.

18. It is not clear whether the Priest is imagined as also keeping the *written* parish records, as was the custom before records were centralised in 1838.

19. Morag Shiach, *Discourse on Popular Culture* (Cambridge, Polity, 1989), ch. 4.

20. Shiach, *Discourse on Popular Culture*, p. 115.

21. Scott, *Minstrelsy of the Scottish Border*, ed. T.F. Henderson (Edinburgh, 1902), I, pp. 119, 129.

22. For Ritson's criticism of Percy, see 'Observations on the Ancient Ballads', prefixed to *Ancient Songs and Ballads* (1790; ed. W.C. Hazlitt, 1877), pp. iii, xviff. Scott's reply is in 'Introductory Remarks on Popular Poetry', *Minstrelsy*, I, p. 30f.

23. Ritson, 'Observations on the Ancient English Minstrels', *Ancient Songs and Ballads*, ed. W.C. Hazlitt, p. xxiv.

24. 'Observations', pp. xxviii–xxiv.

25. 'Observations', pp. xxxi–xxxii. For Scott's view see 'Remarks', p. 46.

26. 'Essay on Imitations of the Ancient Ballads' (1830; a continuation of the 'Introductory Remarks on Popular Poetry'), *Minstrelsy*, IV, pp. 4ff.

27. Robert Crawford's *Devolving English Literature* (Oxford, Clarendon, 1992) is a powerful argument for the importance of Scottish writers in the formation of our concept of 'English Literature'. His discussion of Scott (and Burns), however, seems to take too much for granted. See my review in *English*, 42 (1993), pp. 79ff.

28. Mary Louise Pratt, 'Linguistic Utopias', in *The Linguistics of Writing*, ed. Nigel Fabb and others (Manchester UP, 1987), pp. 54–5.

29. Don Bialostosky's reading of the poems along these lines is often very productive and certainly worth reading, but it undervalues generic and rhetorical differences (*Making Tales: The Poetics of Wordsworth's Narrative Experiments* [Chicago, University of Chicago Press, 1984]).

30. Gill, p. 593.

31. This is the speaker Coleridge had in mind when criticising Wordsworth's theory of diction: 'the rustic . . . aims almost solely to convey *insulated facts*, either those of his scanty experience or his traditional belief; while the educated man chiefly seeks to discover and express those *connections* of things, or those relative *bearings* of fact to fact, from which some more or less general law is deducible.' *Biographia Literaria*, II, p. 39.

32. Mary Jacobus gives the text of 'Des Pfarrers Tochter' in *Tradition and Experiment in Wordsworth's Lyrical Ballads 1798* (Oxford, Clarendon, 1976).

33. Jacobus, *Tradition and Experiment*; S.M. Parrish, *The Art of the Lyrical Ballads* (Cambridge, Mass., Harvard UP, 1973).

34. *Tradition and Experiment*, p. 245.

35. See John Barrell, 'Sir Joshua Reynolds and the Englishness of English Art' in H. Bhabha (ed.), *Nation and Narration*, pp. 154ff. Barrell reminds us that 'locality' is one of the 'principal enemies' of 'the civic ideal of art' in the eighteenth century: an ideal challenged, in Barrell's view, by James Barry and others.

36. Gill, pp. 611–12.

37. 'Auld' appears only in the 1798 and 1800 editions, later replaced by 'old'; 'canty' is italicised in those editions, but, again, not in later ones.

38. *Preface* (1800); Gill, pp. 610–11.

39. *Prose Works*, I, p. 184, and the references given. In addition to Reynold's eleventh Discourse, the seventh is relevant.

40. *Discourses* (VII), p. 136.

41. *Prose Works*, I, p. 184.

42. *Monthly Review*, XXIX, June 1799; quoted in Brett and Jones, p. 322.

43. Cited in Butler (ed.), *Burke, Paine, Godwin and the Revolution Controversy* (Cambridge, CUP, 1984), p. 219.

44. *The Anti-Jacobin*, II, November 1797. Reprinted in L. Sanders (ed.), *Selections from the Anti-Jacobin* (London, 1904), pp. 9–11.

45. The first was published in *Poems* (Bath, 1795) but Southey excluded it from his *Poetical Works* (1838); the second appeared in *Poems*, 1797, and is reprinted in *Poetical Works*, II, p. 141.

46. Quoted from Butler (ed.), *Burke, Paine, Godwin and the Revolution Controversy*, p. 219.

47. Mark Storey, *The Poetry of John Clare* (London, Macmillan, 1974), p. 198.

48. R. Mayo, 'The Contemporaneity of the *Lyrical Ballads*', *PMLA*, 69 (1954), pp. 486–522.

49. I'm thinking of the tone of the second 'Holy Thursday' ('Are such things done on Albion's shore?') or of 'The Mental Traveller'.

50. Compare Wordsworth's defence of repetition on the grounds that it is natural in moments of emotional stress (Preface; Gill, p. 594).

51. Malthus's *Essay on the Principle of Population* was published in 1798.

52. Quoted in Butler (ed.) *Burke, Paine, Godwin and the Revolution Controversy*, (Cambridge, CUP, 1984), p. 216.

53. On the *Guide*, see Chapter 5 below. A relationship between mountainous topography and political republicanism in Switzerland is projected in a number of sonnets written in 1809, at the time when Wordsworth was writing his pamphlet 'The Convention of Cintra' (*PW*, III, pp. 128ff).

54. Paul De Man argued that physical idiosyncracy in the form of sensory deprivation (blindness, dumbness, general infirmity) is central to Wordsworth's presentation of the community of the living and the dead in *The Excursion*. This claim serves a broader argument about the relationship between autobiography and self-defacement ('Autobiography as De-Facement', in *The Rhetoric of Romanticism* [New York, Columbia UP, 1984]).

55. M.H. Abrams, *Natural Supernaturalism* (New York, Norton, 1971).

56. Text quoted from the MS D version in *Home at Grasmere*, p. 43.

57. Jonathan Bate, *Romantic Ecology: Wordsworth and the Environmental Tradition* (London, Routledge, 1991), pp. 112–14.

58. The most cogent argument about the difference between Wordsworth's *Guide* and previous handbooks for the picturesque traveller (Gilpin, West) is Hugh Sykes Davies's in *Wordsworth and the Worth of Words* (Cambridge, CUP, 1987), though one need not agree with his premise that Wordsworth's early attraction to the picturesque was essentially Godwinian.

CHAPTER 3

Power

'Power': the word is not a familiar *literary*-critical term with the cachet of 'form', 'tension' or 'ambiguity' – terms which were dominant when readers could take for granted that there *was* a category named 'literary' – but it has come to be used in writing about culture in a broad sense. When Wordsworth wrote about power he was writing substantially about the effect of literature on readers, though he clearly had other meanings in mind. The difficulty of making power the subject of a chapter on Wordsworth is that the word is likely to slide between quite different meanings; the specific literary meanings Wordsworth, De Quincey and Coleridge gave it and the general authority of dominant cultural formations or the authority that the printed text has over the ways we orally shape and reshape our lives – if indeed our oral consciousness can ever be pre-textual.[1] Both are the subject of negotiation between reader and writer. And there is the broader discourse of ideological power concealed in social structures, which is perhaps less open to negotiation than cultural critics sometimes suggest. The emphasis in this chapter is on uses of 'power' that impinge on reader–writer relations, which I believe are central to Wordsworth's aesthetic. But we cannot begin without considering the dominant aesthetic discourse of power in the late eighteenth century, the discourse of the sublime, which necessarily involves a politics of communication, that is a conception of reader–writer relations. There is a vast literature on the sublime,[2] and I shall concentrate on a few specific points that provide access to Wordsworth's own texts, whether in contrast or continuity.

A central question in discussions of the 'high' doctrine of the sublime in the eighteenth century is the relation between power and fear. Burke's *A Philosophical Enquiry into the Origins of Our Ideas of the Sublime and the Beautiful* is the seminal text, and its images and strategies make interesting contrasts with Wordsworth's.[3] For Burke, terror is 'the common stock of everything that is sublime',[4] and power plays a role in inducing terror, as do other qualities like vastness and obscurity. He distinguishes between pleasant and painful manifestations of power and argues that only the latter can be sublime (because they excite terror); and in any case 'the idea of pain, in its highest degree, is much stronger than the highest degree of pleasure'. This leads to, or is based on, a conviction that 'no great efforts of power are necessary' to 'the enjoyment of pleasure' because 'pleasure follows the will. . . . But pain is always inflicted by a power in some way superior' to us. In short, 'power' is equated with power to harm. Our *immediate* response ('before reflection') to human or animal strength is fear, 'lest this enormous strength should be employed for the purpose of rapine and destruction'.

Since Burke's only interest is to analyse the sublime, it is perhaps not surprising that he defines power exclusively in terms of terror. But it is a very obviously determined argument, and it leads him into difficulties when he briefly considers objections. Can power coexist with affection or love? It cannot, because 'love approaches much nearer to contempt than is commonly imagined', and contempt negates fear and therefore power. The example he offers (again a very determined one) is affection between humans and dogs, which coexists with the common use of 'dog' as a term of contempt. It is a harsh argument, and Burke seems aware of the fact: he has particular trouble with the notion of God, which might, he acknowledges, suggest power without terror. In a passage expanded greatly after the first published version of the *Enquiry*, he draws on Old Testament images of God to prove that '*primos in orbe deos facit timor*', though he feels the awkwardness of using this maxim (from Statius) of a Christian God. He is much less troubled in asserting that 'the power which arises from institution in kings and commanders, has the same connection with terror' as the '*natural* power' of wolves, though the juxtaposition of these images might cause uneasiness in more democratically-minded readers.

Another casualty of Burke's argument is imagination. In the passage about God he remarks:

> Now, though in a just [i.e. reasoned] idea of the Deity, perhaps none of his attributes are predominant, yet to our imagination, his power is by far the most striking. Some reflection, some comparing is necessary to satisfy us of his wisdom, his justice, and his goodness; to be struck with his power, it is only necessary that we should open our eyes.

An equally rational conclusion might be that imagination *confers* power on the idea of God, but Burke circumvents this by saying that imagining is simply like opening our eyes – a mechanical reflex. A less attenuated concept of imagination, one involving effort, would turn the argument on its head: the 'rational' view of God would be the surface view; the imaginative view the higher, the deeper, the more difficult. Burke's strict hierarchy of reason and imagination in this passage is of a kind that is radically challenged in *The Prelude*, in *Biographia Literaria* and almost every other Romantic discussion of imagination.

Passages like these show how tactical Burke's arguments and images are, and for that reason they provide points of entry for alternative views. His rhetoric is more daring, therefore more vulnerable, than his tone sometimes suggests. Although his general doctrine of the sublime had great influence on Romantic writing, his conception of the relation of power and the sublime is only partly reflected in Wordsworth's diverse writing on power.[5] Areas of divergence include the following: first, the experience of literature, even sublime literature, is always accompanied by 'an overbalance of pleasure' over pain; that is, there is a framing effect which in the Preface to *Lyrical Ballads* he ascribes to the power of metre; secondly, 'joy', a more characteristically Romantic word than Burke's passive 'pleasure',[6] suggests a more active, sought condition, one that includes effort and struggle; thirdly, power is not necessarily at odds with affection and domestic relations. It is interesting that Burke makes human / canine relations stand for the domestic and the familiar, whereas Wordsworth explores human domestic relations extensively and is scarcely ever concerned with the domestication of animals.[7] Finally and chiefly, Wordsworth's assertion of the power of literature (and perhaps of power in general) is crossed at every point by a need for complicity, complementarity and negotiation between the reader and the writer. The last point is central to this chapter.

Before turning to these subjects it is worth glancing at Wordsworth's own attempt to write an aesthetic treatise in the Burkean mode, the fragmentary essay 'The Sublime and the Beautiful' designed at one stage to preface what became *A Guide Through the District of the Lakes*. He distinguishes several relationships between the mind and *natural* objects, all involving power. Interestingly, in one case power is thought of as shared ('participated': the notion can be found in Dennis, Burke and Gerard); but in others there is an unequal relationship either of 'triumph', of 'resistance', or of 'humiliation and prostration'.[8] Wordsworth develops all three cases to show that nevertheless *unity* – both in the object and in the mind, the essential quality of sublime experience – is not impaired by these imbalances, though it has a different dynamic in each case. It is the dynamic that is important; for even in the most straightforward case when the mind 'participates [the] force which is acting upon it', it can only 'grasp at something towards which it can make approaches but which it is incapable of attaining'. It is not a question of the mind's union (in some mystic way) with the object, but of a relationship in which the perceived unity of the object is accompanied by a unity of consciousness in the mind of the observer. The different effects of power produce different relationships, though all can be described – with some ingenuity of Wordsworth's part – as involving unity.[9] It is evident that 'The Sublime and the Beautiful' attempts not simply to analyse power, but in a sense to disperse it through a variety of experiences. I suggest the text is so insistent on unity *because* of this, because there is a danger that the subject will dissolve before our eyes. The peculiar tension in this text perhaps reflects its genre: a reasoned discourse on a subject already fully treated by writers of philosophical and academic standing. It is a much more systematic piece of writing than any other he undertook, with the exception perhaps of the *Guide to the Lakes* itself; more focused in its strategies than the various prefaces. For one thing it is explicitly not concerned with the sublime in 'the works of man', which, Wordsworth remarks in passing, need not involve power. Unless he is referring only to non-literary artefacts, this is a surprising exception in view of his analyses of literary power in *The Prelude* and the 1815 'Essay'. But perhaps it is not so surprising: in common with eighteenth-century treatises on the sublime, Wordsworth's essay speaks of 'the mind' as if all minds were alike, and for all the psychological interest of his distinctions between participation, resistance, submission and triumph, he does not here link power to questions of taste, judgement and reading habits as he does elsewhere. The essay is written within generic constraints; the related passages in *The Prelude* and the 1815 'Essay', one slightly earlier and the other ten years later than this text, are both more amorphous and wider-reaching.

Dispersing power: taste

Any discussion of 'power' in Wordsworth's writing must turn sooner or later to his terms of reader–writer relations because it is in that context – the context of reading and judging poetry – that he addresses the topic most explicitly. The chief text is the 'Essay, Supplementary to the Preface', where 'power' is defined both as a quality of poetry and a process in the minds of writer and reader. The test of 'genius' is whether it 'call[s] forth and bestow[s] power' in the mind of the reader. 'Elevated or profound passion cannot exist' without 'a co-operating power in the mind of the Reader'. It is obvious that this is a test of readers as much as writers, as Wordsworth implicitly acknowledges in a long passage speculating on the reasons why poetry readers are often bad readers; so the criterion of 'popularity' is a false one. Passion is evidence of power in both reader and writer. One of the extraordinary things about this argument is that, while dismissing the term 'taste' as naming something *'passive'*, Wordsworth defines 'passion' as *'action'*: it is a strange reversal of logic to draw attention to the etymology linking 'passion' and *'suffering'* and at the same time to assert that suffering implies *'action'*.[10] Deleting the traditional opposition between active and passive has enormous implications for the concept of power; indeed it appears to empty it completely, unless we can think of power as bi-directional and complementary rather than as the simple authority of one concept (or person) over another. It makes us look again at familiar locutions ('over' in my previous sentence reinforces a hierarchy) and perhaps also the way we think about active and passive as grammatical terms. I shall suggest later in this chapter that there are crucial passages in *The Prelude* where Wordsworth's syntax seems to be reversible, others where the subject of a grammatically 'active' verb is replaced or redefined in way that disperses the notion of a single hierarchical relationship between subject and object. This is an area where his poetic practice, even more clearly than his theory, converges with subversive notions of grammar in Horne Tooke's *Diversions of Purley*.[11]

We can usefully compare Wordsworth's texts on power with De Quincey's discussion of 'the literature of power' as distinct from 'the literature of knowledge' in his essay 'The Poetry of Pope'.[12] De Quincey claimed the distinction was Wordsworth's, and although Wordsworth did not use the exact phrases, the separation of knowledge and power is important in his writing too. De Quincey exploits the logical advantage of a distinct opposition between the two terms, but his discussion raises as many questions as it answers. Yet their strategies and metaphors in writing about power have something in common. In this respect De Quincey's argument is interesting both for its representative value (as I see it) and for its peculiar vehemences.

> There is, first, the literature of *knowledge*; and, secondly, the literature of *power*. The function of the first is – to *teach*; the function of the second is – to *move*. . . . What do you learn from 'Paradise Lost'? Nothing at all. What do you learn from a cookery-book? Something new, something that you did not know before, in every paragraph. But would you therefore put the wretched cookery-book on a higher level of estimation than the divine poem? What you owe to Milton is not any knowledge, of which a million separate items are still but a million of advancing steps still on the same earthly level; what you owe is *power*, – that is, exercise and expansion of your own latent capacity of sympathy with the infinite. . . .[13]

The distinction between the instructive and the moving in literature is familiar enough, but De Quincey develops it interestingly. There is a special contempt in his implicitly likening some of Pope's poetry to a cookery book rather than, say, a philosophical treatise or an essay in *The Spectator*. No doubt it is rhetorical exaggeration, but the terms of the contrast between Milton and Pope are not as simple as he suggests. It is at least as untrue that you *learn* nothing from reading *Paradise Lost* as that Pope's poetry, even the 'Essay on Man' (which De Quincey especially finds fault with), reads like a set of instructions: I learned a great deal about mythologies of various kinds, and astronomy, not to mention theology, from reading *Paradise Lost*, and I don't think I am alone. This is a modern perspective, but I imagine many of the first readers of the essay could have said the same (he is addressing readers *as* readers). In this passage as elsewhere his learning perhaps sets him apart from his readers. (Baudelaire likened De Quincey's mind to a Greek lexicon.) I do not suggest his discussion is valueless, but I think it needs placing as essentially scholarly. His praise is as partial, in both senses, as his condemnation. How does his partiality function?

Part of the answer is that, like Wordsworth, Coleridge, Keats and many others (but not Byron), he broadly contrasts the eighteenth century with the seventeenth and finds it lacking in spiritual ambition: he plays a role in the Romantic project of making Milton and his contemporaries 'living at this hour'. But when he characterises what he doesn't like as utilitarian, he is using a historically different argument addressed to his contemporaries generally, not just to those who read poetry: in fact the essay is precisely aimed at *making* readers more ambitious. Writing in the 1840s, he attacks the cult of instruction fostered by mechanics' institutes and bodies like the Society for the Promotion of Useful Knowledge (satirised by Peacock in *Crotchet Castle* [1832] as the 'Steam Intellect Society'). Arguing against the past and the present, in favour of a remoter past and a possible future, he superimposes two distinct historical schemes – which, as we shall see, Wordsworth does also.

The invocation of cookery books has other implications. I've been saying De Quincey uses it as a metonym for *merely* utilitarian writing, supposing a set of instructions comes closest to that function. But when Wordsworth uses a related metaphor to stigmatise passive reading and judgement in the Preface to *Lyrical Ballads* ('as if it were a thing as indifferent as a taste for rope-dancing, or Frontiniac, or Sherry')[14] he writes with a slightly different *animus*: against customs that make an *art* of judging utilitarian or merely frivolous objects and activities, thereby devaluing judgement of the traditional arts. Interestingly the argument has xenophobic overtones: 'rope-dancing' is the kind of activity he condemns in the London of Book VII of *The Prelude* ('Singers, Rope-dancers, Giants and Dwarfs, / Clowns, Conjurors, Posture-masters, Harlequins, / Amid the uproar of the rabblement'). This catalogue of sights is complemented by others that more explicitly link strangeness with foreignness. The metropolis, which in the different language of Book VIII is presented as a metonym for the nation ('The Fountain of my Country's destiny'), is here a parade of 'All out-o'-th'-way, far-fetched, perverted things', which include 'the silver collar'd Negro, . . . Albinos, painted Indians, Dwarfs'. If the primary meaning of 'out-o'-th'-way' is 'unnatural', it also retains a connotation of geographical distance and racial difference. So the heterogeneity of London is not only *visual* heterogeneity and the impossibility of sublime vision, but also communal incoherence. That much is hardly surprising because it is common to register the strange as the unnatural. But Wordsworth goes further (typically) in relating this kind of incoherence to bad taste. London is a scene of false *taste*, where the pastoral tragedy of

Mary of Buttermere becomes a melodrama at Sadler's Wells (a generic muddle), and where rope-dancing remained, in De Selincourt's words, 'evidently one of the most popular items' with the spectators.[15] The chaos of London with its '*chance* spectators' is implicitly contrasted with an idea that there exists or should exist a coherent body of serious spectators, serious users of art: a nation of potential *readers*.

In the 1815 'Essay', 'power' is the index of a community of taste and is contrasted more explicitly with 'European' customs (wines, 'Frontiniac' and sherry, are foreign). Only 'a sinking of the spirit of nations' could bring about a situation where judging art is like judging cuisine. This more explicit xenophobia has to do with a need to restrict the language of judgement to the genuinely aesthetic, and that excludes eating and drinking. Wordsworth's position may not be as absolute as I'm suggesting, but it is interesting that his casual metaphors have specific resonances. In the writings of those, like Peacock and Lamb, who *considered* their views about eating and drinking, there is also a dislike of French finesse (perhaps to some extent dissimulated in Lamb) and a celebration of the good old English ways: gross pieces of meat carved at the table. It is another way of stigmatising foreign customs as unnatural, as if the true cook had no other resource than to present the animal in a condition as near as convenient to its living state. Cooking remained a French art, as far as the English were concerned: the Prince Regent patronised Carême, and Victoria's chief cook was Carême's pupil Francatelli. Carême's art was an art of display; English works such as Thomas Walker's *The Original* (1835) and Eliza Acton's *Modern Cookery for Private Families* (1845) were much more bourgeois and practical. What Peacock and Lamb celebrate, Wordsworth only suggests, but these metaphors are not just peripheral because they point to a paradox in Wordsworth's thinking about the artistic renovation of life in its most common manifestations. He notoriously addressed a sonnet to a spade,[16] and in his analysis of 'taste' and 'passion' he sweeps away a number of class-based associations and prejudices, as he does in his letter to John Wilson about 'The Idiot Boy'.[17] We might expect him, therefore, to welcome any way of extending the area in which aesthetic judgement is appropriate. But he does not, and his mapping of the aesthetic has its specific shape; it includes spinning, for example, but excludes eating.

Wordsworth's writing intrudes into the trivial and the everyday in a peculiarly persuasive and intolerable way, and that is congruent with an obsession with readership and a pervasive doctrine of power: not only that the poet's power can transform everyday objects and activities, but that he can speak for their users.

> Grief, thou hast lost an ever-ready friend
> Now that the cottage Spinning-wheel is mute[.][18]

The obvious response to this sonnet on the demise of the spinning-wheel, composed by 1815 and published in 1819, is that it is a Luddite lament for industrialisation, but a clearer view might question why the poem begins with 'grief' and not contentment or even happiness. The poems accepts that grief is inevitable and presumes to comment upon it; presumes, even, to suggest that the sound of the wheel, mechanical but thought of as individual, can be companionable, a voice for grief as well as the 'joy' that the poem secondarily mentions. Grief cannot be removed but it can be shared and therefore alleviated. In his poems on trivial subjects he seeks companionship that changes the generic into the individual, even when writing a poem about 'The Spade of a Friend'. But Wordsworth's celebration of the trivial is not as innocent as parodists have had to assume. The spade poem is addressed to Thomas Wilkinson, an 'agriculturalist' (as the title names him) but also a writer: he was the author of a *Tour in Scotland*, part of which supplied the last two lines of 'The Solitary Reaper'. The poem does not explore an intimate relation between writing and digging (as Seamus Heaney's poem 'Digging' does) but rather contrasts 'high and low', 'the industry of body and of mind'; but nevertheless it gives an aesthetic value to manual labour by focusing on the spade rather than on the more obviously aesthetic function of *design* in landscape gardening. The spade has dug 'pleasure grounds' (the term is Humphry Repton's and applies only to the life-style of the relatively wealthy),[19] but Wordsworth chooses to focus on the implement rather than the mind. *Here*, it seems, he collaborates with a movement to extend aesthetic criteria into non-traditional activities, but in the case of eating and drinking he refuses to do so. Since the late eighteenth century was an age in which England dominated gardening and France dominated cooking and wine-making, we may suspect that the choice of metaphors in the Preface to *Lyrical Ballads* and the 1815 'Essay' was not casual. But the paradox remains: defining a coherent constituency of competent judges means excluding not only 'bad' taste but taste of any kind applied to inappropriate things.

The cultural differences I have been describing are important when we think of Wordsworth as a poet of the 'ordinary', because the term begs questions about geographical, political and stylistic norms. He insists that ordinariness is a site of power but sometimes turns his back on the actualities of political power, as if the idea that 'there is a world elsewhere', as Shakespeare's Coriolanus put it, were a sufficient answer to government, demagogues and (for example) enclosers. Land enclosure is an interesting case, because Wordsworth's own experience of it – the point at which the peasant is confronted by those who have power over him – is unclear. The remoter parts of the West Country, the scene of some of the 1798 *Lyrical Ballads*, like the Lake district (more prominent in the 1800 volume), were relatively unaffected. Skirting the central agricultural regions of the kingdom, Wordsworth to some extent skirted the issue. The one well-known poem set in a region affected by enclosure, 'Tintern Abbey', is silent on the subject. Yet we should not readily agree with Marjorie Levinson's view that he was in some (unspecified) sense *wrong* to ignore it,[20] because in fact there was very little enclosure in the Wye valley between 1793 and 1798 and *relatively* little anywhere in the 1790s. It was after the General Enclosure Act of 1801 that the pace of enclosure became rapid. The problem is that Wordsworth recognised the operations of imaginative power in so many unconsidered byways of life that we can easily come to expect him to have made a complete map: a recipe for disappointment.

Power and knowledge: (i) history

'Power' is a *radically* unstable term in Wordsworth and De Quincey because one of the points at issue is to determine the kinds of discourse to which the word belongs as an aesthetic term. As I have shown, Wordsworth extends its scope to include sympathetic contemplation of the trivial and the everyday, and he notes that if 'taste' is thought of as appropriate *only* to matters of artistic 'proportion and congruity',[21] it has no place in the central act of communication of power between reader and writer. The 1815 'Essay' analyses taste in specifically exclusive *and* inclusive ways. There are other tensions, real or apparent, one of which is that power is frequently domesticated, but sometimes it is the site of transgression. Another, which has radical implications, springs from the separation of power and knowledge, an opposition in which both terms begin to look unstable. The question 'what counts as knowledge?' is as unavoidable as 'what counts as power?'. These issues surface in many quite different contexts in Wordsworth's writing, both early and late. For the sake of variety (if not perverseness) I shall begin by looking at a sonnet that seems a mere footnote to Wordsworth's more familiar discussions of power:

AT ROME. – REGRETS. IN ALLUSION TO NIEBUHR, AND OTHER MODERN HISTORIANS

Those old credulities, to nature dear,
Shall they no longer bloom upon the stock
Of History, stript naked as a rock
'Mid a dry desert? What is it we hear?
The glory of Infant Rome must disappear,
Her morning splendours vanish, and their place
Know them no more. If Truth, who veiled her face
With those bright beams yet hid it not, must steer
Henceforth a humbler course perplexed and slow;
One solace yet remains for us who came
Into this world in days when story lacked
Severe research, that in our hearts we know
How, for exciting youth's heroic flame,
Assent is power, belief the soul of fact.

Niebuhr's *Römische Geschichte* had been partly translated into English when Wordsworth wrote the sonnet shortly after a trip to Italy in 1837; it became the standard text for a revisionist history of Rome that paralleled the 'higher' (i.e. historical and textual) criticism of the scriptures, dismissing as mere mythology many of the early family annals Livy and other historians had valued equally with 'fact'. The subject is almost a *leitmotiv* in *Memorials of a Tour in Italy, 1837*, the collection of poems in which the sonnet was published. Wordsworth's attitude can be dismissed as merely backward-looking (if that is a reason for dismissal), but, like other negative responses, it can come to seem positive as well. Peacock's Morgana Gryll in *Gryll Grange* (1859) prefers Livy to Niebuhr because 'the History of the early ages of Rome' becomes a 'dry skeleton' when 'told by one who believes nothing that the Romans believed'.

Because their religion is not our religion, we pass over the supernatural part of the matter in silence, or advert to it in a spirit of contemptuous incredulity. We do not give it its proper place, nor present it in its proper colours, as a cause in the production of great effects.[22]

Peacock's argument, and Wordsworth's too, is that we should be sympathetic with the past, understanding its fictions without necessarily agreeing with them. What Peacock's heroine makes plain is that, true or not, fictions have measurable effects that are the province of history, and so the fictions themselves must also be noticed in our histories.

While Peacock makes these opposed views a matter of taste merely, Wordsworth explores fiction more intimately in order to find its relation to fact. Having distinguished between 'History' and 'story', he asserts that 'Assent is power, belief the soul of fact'. The first part of that sentence is the whole argument of the 1815 'Essay, Supplementary to the Preface': power is the meeting place of writer and reader and is *therefore* dependent on assent, and conversely assent is empowering. But the poem goes further in imagining a band of rebels against 'the humbler course' of history, a band that consists, significantly, of both those who came earlier (like the 67-year-old Wordsworth) and the 'heroic' youth of the present. The conviction that old and young might combine against the rationality of what comes between is completely at odds with the more familiar idea of imaginative growth and decay that is the central myth of 'Tintern Abbey', *The Prelude*, the 'Immortality Ode' and other poems, such as 'Peele Castle', that are usually taken as central to his work. (Yet it does occur locally in Book V of *The Prelude* when 'ballad-tunes' are described as 'Food for the hungry ears of little ones, / And of old men who have survived their joy', a conscious echo, perhaps, of Sidney's *Apology for Poetry*. I shall return to this below.) 'Credulities' are 'natural' – a standard trope of nostalgia – but they are also the necessary fictions of heroism in the young. There is an abandon in this poem that is almost Yeatsian.

The striking thing about the poem is that it imagines *recent* history as reversible or cyclical in the act of considering ancient history: the history of readership is as much the subject of the poem as national history, because Niebuhr's radical re-reading provides an opportunity to question the grounds of all readings and shows that the reader's will has an inevitable part in effectual reading.

There is a subtext to this sonnet and its companion-pieces in the same collection,[23] an analogy between early Rome and contemporary Britain that Wordsworth made explicit in a note attached to a similar attack on Niebuhr in 'Musings Near Aquapendente':

> And who – if not a man as cold
> In heart as dull in brain – while pacing ground
> Chosen by Rome's legendary Bards, high minds
> Out of her early struggles well inspired
> To localize heroic acts – could look
> Upon the spots with undelighted eye
> Though even to their last syllable the Lays
> And very names of those who gave them birth
> Have perished?

Wordsworth asked Frederick Faber to write a note on the poem linking early pieties in Rome with the revival of 'a devout deference to the voice of Christian antiquity' in Britain in the 1840s.[24] Though he remained antagonistic to Roman Catholic doctrines, Wordsworth saw in the Tractarian movement a coherence of old and new analogous to his own exploration of the force of tradition, and the sequence is a reinterpretation of affective fictions no less important than the critique of mythology in *The Excursion*.[25]

It is true that this is not a settled view, even within the narrow confines of the *Memorials of a Tour in Italy*. The two sonnets following the one I've discussed draw back from defence of 'old credulities', though in curious ways. The last of the three ('Plea for the Historian') appears simply to reject them as 'dazzling flatteries, / Dear . . . to unsuspecting Youth', but the argument is compromised when he uses the figure of Clio to stand for truth:

> flatteries . . .
> That might have drawn down Clio from the skies
> To vindicate the majesty of truth.
> Such was her office while she walked with men,
> A Muse, who, not unmindful of her Sire
> All-ruling Jove, whate'er the theme might be
> Revered her Mother, sage Mnemosyne,
> And taught her faithful servants how the lyre
> Should animate, but not mislead the pen.

Clio is the Muse of history, which should be the same as truth (as against 'dazzlement'), but she is given a special dependence on

Mnemosyne (memory) that modifies her obedience to 'all-ruling' Jove. She is the offspring of power *and* memory. Wordsworth probably knew that *kleos* is translated by the Latin *gloria* in Lemprière: the etymology points to her function as eulogist of heroic deeds – an earlier concept of history. At all events 'Clio' cannot stand for 'fact' when Jove's *power* is also invoked: the poem's appeal to truth as something simple, mature, and factual is compromised by the mythology in which truth is evoked. This reading can be supported by Wordsworth's footnote quoting most of the first two lines of a poem Horace wrote in praise of Augustus.[26] Horace begins *his* poem by rhetorically asking what man, hero or god Clio should now celebrate, and after the gods, after Romulus, Regulus and Cæsar, Augustus emerges. Horace based his poem on one of Pindar's, the one that Pound invokes ironically in 'Hugh Selwyn Mauberley': 'What god, man, or hero / Shall I place a tin wreath upon!' The force of Wordsworth's footnote, his reference to Horace, is hard to judge, but we can scarcely believe that the association of Clio and eulogy does not complicate the simple scheme of truth *versus* fiction, especially since eulogy of Augustus cannot be dismissed as the fictions of an unscientific age.

The other sonnet ('Complacent fictions were they') also acknowledges that the early lays were flattery, but praises them as 'pure-minded' flattery, evidence of a 'noble' people. As a defining contrast he points to the supposed flattery of violence in the works of 'Runic Scald[s]'. This hackneyed image is, I take it, a metonymy for battle-poetry in general, and the underlying contrast is between the 'blood-thirsty' exercise of power among warring tribes and mytho-logised ancestor-worship of the early books of Livy's *History*. It is significant that here, as well as in his ghosted note on the Tractarians, negotiations between the living and the dead – the subject of the *Essays upon Epitaphs* – are allowed a latitude of fiction he rejects in more (supposedly) blood-thirsty traditions. (Correspondingly, the classical myths he explores in the fourth Book of *The Excursion* are myths of naming, not the tragic and bloody myths of Troy and Thebes.) In both poems the terms in which non-fabular truth can be defined are severely limited by the need to celebrate the dead.

Power and knowledge: (ii) education

These late poems about history have similarities with a much earlier passage in *The Prelude* about romantic fables. The fact is surprising if

we subscribe to the view that Wordsworth's poetry underwent crucial
changes of view after about 1815. In both cases there is a relationship
between companionship and transgression.

> Ye dreamers, then,
> Forgers of lawless tales! We bless you then,
> Impostors, drivellers, dotards, as the ape
> Philosophy will call you: then we feel
> With what, and how great might ye are in league,
> Who make our wish our power, our thought a deed,
> An empire, a possession; Ye whom Time
> And Seasons serve; all Faculties; to whom
> Earth crouches, th'elements are as potter's clay,
> Space like a Heaven filled up with Northern lights;
> Here, nowhere, there, and everywhere at once.
>
> (V, 547–57)

'Tales that charm away the wakeful night' are considered chiefly but
not solely as children's books. The passage is part of a topical debate
about the efficacy of different kinds of literature in education, a
debate disseminated by Rousseau's influence (as much as by his
writings) and evident in, for example, Blake's antagonism in *Songs of
Innocence* to improving, moralising works.[27] Though Blake almost
certainly did not feel the same enthusiasm for the *Arabian Nights* as
Wordsworth, both reject thinking that excludes everything but the
exemplary. More than that, each substitutes his own ideal: to the
extent that Blake's Songs answer Isaac Watts's *Divine Songs for
Children*, they substitute joy for goodness; in a different dialectic,
Wordsworth substitutes power for measurable knowledge ('he must
live / Knowing that he grows wiser every day, / Or else not live at
all'). The ideal expressed here, 'Knowledge not purchased with the
loss of power', implies that knowledge, as commonly defined, *reduces*
power. This calls both terms into question: what *is* knowledge?; what
is power? Bacon's equation '*scientia est potestas*', now familiar as a
school motto throughout the old colonial world, had a particular
political force in the utilitarian ethos of the 1830s, when it became a
slogan among the Chartists ('Knowledge is Power' was the motto of
Henry Hetherington's unlicensed newspaper, *The Poor Man's
Guardian*), and it survived as the leading theme in Lord Brougham's
founding address to the National Association for the Promotion of
Social Science in 1857. I do not think we can assume the phrase had

the same political implications in 1805, though the seeds of utilitarianism were already sown. In rejecting the equation Wordsworth focuses particularly on the question of how learning is institutionalised and gives a powerful analysis of the way institutions replicate themselves.

The issue is prominent in the fifth Book, but before turning to it we should recall Wordsworth's own educational experience. He attended a respected grammar school that led successful pupils to university, which put him potentially in the main stream of English culture – and, incidentally, separated him formally from non-conformist associations.[28] The fact that he writes of opting out in some respects at Cambridge ('I was not for that hour, / Nor for that place') need not obscure his earlier sense of a companionship through literature that replaced, perhaps, a familial companionship. *The Prelude* tells of sharing 'favorite verses with one voice' with a friend, at the time of life when companions are chosen. There is no chosen companion in Wordsworth's representation of life at Cambridge in Book III, but later, in the alpine crossing in Book VI, we learn of a friendship suppressed in the earlier account. It is clear that the poem is structured on a pattern of engagement and solitude that is designed to give special value to the latter. To return to a point I made above, the relation between society and solitude (in Miltonic terms) can be read as a relationship between enabling circumstance and true insight – society is a ladder that can be kicked away – but if we read Wordsworth this way we ignore most of what he wrote.

The dominant image of institutionalised knowledge in Book V, the 'dwarf man' who represents the utilitarians' ideal pupil, is an image of both obedience and solitude. Surrounded by teachers and other admiring adults, the boy is companionless: a boy with private tutors belonging to a family that could afford them. It is hard to separate the philosophic ideal from the social circumstances that allow it, because the passage is dominated by images of enclosure. 'His discourse moves slow, / Massy and ponderous as a prison door':

> Vanity
> That is his soul, there lives he, and there moves;
> It is the soul of everything he seeks;
> That gone, nothing is left which he can love.
> Nay, if a thought of purer birth should rise
> To carry him towards a better clime

Some busy helper still is on the watch
To drive him back and pound him like a Stray
Within the pinfold of his own conceit;
Which is his home, his natural dwelling place.

(V, 354–63)

The pupil is enclosed by both the teacher's authority and his own self-congratulation. In fact there is a curiously reflexive relationship between the two, as if the pupil is a distorted image of the teacher: 'His Teachers stare' at their own creation, as Frankenstein does. A more grotesque image of enclosure precedes the lines quoted above: exhumation, the opening of the coffin, an image reminiscent of Gothic fiction (a mode which, incidentally, trades on simplified power structures, especially those based on fear):

Forth bring him to the light of common sense
And, fresh and shewy as it is, the Corps
Slips from us into powder.

(V, 352–4)

But this remains within the context of a simple one-directional authority that keeps the pupil within the 'pinfold' of what he knows. He has no power outside it; knowledge and power are separated completely. In this way the passage contrasts strongly with those in which power is domesticated ('Visionary power / Attends upon the motion of the winds . . .'), where 'shadowy things' are said to 'make their *abode*': here, 'home' signifies only the known and the measured; there, it is a site where the uncalculated is understood.

I've been suggesting that Wordsworth's discourse of power involves relationship, whether of reader and writer or in images of companionship. The idea seems to be common to his strategies for domesticating power and thinking of it as transgression. Although the discussion of *nature's* power in *The Prelude* and the essay on 'The Sublime and the Beautiful' is generally from the viewpoint of solitude or in the voice of the representative mind, there is a strong sense of collective experience in his discussion of the power of literature in Books V and VI – in spite of the chilling image of isolation and impotence the former begins with, the dream of the Arab rider with his book and shell.

Yet the figure contrasting with the 'dwarf man' in Book V is the 'boy of Winander' who blows 'mimic hootings' to the listening owls, and he is also companionless in life, becoming part of a community only in 'the silent neighbourhood of graves'. The terms of the contrast are quite close: the boy 'mimics' owls as the pupil mimics his teachers. The simple way of expressing the difference between them is to say that one mimics nature and the other men and books, and Wordsworth elsewhere exploits the jingle between 'nature' and 'teacher'.[29] But that is not a sufficient explanation, if only because 'Nature' is so opaque a term. A more fundamental distinction is the relation between ends and means and the shift of power between the self and whatever 'other' is involved. The boy of Winander imitates without calculation – he assumes, I suppose, human mastery in that he can ape the language of owls whereas owls have few means of aping human speech, supposing they wanted to, but he is mastered through his own receptiveness. He begins as the subject of Wordsworth's sentences and becomes the object. In contrast the dwarf man is an object of instruction though he goes on believing in his own power, as long as he is driven back 'like a Stray / Within the pinfold of his own conceit'.

There are ironies in both cases, and my description in the previous paragraph has distinguished them perhaps too flatly. Wordsworth's thinking about power, and about relationship in general, is complicated by a fluid but crucial distinction between childhood and adulthood. Revisions of *The Prelude* often involve changing dates in the explicitly autobiographical sections or changing the ages of figures presented as other than the author. The boy of Winander died at nine according to the earliest manuscript (1798) – in which part of the passage is in the first person, not the third – at ten when the passage was first published in *Lyrical Ballads* (1800), and at eleven when the poem was published as a whole (1850).[30] The discrepancies may be unimportant, but the fact that he took the trouble to revise suggests he had changing views about the point at which childhood should be distinguished from self-consciousness. In the 1798 version the boy is just younger than Wordsworth was when he entered Hawkshead grammar school, an entirely different milieu from any he had previously experienced, where he claimed later to have learned more in two months than in the previous two years.[31] I suggest that in this context the age where serious schooling begins is taken as a point of transition from the 'wildness' of childhood to the more consciously social ethos of early maturity. The boy of Winander is a village boy who never becomes old enough to be institutionalised and who seems to lack even a family: only the narrator mourns for him.

What I'm suggesting is that the power of writing is not *simply* contrasted with the power of nature in this text: another contrast cuts across it, which itself is unstable. Wordsworth insists that early childhood must be distinguished from later years with their consciousness of a dynamic of choice of companionship – their sense of society – whether personal or literary, but the freedom and power of early years when romances 'make our wish our deed' are a model of communication that adult experience should incorporate, not reject. He praises romances in language that is plural, and his first literary ambition, to own a complete copy of the *Arabian Nights*, is 'a league, a covenant' with a friend. Reading is shared. We may want to understand the language as a political reference to the 'solemn league and covenant' of the Scottish Dissenters: if so, it must surely be a joke, but even then – perhaps particularly then – the passage is about the power that comes of sharing, especially when sharing is consciousness of dissent. In the lines quoted above, Romances are 'in league' with 'might', wish becomes power, thought becomes 'An empire, a possession'. And Romances are 'lawless' according to 'the ape / Philosophy': they have their own laws and their own area of jurisdiction; they create an empire that competes with the economic and political empire that validates measurable education. The phrase 'the ape / Philosophy' repeats the idea of mere reflection, mimicry, that is prominent in the 'dwarf man' section.

Sequence and syntax

Visionary Power
Attends upon the motion of the winds
Embodied in the mystery of words.
There darkness makes abode, and all the host
Of shadowy things do work their changes there,
As in a mansion like their proper home:
Even forms and substances are circumfus'd
By that transparent veil with light divine;
And through the turnings intricate of Verse,
Present themselves as objects recognis'd
In flashes, with a glory scarce their own.

(V, 619–29)

Whatever else this climactic passage signifies,[32] it is about the known and the unknown, developing and complicating the discourse of knowledge and power earlier in the same book of *The Prelude*. Power 'attends upon', waits upon, serves: Wordsworth's first emphasis is on power *corresponding* (to use the word in the 1815 'Essay') rather than authorising. The entities to which power is ascribed ('darkness', 'shadowy things') are housed in images of familiarity, though the traditional discourse of the sublime makes them unfamiliar and authoritative. The simile of 'home' suggests this transformation of the sublime, but it is only a partial transformation because the 'shadowy things' (the powers that work changes) are in fact in a 'mansion' which is *not* 'their proper home', only 'like' it. There is a curious sense of their being guests so welcome that they are deluded into thinking themselves at home. Perhaps this is an unduly anthropocentric way of putting it, but Wordsworth elsewhere uses 'mansion' and 'home' in precise ways ('thy mind / Shall be a mansion for all lovely forms, / Thy memory be as a dwelling-place / For all sweet sounds and harmonies'), and the use of both terms in this line creates a distinction between them. Language, if 'There' means *in* language, is a mansion like home, both familiar and unfamiliar, home and not home, our possession and yet a place we visit.

This doubleness is worth dwelling on because the grand narratives about Romantic poetry in the work of, for example, M.H. Abrams,[33] describe a quest and a return, a fall and a redemption, a journey that brings us home. Whether this broad context is in itself helpful or not, we should note that what looks like its corollary at the textual level – ambivalent location of origins, motion this way and that – actually destabilises language in a way that makes grand narratives look dubious. Passages like this are *about* language and power and bring into question the causal and hierarchical structures narratives need.

There are many other oppositions that are not quite paradoxes, or, to be more precise, not stable paradoxes. Language is a 'transparent veil' that nevertheless *adds* light; 'recognition' occurs in 'flashes'. Does the latter phrase mean that objects become *un*recognisable again after the flash, so that recognition is not an achieved stability but a momentary, possibly illusory perspective? Such a reading strains the meaning of 'recognition', but the text *works* under strain: if, instead of 'recognis'd', Wordsworth had written 'perceived anew' there would have been no such strain. But similarly there would have been no such radical questioning of the origins of power.

This is not an isolated example. The equally well-known passage about imagination embedded in the narrative of the Alpine crossing

also constructs a series of unstable relations concerning power,
authority, vision and familiarity:

> In such strength
> Of usurpation, in such visitings
> Of awful promise, when the light of sense
> Goes out in flashes that have shewn to us
> The invisible world, doth Greatness make abode,
> There harbours whether we be young or old.
> Our destiny, our nature, and our home
> Is with infinitude and only there . . .
>
> (VI, 532–9)

'Flashes' appears to be an image both of extraordinary insight made
possible by the passing of ordinary light, and of an intensification of
the ordinary.[34]

Power is problematised in syntax as well as in theme. This is
nowhere more true than in *The Prelude*, where the self is subject *and*
object, both philosophically and grammatically. As in other autobio-
graphies, there is a need to objectify the self in the past and to
maintain a fluid viewpoint at the 'moment' of writing, but each of
these goals is potentially a trap: the first might lead to constraint, the
second to incoherence. To avoid the trap Wordsworth perpetually
revises the past and occasionally condenses the present (in addresses
to Coleridge or to himself, as in the apostrophe to 'Imagination' in
Book VI). What happens repeatedly in the poem is the causal
relationship between past and present, its power structure, is inverted
or erased. One of the fictions of the poem is that the past governs the
present (as 'the child is father of the man'), but the authority of
writing reverses the balance: the present after all constructs the past
even in representing it as authoritative.

I suggest we understand the dynamic of past and present in *The
Prelude* as a limiting case of the broader dynamic of subject and
object, self and other, inner and outer, elsewhere in his work: all these
terms are radically destabilised. But if so, why use them at all? The
answer is that 'power' is so commonly seen as a term *implying* a binary
opposition (*x* has power over *y*) that it is necessary to examine how
Wordsworth's particular use of the word dissolves or disperses
oppositions.

One way he does it is to make terms ambiguous by mixing
established categories; another is to reverse the hierarchy typical of

abstract texts where substantives are valued above verbs –
Wordsworth frequently values verbs over substantives, process over
product or agent.[35] Something of the first is evident in passages like
this:

> Whose truth is not a motion or a shape
> Instinct with vital functions, but a block
> Or waxen image which yourselves have made . . .

'Motion' and 'shape' name different concepts in empirical reasoning,
but they seem to be in apposition here. If not – if they are alternatives
– the *categoric* significance of 'shape' is still pushed into the background by the following phrase: what matters is not the spatial
particularity of shape but its content and potency. By contrast the
'block or waxen image' signifies purely *as* a shape; a shape manu-
factured to determine a concept. Wordsworth's critique of false 'truth'
is in the sceptical tradition of Bacon, the 'waxen image' a later 'idol',
but the analytic tool can be used to different ends: the passage
functions as a whole by denying or backgrounding primary meanings
in the technical language of philosophy. Coleridge's urge to desynony-
mise aesthetic terms – 'fancy' and 'imagination', for example – works
in an opposite direction but perhaps has the same origin in mistrust of
received terminology. His work takes a place in a tradition of
systematic idealist philosophy where the crucial distinctions are
between substantives (like Kant's *Vernunft* and *Verstand*). Much of
The Prelude is not unsystematic but *anti*systematic, and grammatical
apposition is a frequent and powerful method.

There is a similar emphasis on other relational terms:[36]

> hence religion, faith
> And endless occupation for the soul
> Whether discursive or intuitive
> Hence sovereignty within and peace at will
> Emotion which best foresight need not fear
> Most worthy then of trust when most intense.
> Hence cheerfulness in every act of life
> Hence truth in moral judgements and delight
> That fails not in the external universe.
>
> (XIII, 111–19)

'Hence': a sign of logical deduction; but what is deduced is far from
logically entailed in the 'meditation', preceding these lines, on the

'image of a mighty mind' following the ascent of Snowdon. Such minds are named 'Powers' because, though especially sensitive to impressions from the outer world they are also exceptionally self-conscious and self-disciplined. It is usually argued that the episode as a whole emphasises the power of mind *over* nature, disappointingly disturbing the balance of mind and nature in Book III and, less emphatically, in Book XII.[37] But though these minds are indeed named 'Powers', the actions that characterise them are written as grammatically passive ('not enthralled . . . quickened . . . rouz'd and made thereby more fit' [103–5]). The assertion of mastery is contradicted by the conditions that guarantee it. And there is a similar difficulty with 'hence', though it works in the opposite way. The term implies that the subsequent follows (logically) the precedent, but in fact the multiple subsequents here broaden the frame of reference. Huge things follow from comparatively little things. To say that *a religious sense* follows from analytic self-consciousness has an air of plausibility; to say 'religion' does is to tempt disbelief. Other things that are said to follow (logically) are distinctly paradoxical: 'peace at will', 'emotion . . . Most worthy then of trust when most intense'.

There are philosophies that embrace paradoxes and call them mysteries, but I do not think that is the force of this passage. The lines imitate logic but subvert it (daringly, enthusiastically, not cynically). The effect of the whole Snowdon episode is to revalue the *un*foreseen (the sudden revelation of a night landscape), to break the logic of cause and consequence that logical signifiers like 'hence' invoke.

In a way this passage is exceptional because it marks the beginning of the end of the poem,[38] and Wordsworth is looking for summary devices to recall past matter – a musical coda crammed with earlier motifs, or, in a less exalted metaphor, the conventional 'thus' in the last paragraph of an essay. But perhaps it is not so exceptional. One of the functions of endings is to bring into prominence the connective strategies that have been implicit or less obvious all along, devices that imply cause or sequence or, as often in *The Prelude*, both at once. Further, in many individual episodes the text moves towards closure but simultaneously acknowledges that there is no end, neither to the causal sequence of experience nor to its own acts of redefinition. Here is an example from Book III, a passage in which Wordsworth speaks of a growing self-consciousness in his perception of nature:

> Let me dare to speak
> A higher language, say that now I felt
> The strength and consolation which were mine.
> As if awakened, summoned, rouzed, constrained,
> I looked for universal things, perused
> The common countenance of earth and heaven,
> And, turning the mind in upon itself,
> Pored, watched, expected, listened, spread my thoughts,
> And spread them with a wider creeping, felt
> Incumbences more awful, visitings
> Of the upholder, of the tranquil soul,
> Which underneath all passion lives secure
> A steadfast life. But peace, it is enough
> To notice that I was ascending now
> To such community with highest truth.

(III, 106–20)

The first sentence announces an act of redefinition, specifically a change of linguistic frame or register. It marks a stage in the argument as well as the autobiographical narrative but also a change of medium. The language is heterogeneously sorted. The nouns are opaque and diffuse ('things', 'incumbences', 'upholder'), the verbs contrastingly specific, powerful and more numerous, both active and passive (the gerund 'visitings' slides between the two). The 'mind' is given an almost tactile quality, as if *it* 'pored' and 'spread', but what it feels is a sequence of abstractions: 'universal things', 'common countenance', 'incumbences', 'upholder'. The passage communicates a remarkable sense of intellectual *expectancy*, something ever more about to be, built upon what seems solid physical experience. Its power, I think, comes from a double textual source, the opposition of concreteness and abstraction in verbs and nouns, and the way in which it plays with finality and continuity, definition and openness. There is a huge forward momentum but at the same time a sense of marking off distinctive stages of a journey. An act of closure ('peace, it is enough') is complemented by a re-opening ('I was ascending now'). The overarching metaphor of ascent and descent invokes an archetypal scene of sublime instruction (Moses on Sinai), but inside that structure there are moments which combine movement and stasis. Such moments have an important *narrative* function in giving shape to poem, but also the intellectual, perhaps I should say the ideological, function of invoking and destabilising sequence and, implicitly, logic and the direction of power. These things create power without specific origin; they make it possible to *report* on experience (not just facts) without ascribing an origin, an enabling process that needs strenuous acts of negation to arrive at its goal: the dream of self-sufficient language, a transcription of the spiritual self.

The discourse of relationship

Reading *The Prelude*'s syntax as *ambiguously* logical perhaps seems perverse or simple-minded, but I believe it is unavoidable and in fact productive. The reason is that the poem *by nature* lacks its 'proper' discourse, lacks generic definition. It was 'a thing unprecedented', as Wordsworth acknowledged to Beaumont,[39] just as Rousseau thought his *Confessions* 'an enterprise that has no precedent'. We categorise both works as autobiography, but the term did not enter the language until the 1790s.[40] Yet the genre established itself quickly, and within forty years Carlyle was complaining about 'These Autobiographical times of ours'.[41] When Wordsworth decided in 1804 to fill the gap between childhood and adult experiences in the existing text of *The Prelude*, generic problems arose. Any simple distinction between the two states becomes much more complex when the past approaches the present; and it's a quality of many autobiographical texts, whether fictional or 'direct' – Gosse's *Father and Son*, Joyce's *Portrait* – that they record greater difficulty in distinguishing past and present at the end than at the beginning. If that seems obvious, we should ask ourselves why, because it is by no means obvious that such texts should proceed as a simple temporal convergence. That they do so is a legacy of Romantic autobiography. More important, a new genre adapts the devices of existing genres for its own purposes. Wordsworth combined in *The Prelude* matters that 'belong' to differing kinds of writing: loco-descriptive verse, heroic narrative, aesthetic treatise, and many others.

His use of logical terms is an example. Logical markers like 'hence' and 'thus' are necessary to construct abstract distinctions in the first place. His texts create unexpected relationships, but relationship of any kind requires prior distinction between its terms. The reciprocal relations so prominent in *The Prelude* made by invoking and undermining hierarchies of past and present, subject and object, inner and outer and (as we have seen in the Book III passage) higher and lower, represent an *approach* to unity or identity that stops short of erasing the discourse of relationship; stops short, that is, of simply invoking a mystic presence. They recognise that reciprocity is the textual shadow of identity.

This leads us back to power. The ideal in the 1815 'Essay' is a mutual relationship between reader and writer, the 'calling forth and bestowing of power'. It is an aesthetic of community in which multiple relationships meet in the text. The argument for it has a weakness and a strength. It is weak because when translated into the actual circumstances of the publishing trade in 1815 it doesn't stand up. Wordsworth attempts to reach 'the People' (who will read sympathetically, that is, powerfully) and bypass the miseducated 'Public' who are in the grip of the reviewers; but it was largely the public, so defined, who bought volumes of poetry, including, of course the edition in which Wordsworth published the 'Essay'. (My sketch leaves out cheaply produced, often pirated pamphlets of ballads that circulated in provincial towns as well as London; a mode of distribution Wordsworth sometimes envied).[42] But the argument is strong in that it does not slide into metaphysics but points towards a psychology and a socio-dynamics of reading, the survey of literary taste Wordsworth had claimed as early as 1800 was necessary for an understanding of poetic reputation and communication.[43] The 1815 'Essay' is such a survey, limited though it is by Wordsworth's overwhelming mistrust of his readers.

That mistrust needs to be acknowledged, because it haunts his aesthetic of communication. I use the word 'communication' in spite of its antiquated associations because it is part of his Romantic ideology *and* it has become a tendentious term in literary criticism and sociology in the last two decades. It is a framework for dispersing power. If we find it utopian in the end, we must nevertheless understand the way Wordsworth explored it, especially in *The Prelude*. In a crucial, difficult passage in Book XII (lines 145–312) Wordsworth discovers that the people he writes about will be the people he writes for; further, he will achieve this by essentially becoming one of them. Subject, audience and writer coalesce. In this retrospective account, written in 1805, he is clearly thinking of a much earlier period, before collaborating with Coleridge on *Lyrical Ballads*, the period of the Salisbury Plain poem, in which Wordsworth's radicalism is shown in a relatively uncomplicated identification with a man forced into crime by poverty. Why should a model of poetic communication that recalls *this* period be so potent in 1805? I don't think we can dismiss it as merely a stage he passed through, because it is the most explicit consideration of the social role of the poet in the whole poem, far more explicit than the better known passage in Book IV, often referred to as Wordsworth's 'poetic dedication', where the young man celebrates 'all the sweetness of a common dawn' and 'vows / Were then made for me . . .' (IV, 330–45). What this passage lacks is a specific sense of the author *as writer*: for that we must turn to Book XII.[44]

> When I began to enquire,
> To watch and question those I met, and held
> Familiar talk with them, the lonely roads
> Were schools to me in which I daily read
> With most delight the passions of mankind,
> There saw into the depth of human souls –
> Souls that appear to have no depth at all
> To vulgar eyes. And now, convinced at heart
> How little that to which alone we give
> The name of education hath to do
> With real feeling and just sense, how vain
> A correspondence with the talking world
> Proves to the most . . .
> I prized such walks the more . . .
>
> (XII, 161–78)

The scene the lines point to is almost identical with that in the Book IV passage, a lonely road and chance encounters, but it is conceptualised quite differently, as 'familiar talk' *with* people rather than aesthetic contemplation *of* them. The contrast is developed in terms of language as contact and language as social currency, but in a complicated way. *Speech* is equated with familiarity, but the opposite term is not written language, as one might expect, but 'a correspondence with the talking world'. 'Correspondence' is communication generally, not necessarily in writing,[45] but 'the talking world' suggests literate society (the 'chattering classes'), those who communicate in confidence that they will be understood. So 'the talking world' comprises those for whom writing and speaking are *not* opposed activities, but it excludes those, the majority, for whom speaking is familiar but writing remote. If this *is* what the passage means, it contrasts two kinds of familiarity: one based on convention, education, social exclusion and an easiness with the written language;

the other on chance face to face meeting, negotiation, inclusion, the familiarity that might (potentially) exists among all pedestrian road-users, whether or not they are able to write. Wordsworth defines his poetic self as a meeting point between literacy and illiteracy.

It is important *not* to see this in over-simple political terms, as though a poet writing for the illiterate *must* be of the radical and possibly revolutionary left. Cobbett should remind us that simple politicisations are meaningless. What matters is that, writing at the heart of Romantic idealisation of the primitive, Wordsworth gives us a significant sociology of reading and speaking. The broad context of this passage in Book XII intertwines literal and metaphorical references to speaking and writing in a way that brings both terms into question, especially by showing how the usage of the literate community conceals a distinction that is crucial to the lives of the illiterate.

Clearly *The Prelude* invokes a general opposition between speaking and writing – as if the first could guarantee communication in a way the second cannot – and also acknowledges the logical absurdity, if that's what it is, of writing in favour of speaking and against writing. This dilemma is central to the Romantic version of the so-called 'logocentric fallacy'. We should acknowledge in turn that Wordsworth explores it as well as making use of it. More important, he explores the metaphoric vehicle as well as the tenor, defining kinds of speaking as well as kinds of writing. *The Prelude* is very much a poem built on recorded and unrecorded conversations: with Coleridge first and last, but also with the discharged soldier in Book IV, Beaupuis, Mary, Dorothy and these 'lowly men' with whom he 'held familiar talk'. At crucial points his education is furthered by communion with men as much as with nature, communion through speaking and hearing rather than reading. It is entirely characteristic that his political education in 1792 is represented as developing in repeated conversations with Beaupuis, even though their themes are literary in origin: Seneca, Cicero, Tacitus, Plutarch. Different kinds of speaking and listening serve different intellectual purposes, and Wordsworth discovers his central purpose by choosing a kind of conversation.

The poet as writer, speaker and listener: defining a poetic ideal entails finding / defining a readership as well as subject matter and style. It is in this passage above all others that Wordsworth theorises about art as communication, not mimesis or expression. 'Theorise' is probably too specific a term, because Wordsworth was not a consistent or rigorous thinker about poetry: indeed his virtues as a thinker are alertness and opportunism, the imagination always asserting itself over logic where his allegiances demand it. But as far as there *is* a central act of reorientation in *The Prelude*, it is here in Book XII, and it cannot be seen simply as a return, a *re*assertion, a *re*definition, even though the personal praise of Dorothy it contains ('Thou, midst all . . . preserved me still a poet') suggests this. In fact the Book troubles itself to find a way *beyond* the personal in an image of meeting others, of negotiated contact, and it is on this basis that Wordsworth writes about poetry that draws on and feeds a common pool of power. His programme is to

>   teach,
> Inspire, through unadulterated ears
> Pour rapture, tenderness, and hope . . .

and he defines 'unadulterated ears' first negatively, in defining the adulterated –

>   men adroit
> In speech, and for communion with the world
> Accomplished . . .

– and then positively as men 'unpractised in the strife of phrase', whose language is

> the language of the heavens, the power,
> The thought, the image and the silent joy;
> Words are but under-agents in their souls –
> When they are grasping with their greatest strength
> They do not breathe among them.

In classifying men as users of language he writes of them primarily as speakers, but he is classifying them as listeners too. Syntactical ambiguities point to this double intent:

>   by those
> Who to the letter of the outward promise
> Do read the invisible soul, by men adroit
> In speech, and for communion with the world
> Accomplished . . .

The parallel constructions – 'by those . . .' and 'by men . . .' –
bring together a kind of reading (i.e. superficial) and a kind of
speaking, suggesting an unstated relationship, perhaps a causal one,
between the two; as if habits of speech and habits of understanding
have a common mental root. But it is equally clear that throughout
the whole paragraph Wordsworth is writing about his subject matter
too:

> 'Of these,' said I, 'shall be my song. Of these,
> If future years mature me for the task,
> Will I record the praises, making verse
> Deal boldly with substantial things . . .'

'Song' conventionally signifies poetry, whether sung or not, but it has
a special resonance in this passage: neither speech nor writing, it will
have authority because it will be authentic. The lines also echo
another discussion of textual authority, that in II Corinthians, 3: 'For
the letter killeth, but the spirit giveth life . . . seeing then that we
have such hope, we use great plainness [alternative reading, 'boldness']
of speech.' Wordsworth similarly emphasises 'hope' (line 179), and
builds on and modifies Paul's contrast between written language, 'the
ministration of death, written and engraven in stones' (II Corinthians,
3, 7), with the 'speech' of inspiration.

I remarked above that Wordsworth's writing on language and
power is fascinating because it has psychological and even sociological
dimensions and is not merely metaphysical, but I do not want to
ignore altogether the visionary nature of 'visionary power', not least
because this is an area where metaphysics and politics could overlap
in the Romantic period. J.G. Herder's doctrine of Kraft ('power') may
have had no direct or conscious influence on Wordsworth's thinking,
but it makes a useful comparison with Wordsworth's 'power'. I
translate the word as 'power', although 'force' and 'energy' are also
philosophical equivalents in the eighteenth century.[46] Kraft is the
basis of Herder's philosophy of organism[47] and is the metaphysical
means of overcoming the dualisms: soul/body, mind/matter, subject/
object.[48] It exists prior to reason or any other specific mental faculty,
and because of its presence and operation, the universe is an
organism, not a mechanism, the interaction of organisms, a network
of relations, each of which is not distinct from the things it relates but
is inherent in them. Herder writes of causative powers, rejecting

Hume's claim that causation cannot be known, and sometimes associates power in general with God's power. For our purposes the social meanings of the word are more important. Challenging Rousseau, Herder argues that man is born into a pre-existing society and that it is meaningless to speak of a *contract* between the individual and society, because the two are 'inseparable; they are complementaries, not opposites'.[49] The organic nature of society can be seen in the central role that language plays. Language is not God-given, but nor is it invented by reason. Reason and language are co-terminous: 'Each nation speaks in the manner it thinks and thinks in the manner it speaks. . . . We cannot think without words.'[50] This led to a definition of 'national character', which, according to Herder, cannot exist without a folk-song tradition. The connection between poetry and national feeling is explicit, but there is also an implicit link between poetry and power. Herder supposes that poetry, like religion, originated in the worship of powers (*Kräfte*) rather than forms, as the imagination (*Einbildung*) tried to discover and give shape to unseen powers;[51] and in another early essay on the arts Herder specifically associated the visual arts with space, music with time, and poetry with *Kraft*.[52]

As to the function of poetry in society, Herder sees it as the expression of original power: not the power of the individual writer, but a socially or nationally shared consciousness. (He is now remembered chiefly for his collections of folk-songs and essays upon them.) Just as *Kraft* unites subject and object, so it – in some unspecified way – unites reader and writer, provided they share a language or, as we would say now, belong to the same language community. The *Volk* ('people') in Herder is specifically a language community *and* a nation.

Herder's concept of power is often criticised as being so broad that it is indefinable. What matters to readers of Wordsworth, I think, is that it is a way of placing language and social relations at the centre of metaphysics, a way of challenging the assumption (which we perhaps automatically associate with the philosophical idealism of the Romantic period) that questions of perception and knowledge are naturally and properly formulated in relation to the individual mind rather than to social consciousness. At the same time, where Herder is metaphysical, Wordsworth is pragmatic: his 'power' is never the *equivalent* of Herder's *Kraft* because Wordsworth is concerned with the dynamics of varying relationships, not with finding a term that defines all relatedness whatever. Looking at Herder's conception of the language community sharpens our sense that Wordsworth's is an altogether more tentative and yet more real thing: the 'Poems on the Naming of Places', for example, do *imagine* language communities where speaker and audience, reader and writer communicate completely, but they probe the idea too and are energised by recognitions of incompleteness. Readers' and writers' 'powers' may meet only partially.

The political dimensions of 'power' and *Kraft* also differ. In his early writing Herder used a cultural model based on linguistic and aesthetic homogeneity, and this led to racial definitions of nationhood. Later Herder had difficulty reconciling this model of a unified community with the conviction that power is a universal human attribute.[53] That difficulty seems to me *essentially* Romantic, a paradox of homogeneity and universality. Human history is the history of universal powers but particular peoples have particular histories *necessarily* connected with their particular languages. Put this way, the problem I've identified in Herder is recognisable by readers of Wordsworth, except that Wordsworth wrote less overtly politically and reflected more intimately the social context of Britain – the circumstances of actual readers, circumstances that led him to separate aesthetic community from linguistic community and consider the role of education and class.

A broad difference is that in Herder's case we are thinking of writing of the early 1770s and 1780s that became extremely influential in the next three decades because of the political need for a German nationalist consciousness to organise opposition to Napoleonic expansion. In Britain nationhood could be taken for granted in the 1780s, but the political events of the next three decades made any culturally decentralising force politically dangerous. I would include in that category Wordsworth's distinct regionalism in the second edition of *Lyrical Ballads* (1800) as well as his arguments against the centralisation of literary taste in the metropolis in the 1800 Preface and the 'Essay, Supplementary to the Preface' (1815). In the latter he was faced with Scottish and English critics who (except in the case of Burns) assumed that standards of language and taste were valid throughout the kingdom, yet who at the slightest occasion accused poets of deviating from accepted standards *in ways that signified class differences*. We can contrast Wordsworth with Scott, who imagined in the essay that accompanied *Minstrelsy of the Scottish*

Borders a coherent society based on the supposed ethos of the ballads – a distinctly Herderian project – which now, in fact, reads like a nostalgic, exotic world with little direct relation to political realities.[54]

Herder's work, particularly the essay *Ueber die Ursprung der Sprache*, has been revalued in the last two decades because it represent the beginnings of a sociology of language, for all the mystic nature of his central concept. It is reflected, I think, in recent German discussions of the subject, in the work of Jürgen Habermas for example, who seems to me to be much influenced by Kantian and Romantic theory generally. As an attempt to put communication at the centre of the discussion, Habermas's work makes a stimulating contrast with the predominantly logically oriented work of Derrida. His concept of 'communicative competence' is important because he recognises that there must be certain kinds of agreement – beyond the mere assent to Aristotelean logic that Derrida (following Nietzsche) assumes to be a cornerstone of Western civilisation – among users of language who believe its first *purpose* is to communicate. He specifies four conditions that speech acts must fulfil: they must be 'comprehensible, true, truthful and socially appropriate'. ('True' and 'truthful' differ in that the first means an accurate reflection of reality and the second, roughly, sincerity.) Habermas imagines 'consensual speech actions'[55] among a group of language users who share a *will* to understand and be understood. Now, although that corresponds to what many of us would call ordinary experience within our own circle, it becomes problematic when we try to generalise it in relation to (say) all speakers of English, or even all English speakers of English. It is difficult to see what force could *produce* such a will on a wider basis except an appeal to political identity.

This aspect of his work has been much criticised. Mary Louise Pratt, for example, suggests that Habermas's 'linguistics of community' should be replaced by a 'linguistics of contact', an account of the way language works in everyday life *across* cultural and linguistic boundaries.[56] Pratt writes from the point of view of contemporary multiculturalism and inevitably stresses heterogeneity among users of a particular language, not potential homogeneity. It is the balance between the two – or rather, the way we conceptualise them – that is the central problem of communicative theories of language, including Wordsworth's. From one point of view Habermas's theory is perhaps *too* well designed for readers of Wordsworth, because it repeats Romantic preoccupations and strategies. But it does have things to say about negotiating the differences between individuals and about historical change, and it is important to see that such things can be done within the Romantic tradition. It is too easy to equate Romanticism, perhaps British Romanticism especially, with a search for the one true, authentic voice (the 'original' version of *The Prelude*, for example), or, to put it differently, the lyric voice or, in Bakhtinian terms, the authority of monologism.

Bakhtin is relevant here because the antiformalist text, *Marxism and the Philosophy of Language*, ascribed to V.N. Volosinov but possibly by Bakhtin, defines what I read as Wordsworth's understanding of the problems of communication, but defines it as *anti*-Romantic, as I remarked above in the first chapter. For Volosinov the Romantic hypothesis is that 'monologic utterance . . . [is] the ultimate reality and the point of departure for all thinking about language'.[57] For Wordsworth, as I read him, this is untrue, though other Romantic poets, Novalis for example and possibly Shelley, did explore the idea that poetry was essentially oracular. Volosinov's 'anti-Romantic' argument is that thought is always, as it were, pre-socialised through language, and that the 'inner world' of the individual has a 'stabilised social audience', an environment that shapes reasons and values. Art is not so much a matter of expression accommodating itself to the inner world but vice versa: the inner world realises itself in the potentialities of expression.[58]

For both Volosinov and Habermas the question of historical change in language is crucial. If the inner world, as Volosinov puts it, reflects a stabilised *social* audience, it follows that as social values change, so the inner world changes too. What is wrong with merely linguistic descriptions of language (like Saussure's) as distinct from sociolinguistic descriptions, is that they have no way of accounting for language change. The issue is fundamental to Habermas as well (it is at the centre of his argument with Gadamer), and unavoidable in Wordsworth's poetry and theory, appearing with different emphases in different texts. The 'Essay, Supplementary to the Preface' is about the history of popularity in poetry, and is written as a history of bad taste, just as the Preface to *Lyrical Ballads* is in part a history of change in linguistic fashion. There is more dramatic evidence of Wordsworth's concern with language change in the dream of the Arab horseman at the beginning of Book V of *The Prelude*, where he laments the fragility of poetry in terms that refer to both the physical survival of texts (printed on paper) and aesthetic survival, that is survival through the vicissitudes of taste. His wish for an 'adamantine' medium for recording verse expresses both anxieties: adamant represents hardness, ineffaceability, but since adamant was synonymous with 'loadstone', 'adamantine' also means unwavering, true to the magnetic north. It is not clear how aesthetic change relates to linguistic change in Wordsworth's writing (it would be very surprising if it were clear), but a consciousness of both seems clearly to lie behind this passage. We should relate it to his unfashionable insistence that Chaucer was both great and comprehensible[59] and that Shakespeare's sonnets were poetically valuable (the prevalent idea was that they were worthless). The fact that Wordsworth's praise of Shakespeare is itself very Romantic ('With this key / Shakespeare unlocked his heart') reminds us how positive he was that language differences could be negotiated. His translations of Chaucer's 'Prioress's Tale' and part of 'Troilus and Cresida' (as he names it) and the pseudo-Chaucerian 'The Cuckoo and the Nightingale' are clearly works of love, but they show too great an admiration of the original, and he is content too often to repeat Chaucer's syntax, knowing it would be understood by antiquarian readers but not sufficiently acknowledging the reading habits of others. They are bad translations because they are too reverential.

But if his own dealings with earlier English poetry were difficult, it is important to recognise that they happened, and that they represent to us a part of his probing the functions of poetry and the conditions of its survival. I have been arguing that his texts embody a tentative, pragmatic, but none the less radical conception of power, one that imagines far-reaching negotiations between writer and reader. I think this applies diachronically as well as synchronically, as I indicated in my discussion of cultural bequest in Chapter 1. For this reason theories of language that deal explicitly with language *change* give us a more useful perspective on Wordsworth's writing about writing than those concerned only with logic and binary oppositions. Habermas fruitfully adopts the terms of speech-act theory in thinking about change: it is likely that 'constative' and 'illocutionary' significance (the former describes, broadly, 'dictionary meaning'; the latter describes performance) change historically in different if not entirely unrelated ways, and that, broadly speaking, constative changes are more easily traced – through dictionaries – than illocutionary ones. The latter can be deduced from representations of oral language in fiction, often, of course, in ways that relate to class and education, and for this reason we can usefully compare Wordsworth's representations of speech with those of, say, Jane Austen or Frances Burney, as I suggested in the previous chapter. From this point of view it is not only proper but necessary to read poetry against fiction, and vice versa: language differences that we read as generic or social can also indicate historic change. It would be fascinating to guess how long it takes a particular colloquialism (say) to move from speech into fiction and then into poetry.

Like *The Prelude*, a discussion of power should end with the future not the past. The end of the poem is a very special interface between the public and the private, between a known reader (Coleridge) and the unknown. Address to Coleridge could be personal, in a style that imitated oral language, even though Coleridge was physically absent during the composition of most of the poem; but the more Wordsworth committed himself to trust in Coleridge's sympathetic reading, the less he could regard him as the typical reader. Many passages in the poem report or imitate conversations, as if conversation were the true image of communication, the interchange of power, but we find a curious doubleness in *The Prelude*'s codas in Books X, XII and XIII, because though they are addressed to Coleridge they are also awkward (unpractised) addresses to the public.

> To thee . . .
> It will be known – by thee at least, my friend,
> Felt – that he history of a poet's mind
> Is labour not unworthy of regard:
> To thee the work shall justify itself.
>
> (XIII, 406–10)

The speaker exhorts and concedes in the manner of someone not sure of his audience. We can read these illocutionary acts as signs of the drama of a particular relationship, but passages like this suggest a speaker with one eye on intimacy and another on the world at large. Their explanatory gestures, multiplying in proportion to the speaker's sense of possible misunderstanding in an immediate audience, perhaps account for the divergent emphases on *both* prosiness (Macaulay) and passion (F.D. Maurice) when the poem was published forty-five years later[60] and for the even more radical estrangements of postmodernist readers. Wordsworth can assert too much to be persuasive and concede too much to be comprehensible. Authority is continually asserted *and* craved: self-revision is self-effacement and self-assertion.

Notes and references

1. Jerome Bruner and Susan Weisser give a brief summary of the arguments against such a supposition in 'The invention of the self: autobiography and its forms', in *Orality and Literacy*, ed. David R. Olson and Nancy Torrance (Cambridge, CUP, 1991), pp. 129–48.

2. The most influential of recent works are Thomas Weiskel, *The Romantic Sublime* (Baltimore, Johns Hopkins UP, 1976); Theresa Kelley, *Wordsworth's Revisionary Aesthetics* (Cambridge, CUP, 1988); Peter De Bolla, *The Discourse of the Sublime* (London, Routledge, 1989).

3. Wordsworth's admiration for Burke in *The Prelude* (post-1805 versions) is well known, but compare the comment (possibly dictated by Coleridge) on Burke's *Enquiry* in his handwriting in an annotation to Coleridge's copy of Knight's *Analytical Inquiry*: 'little better than a tissue of trifles' (quoted in P. De Bolla, *The Discourse of the Sublime* [London, Routledge, 1989], p. 282).

4. *A Philosophical Enquiry into the Origin of Our Ideas of the Sublime and the Beautiful*, ed. James T. Boulton (London, Routledge and Kegan Paul, 1958; rev. edn, Oxford, Basil Blackwell, 1987), Section 5, pp. 64–70.

5. Wordsworth's ideas about the sublime were not all formed by direct contact with Burke's writing. Richard Payne Knight's *Analytical Enquiry into the Principles of Taste* (a copy of which Wordsworth owned) specifically severs Burke's connection between power and terror. See W.J.B. Owen, *Wordsworth as Critic* (London, OUP, 1969), pp. 203ff.

6. I have in mind the emphasis on 'joy' (as against moral utility) in Blake's *Songs of Innocence*, as well as in *The Prelude* and the 'Immortality Ode'.

7. 'Fidelity', beloved of Victorian anthologists, is the exception that proves the rule; 'Peter Bell' is an ironic exploration of man's supposedly natural superiority to animals, which could itself provide a critique of Burke's imagery. Doubtless Wordsworth had other things in mind.

8. *Prose Works*, II, pp. 349ff.

9. For a summary of the argument see Owen, pp. 203ff.

10. All phrases quoted from Gill, p. 659.

11. For a discussion of the implications of Tooke's grammar see Olivia Smith, *The Politics of Language 1791–1819* (Oxford, Clarendon, 1984) and Tony Crowley, *The Politics of Discourse* (London, Macmillan, 1989).

12. First published in the *North British Review*, August 1848. Passages quoted are from David Bromwich's partial reprint in *Romantic Critical Essays* (Cambridge, CUP, 1987).

13. Bromwich, pp. 174–5.

14. Gill, p. 605.

15. *The Prelude*, p. 632.

16. Milton's sonnet to a university porter could be said to be a parallel case, and Wordsworth may have had it in mind.

17. *Letters*, I, pp. 354–8.

18. *PW*, III, p. 11.

19. Humphry Repton, *Sketches and Hints on Landscape Gardening* (London, 1794), *passim*. See also Richard Payne Knight's pointed satire on the phrase in *The Landscape* (second edn, London, 1795), ll. 227–8. The debate was given new life on the publication of Uvedale Price's *Essays on the Picturesque* (London, 1810).

20. Marjorie Levinson, *Wordsworth's Great Period Poems* (Cambridge, CUP, 1986).

21. 'Essay, Supplementary to the Preface' (Gill, pp. 658–9).

22. T.L. Peacock, *'Headlong Hall' and 'Gryll Grange'*, ed. M. Baron and M. Slater (Oxford, OUP, 1987), pp. 219–20.

23. Noted by de Selincourt, *PW*, III, p. 494.

24. *PW*, III, p. 493.

25. Wordsworth became sympathetic to prayers for the welfare of the dead in his later years, a fact to which Faber drew attention in *Lives of the English Saints* (1844), in which he reprinted Wordsworth's 'Stanzas suggested in a Steamboat off Saint Bees' Head'. See *PW*, IV, pp. 402–3. In view of Wordsworth's persistent explorations of communities of the living and the dead, it is not surprising this particular custom should be the meeting point of his Anglicanism and Roman practices.

26. The reference is given in *PW*, III, p. 494.

27. David Erdman discusses Thomas Wedgwood's attempt to get Wordsworth involved in a rational system of education in 'Coleridge, Wordsworth and the Wedgwood Fund', *Bulletin of the New York Public Library*, 60 (1956), pp. 425–43, 487–507.

28. The case for deep conceptual relations between Wordsworth's poetry and non-conformist texts has been argued vigorously but not entirely convincingly by Richard Brantley in *Wordsworth's 'Natural Methodism'* (New Haven, Yale UP, 1975). See my review in *English*, 25 (1976), pp. 48ff.

29. In 'The Tables Turned'. See Chapter 1 above.

30. *The Prelude*, pp. 158–9.

31. The sense of community in the early 'Lines written as a school exercise at Hawkshead, Anno Aetatis 14' is hardly surprisingly in a school exercise, but even here he negotiates a path between monastic seclusion and martial solidarity (*PW*, I, pp. 259–61).

32. See especially Isobel Armstrong, *Language as Living Form in Nineteenth-Century Poetry* (Brighton, Harvester, 1982), pp. 65ff.

33. M.H. Abrams, *Natural Supernaturalism* (New York, Norton, 1971).

34. Jonathan Wordsworth relates what I have called an instability to a particular phase of Wordsworth's interior life (*William Wordsworth: The Borders of Vision*, pp. 33ff), but biographical reference does not exhaust its interest.

35. As A.N. Whitehead argued many years ago in *Science and the Modern World* (Cambridge, 1926).

36. See Christopher Ricks, 'A sinking inwards into ourselves from thought to thought', in *Harvard Studies in English*, 2 (1971) ed. R. Brower (reprinted in *The Force of Poetry* [Oxford, Clarendon, 1984], pp. 117ff) for a fruitful examination of Wordsworth's use of prepositions.

37. See for example Jonathan Wordsworth, *William Wordsworth: The Borders of Vision*, ch. 10.

38. Jonathan Wordsworth's view that this passage was to end a five-book version of *The Prelude* completed in the Spring of 1804 (J. Wordsworth, 'The Five-Book Prelude of Early Spring 1804', *JEGP*, 76 [1977], pp. 1–25) is refuted by Mark L. Reed in the introduction to his edition, *The Thirteen-Book Prelude* (Ithaca, Cornell UP, 1992).

39. Wordsworth to Beaumont, 1.5.1805 (*Letters*, I p. 586).

40. Recent discussions of the genre keep alive the question whether it is in fact a genre. The positive view can be found in W. Spengemann, *The Forms of Autobiography* (New Haven, Yale UP, 1980); the negative in J. Olney, *Metaphors of Self: The Meaning of Autobiography* (Princeton, N.J., Princeton UP, 1972).

41. *Sartor Resartus*, II, ii (Centenary Edition [London, 1896], I, p. 75).

42. Wordsworth to Francis Wrangham, 5.6.1808 (*Letters*, II, p. 248).

43. Preface to *Lyrical Ballads* (Gill, pp. 595–6).

44. Some of the following paragraphs develop ideas in my 'Speaking and Writing: Wordsworth's "Fit Audience" ', *English*, 32 (1983), pp. 217–50.

45. OED, s.v., 5.

46. Maupertuis used the French 'force' in referring to Herder's *Kraft*; and R.T. Clark has argued that Herder's *Kraft* is influenced by James Harris's use of the Aristotelian idea of poetic 'energy': see H.B. Nisbet, *Herder and Scientific Thought* (Cambridge, Modern Humanities Research Association, 1970), pp. 10, 14.

47. F.M. Barnard, *Herder's Social and Political Thought* (Oxford, Clarendon, 1965), ch. III.

48. Nisbet, *Herder and Scientific Thought*, p. 9.

49. Barnard, p. 55, paraphrasing Herder's *An Prediger* (1774) and *Ideen zur Philosophie der Geschichte der Menschheit* (1785).

50. Barnard, p. 56, paraphrasing *Ueber die neuere Deutsche Literatur* (1767, 1768).

51. Nisbet, pp. 13–14, quoting Herder's *Aelteste Urkunde des Menschengeschlechts* (vol. 1, 1774).

52. Nisbet, p. 14, referring to *Kritische Wälder* (1770).

53. *Humanität* is a crucial concept in Herder's movement from nationalism to internationalism. See Barnard, ch. v.

54. See above, Chapter 1.

55. On this term see T. McCarthy, *The Critical Theory of Jürgen Habermas* (London, Hutchinson, 1978), p. 288. My brief sketch of Habermas largely follows McCarthy. For a more recent critique of Habermas, see Robert C. Holub, *Jürgen Habermas, Critic in the Public Sphere* (London, Routledge, 1991).

56. Mary Louise Pratt, 'Linguistic Utopias', in Nigel Fabb and others (eds), *The Linguistics of Writing* (Manchester UP, 1987), pp. 48–66.

57. V.N. Volosinov, *Marxism and the Philosophy of Language* (1929, 1930), trans L. Matejka and I.R. Titunik (New York, Seminar Press, 1973), p. 84.

58. Volosinov, p. 90.

59. 'It is worth while here to observe that the affecting parts of Chaucer are almost always expressed in language pure and universally intelligible even to this day' (Preface to *Lyrical Ballads* [Gill, p. 597]).

50. Macaulay's and Maurice's private comments on the poem are reprinted in *The Prelude* (ed. J. Wordsworth, M.H. Abrams and S. Gill), p. 560.

CHAPTER 4
Familial authority

Wordsworth's writing engages with language differences reflecting region and class, not directly revealing or even adumbrating our twentieth-century preoccupations with these matters, but touching on wider debates about the nature of language and society. So it is, I think, with the language differences that mark and constitute familial relations. This is an area where we have many handy images, in Wordsworth's case that of a circle, a family circle, implicitly a circle of equals. Its main function is to erase or at least enclose familial differences, and that is important not only in Wordsworth's representation of family relationships but also as a model for broader emotional relationships, including that of reader and writer: Dorothy's journals and letters, Sarah Hutchinson's too, show that Wordsworth's circle was partly, perhaps primarily, a circle of *readers*. On this factual basis the image or myth of the Wordsworth circle[1] has been elaborated in literary accounts of his life; first by Wordsworth himself in the 'Poems on the Naming of Places' and by Coleridge in a number of poems written in 1801 and 1802 ('The Day-Dream', 'A Day-Dream', 'Letter to Sara Hutchinson'), and later by De Quincey in his *Recollections of the Lake Poets*. Wordsworth used his sister, his wife, his sister-in-law Sara and later his daughter Dora as amanuenses, occasional muses and sometimes silent collaborators. Edward Quillinan, Dora's husband, took up the pen when she died. Two of Wordsworth's most famous lines –

> They flash upon that inward eye
> Which is the bliss of solitude

– were not written by Wordsworth at all, but by Mary, and the same poem ('I wandered lonely as a cloud') draws heavily on Dorothy's journals, yet Wordsworth never acknowledged the second fact publicly and only in 1842 announced that 'the two best lines . . .

are by Mary', leaving his readers to guess which lines he meant.[2] As Dale Spender remarked, Wordsworth is among 'the great writers known to have . . . propensities for taking the writing of women and using it for their own ends'.[3] Spender's comment is made from a *general* feminist point of view and does not concern the distinctions society makes between wife, sister, daughter, lover, friend. Wordsworth's poems do, however, deal in such distinctions, often in curious, disguised and challenging ways, and we need to be aware in probing the concept of the Wordsworth circle that a simple gender distinction is not a sufficiently subtle means of analysis. Familial and quasi-familial structures involve gender distinctions, consciously or unconsciously, but other distinctions are equally important. All of them complicate – enrich, compromise – the image of the circle.

As a descriptive term 'the Wordsworth circle' overlaps partially with the more explicitly literary historical term, 'The Lake poets', because Wordsworth and Coleridge publicly addressed each other as 'brother' in their poems.[4] Coleridge was 'twin, almost', as well as being a collaborator over the first edition of *Lyrical Ballads* and an imagined collaborator at crucial points in *The Prelude*. The glaring difference between the two terms is, of course, that the first largely signifies women and the second, men (Southey as well as Wordsworth and Coleridge; and sometimes Charles Lamb, Charles Lloyd and John Wilson). When the word 'sister' occurs in *Lyrical Ballads* and the *Poems in Two Volumes* of 1807 it generally points to a private relationship, not a public one. I shall discuss the difference later in this chapter, but for the moment I want to emphasise that both terms – and indeed other familial terms – can be used as metaphors for intellectual and emotional relations, and that it is the nature of metaphors that they can be modified or erased. Simply, the terms are to be examined in the context of both the needs of particular poems and the conventions of naming and addressing dominant when they were written.

Before turning to the particularities of the Wordsworth circle, real and imagined, I note briefly that the image has political uses, and some are especially relevant to Wordsworth. Circles have centres, which can be imagined as sources of authority ('Turning and turning in the widening gyre . . .'), but a circle can also inscribe dispersal of power, so that each member has allegiance to the others in a non-hierarchical way, even if there is also allegiance to a transcendental ideal within or outside the circle.[5] There is plenty of evidence that Wordsworth read seventeenth-century debates in which the image had a political reality,[6] and it persists in eighteenth-century non-conformist religious texts.[7] Clearly this can be related to Wordsworth's imagined communities, which I discussed above in Chapter 2, and to representations of the extended family as a circle. But in this chapter I shall concentrate as much on affection and sexual attraction as on power and look beyond the abstract patterns congenial to discussions of power.

Domestic relations in Wordsworth's writing can often be surprisingly interesting – surprising because we tend to think of the domestic as simple compared with the transcendental meditations of solitude. But the domestic is unavoidably *there* as a central part of his imagination, and it is an area in which distinctions of gender and generation (and therefore self and other) are prominent, therefore questionable. Lawrence Lipking wrote astutely that the 'willingness of the young Wordsworth to entertain the most womanish, unmanly, or agitated points of view, even at the risk of looking ridiculous, is among his most admirable traits'.[8] He referred to such poems as 'The Female Vagrant', 'The Mad Mother' and 'Complaint of the Forsaken Indian Woman' in *Lyrical Ballads*, but the trait is evident in Wordsworth's domestic poems as well, and there is something maternal as well as paternal about his care for his readers, as Arnold perhaps felt in defining Wordsworth's power in an image of nurturing:

> He laid us as we lay at birth,
> On the cool, flowery lap of earth[:][9]

Wordsworth as (male) midwife, presents the reborn reader to her or his natural parent; a sense of original though vicarious strength. Gendering of the self in Romantic poetry can often be seen as a matter of constructing a heroic (and therefore masculine) image, autogenetic and solitary. But Arnold's image reminds us of the link between the transcendental (whether heroic or masculine, or both) and the domestic, with its more complex constructions of self (and gender) and relationship. Still, the real appropriateness of the circle as an image of the domestic in Wordsworth is that it is a way of imagining a group of overlapping non-hierarchical relationships. Of course, other images and discourses impose other relations, but the circle can remain a powerful imaginative force nevertheless.

Perhaps the greatest power of the circle as image is its attraction to those who feel themselves *outside* it. We speak of 'charmed circles' when we see a wholeness in them and feel a corresponding incompleteness or failing outside, and we perhaps speak most forcibly when we are uncertain whether we are within or without. This is the chief focus, I think, of Coleridge's so-called 'Asra poems', a group of poems to Sara Hutchinson, including the two mentioned above, and it is *because* they play over modes of inclusion and exclusion that they so fully project the idea of the circle.[10] What Coleridge was stimulated to imagine in the Wordsworth circle was a kind of peace that reconciled (while in some way still preserving) the differences between male and female, adult and child, self and other: more particularly, between sexual and familial feeling.

> My eyes make pictures, when they are shut:
>   I see a fountain, large and fair,
> A willow and a ruined hut,
>   And thee, and me and Mary there.
> O Mary! make thy gentle lap our pillow!
> Bend o'er us, like a bower, my beautiful green willow! . . .
>
>   Thine eyelash on my cheek doth play—
>   'Tis Mary's hand upon my brow!
>   ('A Day-Dream', 1–6, 31–2)[11]

The central image of the fountain[12] focuses (unifies) a relationship between one man and two women. Though the lap and the eyelash are distinguished as features of different women, each symbolising a different kind of ministration, maternal in one case and erotic in the other, the overall effect is not so simple. Like many of Coleridge's fantasies in his notebooks this poem *essentially* blurs socially defined family relations, playing instead with *self-imposed* boundaries of transgression and guilt: daring (or not daring) to enter a circle where these things are simplified. The female breast, with its ambiguous attractions, seems to be an important incarnation of the circle in the notebooks.[13] Coleridge's feelings about the 'circle' could also issue in jealousy, as they did when in 1806 he fantasised (surely) a scene in which he saw Wordsworth and Sara Hutchinson in bed together.[14] Desire, guilt and jealousy seems to be involved in his representation of the Wordsworth circle in the 'Letter to Sara Hutchinson' and its derivative poem 'Dejection, an Ode', which in its first published version was addressed not to a 'Lady' but to 'Edward'. Whether or not we assume 'Edward' is in some sense Wordsworth, the change of gender is a crucial ambivalence: Coleridge sought (among other things no doubt) a wholeness that he could at different times attribute to the desired woman or the envied man. The circle and the related idea of reciprocity (which underlies the whole poem) are the outer and inner projections of desire. However we read Coleridge's reflections on familial and sexual life (and they are certainly more complex than I have suggested), we can't help but notice that Wordsworth's constructions or fantasies of the family are much less *overtly* concerned with sex. But I shall be arguing that his poems are not as sexless as they are often thought to be, and that sexuality and family feeling *are* related in his poems, though not as they are in Coleridge's. Shelley's 'Peter Bell the Third' contains powerful critical images of Wordsworth, especially in relation to sexuality, but, as Leavis argued many years ago, they are powerful because they link strengths and weaknesses inextricably.[15] These lines don't quite say what they seem to mean:

> But from the first 'twas Peter's drift
> To be a kind of moral eunuch.
> He touched the hem of Nature's shift,
> Felt faint – and never dared uplift
> The closest, all-concealing tunic.

> She laughed the while, with an arch smile,
> And kissed him with a sister's kiss . . .

Part of the gibe at Wordsworth's relationship with his sister lies in the fact that the passage *does* acknowledge desire, though it is crossed by fear (' 'twixt love and fear, / He looked, as he no doubt felt, queer, / And in his dream sat down'), so that Peter is no more than *a kind of* eunuch. It is a caricature, of course (which Shelley might have written quite differently if he had known about Annette Vallon), and contradicted in the same poem by the fantasy that Peter / Wordsworth was the adulterous father of the Idiot Boy. But there is a truth in Shelley's characterisation of Wordsworth as *fearfully* exploratory, *tentatively* persistent in his representation of family and sexual relations: a tone quite different from Coleridge's powerful fears, confidings and (in the other sense) confidences.

Nature, desire and guilt

Wordsworth seldom wrote explicitly about male sexuality and guilt, but there are important exceptions, and the early poem 'Ruth', published in 1798 in *Lyrical Ballads*, is one of ·them. It is usually grouped with Wordsworth's other early tales about abandoned mothers ('The Female Vagrant', 'The Mad Mother', 'The Complaint of the Forsaken Indian Woman'), poems which focus chiefly on the mother–child relationship, generally stressing the biological basis of motherly feeling. 'Ruth' is certainly about abandonment, but it differs from these poems in exploring the sexual guilt of the (male) seducer in a very particular way, asking specifically what is the place of male desire in nature.[16] The long 'Salisbury Plain' poem, unpublished in its entirety in Wordsworth's lifetime,[17] deals with male guilt, but not specifically sexual guilt, and it does not suggest, as 'Ruth' does, that guilty thoughts and acts can be fostered by different kinds of landscape. The oddity about 'Ruth' is that Wordsworth was tempted, especially in the 1802 version of a much revised poem, to use images of subtropical, exotic, abundance to suggest immoderate appetites: a familiar gothic and Byronic motif, but not one that is easily reconciled with the Wordsworthian notions that 'nature never did betray / The heart that loved her' and that the 'grand and permanent forms of nature' represent what is common, best and noblest in human nature. Landscape signals difference, not similarity; and Wordsworth goes to some lengths to show its workings:

> 'Whatever in those Climes I found
> Irregular in sight or sound
> Did to my mind impart
> A kindred impulse, seem'd allied
> To my own powers, and justified
> The workings of my heart.
>
> Nor less to feed unhallow'd thoughts
> The beauteous forms of nature wrought,
> Fair trees and lovely flowers;
> The breezes their own langour lent;
> The stars had feelings which they sent
> Into those magic bowers.'

The stanza form and imagery are extraordinarily reminiscent of 'Three years she grew':

> The floating clouds their state shall lend
> To her, for her the willow bend,
> Nor shall she fail to see

Even in the motions of the storm
A beauty that shall mould her form
By silent sympathy.

The stars of midnight shall be dear
To her, and she shall lean her ear
In many a secret place
Where rivulets dance their wayward round
And beauty born of murmuring sound
Shall pass into her face.

'Three years' is another poem about seduction, as I argued in the first chapter, though we are encouraged to see *that* seduction as benevolent. There, Nature seduces 'Lucy', and the poem is haunted by the thought that Nature was right to do so, even if the act leaves the speaker bereft. Here it's a different kind of seduction involving 'magic bowers' (perhaps recalling Spenser's magic seductions) that seduce the speaker himself, and there is a deep ambivalence about nature. To give it a simpler, more modern perspective, the poem wonders whether nature, in the form of desire, may after all be amoral. The focus of wonder is *foreignness*. There is an implicit opposition between 'nature' and the foreign (how can the natural be foreign?) which probably reflects Wordsworth's reading of travel literature. Michael Mason has shown that William Bartram's *Travels through North and South Carolina* (1792) – a book long known to have influenced Coleridge – combines a naturalist's interest in flora and fauna with a distinctly prurient interest in Cherokee sexual customs, especially the apparently welcoming gestures of 'young, innocent Cherokee virgins, some busy gathering rich fragrant fruit . . . whilst other parties more gay and libertine, were yet collecting strawberries, or wantonly chasing their companions, tantalising them, staining their lips and cheeks with the rich fruit'.[18]

'Ruth' may be alone among Wordsworth's poems in bringing out so explicitly the related ambiguities of male desire and colonial appropriation (interpretation) of customs,[19] but it is not a freakish poem: it could be read *against* poems like 'Lines left upon a seat in a yew tree', which Hartman thought of as typically Wordsworthian, prompting again the question of how physical nature can provide metaphors for moral imperatives, especially in the framework of sexual and familial relations. The foreign should be seen in relation to the 'wild', a favourite Romantic term of praise: the doctrine of the picturesque made rules about 'the wild' but did not encompass the foreign. My understanding of the Wordsworth circle as fact and image is that it involves both, though in differently conceptualised ways.

'Ruth' seems to have given Wordsworth special problems: it was repeatedly and heavily revised, especially in relation to the narrative point of view. Wordsworth introduced direct speech in 1802 for the stanzas about nature's influence but reverted to indirect narration in 1805. What does the difference amount to? Initially the youth had accused himself of nothing, and the narrator credited him with 'voluptuous thoughts' (not 'unhallow'd thoughts'), vices and low desires. In 1802 Wordsworth explored the youth's mind through direct speech in which he accused himself of 'unhallow'd thoughts', and then the narrator adds the same vices and low desires. Finally, in 1805, the youth acknowledges neither 'unhallow'd' nor 'voluptuous' thoughts but a (false) sense of *liberty*, and the narrator adds his judgements as in the first version. This last revision brings into the poem an overt political dimension previously missing, and it is easy to relate this new critique of liberty to other poems of 1805, notably the 'Ode to Duty'; but this does not answer the questions posed by Wordsworth's experimenting with direct and indirect speech. In fact the strength of the 1802 version lies precisely in the youth's puzzled enthusiasm for a new view of human nature: though it proved delusive, yet its power (in this version) is explicit. It is a more dangerous vision than in either of the other more morally controlled versions.

What has this to do with family relations? Mason noted that the poem revolves around two acts of desertion, the first by Ruth's father, the second by her lover, and that the passage in which the lover imagines his future with Ruth ambiguously combines a restoration of paternal affection with spousal companionship:

> And then he sometimes interwove
> Dear thoughts about a father's love,
> 'For there', he said, 'are spun
> Around the heart such tender ties,
> That our own children to our eyes
> Are dearer than the sun.'[20]

'There': in *that* place nature could produce this effect. There are landscapes, that is, that peculiarly foster particular relations. The problem is that in this poem the landscape of Georgia, described in some detail (borrowed from Bartram), corresponds to two different kinds of relationship: masculine liberty, sexuality and sexual guilt on the one hand, and paternal nurturing on the other. They conflict head-on in the 1802 text because both correspondences exist in the mind of the young man. In earlier and later versions sexuality and guilt are projected in the words of the narrator, so that the conflict is not so acute: we can place the lover's talk of liberty as self-delusion. But the two readings of nature persist, and the relation of 'liberty' and licence is problematic. And the terms are unavoidably political as well as moral. Bartram represents Cherokee society as *open*, unconstrained by social structures that (like the family) impose personal relations in the name of social rights and duties, but it's clear that he's also writing about his own (fantasised) sexual licence. The 'natural republicanism' imagined by European Romantics to have existed among American Indians is shot through with ideas of sexual freedom (I'm thinking of Chateaubriand's *Atala* as well as Blake's *America*); it is a utopia that replaces hierarchical structures (such as the family) with a loose idea of community in which women and men are typically seen in groups rather than as individuals. Such is the perspective of travellers' tales. It is opposite to the one-to-one perspective we find in most of Wordsworth's poems about the dispossessed: 'The Thorn', 'The Old Cumberland Beggar', 'The Sailor's Mother', 'The Last of the Flock'. But it is Wordsworth's equivalent of the utopian plan for a pantisocratic community on the banks of the Susquehanna that Coleridge and Southey had planned in 1794. Ironically Wordsworth's life at Grasmere eight years later, when his devoted sister was joined by his wife and sister-in-law, was a near equivalent of Coleridge's ideal: hence perhaps its magnetism.

Still, 'Ruth' *is* a poem about a woman abandoned twice, by her father and by her lover, and it has a double emphasis on mis-made families. Paternity has a doubly negative image, compounding the idea of paternal irresponsibility in Wordsworth's other poems about abandoned mothers. Why were poems about abandoned mothers so popular in the 1790s? The answer has much to do, no doubt, with historical circumstance, particularly with the plight of soldiers' and sailors' wives, as in 'The Ruined Cottage', the most extended and powerful among Wordsworth's early representations of broken family life. But it is surely no coincidence that these narratives flourished at the moment when writers, Wordsworth particularly, explored the idea of autogenesis, which means imagining one's father absent.

Paternity and its discontents

For a poet strongly associated with a domestic circle Wordsworth wrote surprisingly little about his immediate family, apart from Dorothy. His father is mentioned chiefly as a source of guilt in Book XI of *The Prelude*, though there are passing generalised references elsewhere;[21] his mother has a more extended tribute in Book V; he wrote nothing about his three sons beyond a six-line epitaph on Thomas; and there are two short poems about Catherine, two loosely 'about' Annette's daughter Caroline, a couple about Mary, and a handful about Dora, who in some ways became a replacement for her aunt Dorothy, both as amanuensis and as a figure of maidenliness and at the same time womanliness. There are three elegies about his brother John, but no poem about his other brothers, Richard and Christopher. Clearly females dominate. An equally striking fact is that he wrote more extensively and enquiringly about his own generation (John, the Hutchinson cousins, Dorothy) than about his parents or his children; there is a greater emphasis on 'horizontal' relations than on 'vertical' ones, with their potential for exploring issues of ancestor-worship, inheritance and genetics.[22] Biographical reasons for his relative silence about his parents (he was an orphan) hardly explain an almost complete absence of interest in lineage. Correspondingly, Romantic offspring tend to be presented as *un*fathered, children of Nature rather than members of a genetically linked hierarchy. Wordsworth did not, indeed, write about his own children as Coleridge did in 'Frost at Midnight' – in many ways a mere antitype of the self – but there is a strange lack of specifically familial (even less, paternal) feeling even in his best known, the sonnet 'Surprised by joy', written after Catherine's death in her fourth year. It is so unspecific about formal relations that it might have been written about a person of either sex and almost any age.

> Surprized by joy – impatient as the Wind
> I wished to share the transport – Oh! with whom
> But Thee, long buried in the silent Tomb,
> That spot which no vicissitude can find?
> Love, faithful love recalled thee to my mind –
> But how could I forget thee! Through what power
> Even for the least division of an hour,
> Have I been so beguiled as to be blind
> To my most grievous loss? – That thought's return

Was the worst pang that sorrow ever bore,
Save one, one only, when I stood forlorn,
Knowing my heart's best treasure was no more;
That neither present time, nor years unborn
Could to my sight that heavenly face restore.

The poem's terms of endearment ('my heart's best treasure', 'that heavenly face') seem to come from the common stock of amorous hyperbole, though 'treasure' may have a particular application to a child: something stored up for the future. But the weight of anxiety in the poem is not concerned with these particulars, but with an acute paradox of emotional fidelity. 'Love, faithful love' recalled her as alive, yet love ought not to have let him forget her death. There is no etymological connection between 'beguiled' and 'guilt', but the poem emphasises guilt in the form of impatience, and in this respect may recall the association of death and guilt in the passage about Wordsworth's father in Book XI of *The Prelude*.

It is true that one of Wordsworth's best-known poems, 'Michael', *is* about paternity and lineage, at least in the legal sense of inherited land. I have discussed it in relation to images of community in Chapter 2, but it is worth re-emphasising that Wordsworth creates in it a problematic relation between father and son, especially problematic because the son is hardly imagined as having his own life. He is, as it were, a victim of his father's need for property. Notoriously, the narrative of Luke's waywardness in 'the city' and subsequent emigration is narrated in five lines, as if it were inevitable after he left the land. But the poem *makes* it inevitable because it is about *Michael's* life and mind, not Luke's. The poem is to my mind a brilliant critique of Romantic landscape values, of the relation between aesthetic and legal ownership of land. We need not complain that this emphasis leaves room for only a very constrained presentation of father–son relations.

The most convenient way of explaining a general lack of interest in paternity in the poems lies, again, in the Romantic myth of autogenesis that shapes the whole project of *The Prelude*. Among other things that follow from this is the subordination of parenthood, which in turn may affect the representation of sibling relations. So, for example, when we read Byron, Shelley and Wordsworth, brother–sister incest is respectively a fact, a theme, and a suspicion. Explaining this as narcissistic projection[23] or the symbolic absence of the superego gets us some way towards understanding how the texts work, but it says little about the specific terms in which these relationships are socially constructed. Juliet Flower MacCannell has recently argued that 'utopian treatment[s] of an artificial society formed after the death of the father', such as Rousseau's *La nouvelle Héloïse*, reflect 'The Regime of the Brother',[24] and that is a suggestive framework, though MacCannell is not concerned with historicising it in any detail. Shelley's 'Spouse! Sister! Angel!' ('Epipsychidion') is clearly an object of erotic attraction, but the concept of a coexisting sisterhood remains, and not merely as a flimsy disguise. Wordsworth addresses Dorothy as 'Sister of my soul' in *The Prelude* (XIII, 211), so that a biological sister is also a metaphorical one. In both contexts the word becomes multivalent and questionable. I suggest that words naming family relations are not stable in meaning because social customs regarding brother–sister relations, for example, in 1802 were different from our own. In noting absences in Romantic poetry, we must also try to be precise about what is present. The point can be generalised: if we read Romantic poetry as celebration of the transcendent self freed of familial and social relations, we miss its struggles for freedom and confuse our own struggles to make sense of it. We lose the sense of difference. But we run up against the same problem if we deconstruct transcendence in simplified, binary terms (male / female, conservative / progressive).[25] Wordsworth's poetry engages with familial and social dynamics in a *literal* sense, just as his poetry of nature notoriously mingles the literal with the transcendental.[26] Where transcendence replaces or erases literalness, it leaves traces that need historical and critical analysis.

It is striking that Wordsworth's *least* overtly autobiographical narratives are about family structures, especially father-child relations. They are also among the least read: *The Borderers* and 'Vaudracour and Julia'. The latter is an episode told in the 1805 version of *The Prelude* as an instance of political interference with 'natural' family relations, with the natural obedience of a son or, from the opposite point of view, with his individual rights. *The Borderers* has a different focus and a different setting, but Wordsworth appended a note on its first publication in 1842 to the effect that its psycholgical interest in man's readiness to murder others owed much to his experiences in France in 1792.[27] Both lay in manuscript for many years: 'The Borderers' was completed in 1797; 'Vaudracour and Julia' was first published (as a separate narrative poem) in 1820. Both were substantially revised before publication, and both are crucially poems about the place of family feeling in political thinking and, conversely (and perhaps more truly) the place of politics in family feeling.

The society of *The Borderers* is strikingly different from Scott's depiction of Border culture in *Border Minstrelsy*, where the power of the family (clannishness) is in some degree the guarantee of its truthfulness and naturalness, however violent inter-familial antipathies might be: indeed, the more violence is defined by tribal antipathies the more solidly based it is: such is the implication. Scott's Borderers are feudal (and his feudal imagination has a lot to do with the early nineteenth-century clan-consciousness), whereas Wordsworth's are much more in a state of uncivilisation such as that imagined by Hobbes, a state where strength is right. For Wordsworth the Border culture is no fantasy of a natural order, but rather a nightmare of disorder ruled only by *le droit du plus fort*. I think this an important general truth about the relation of family and politics in Wordsworth. He had the opportunity to indulge in nostalgic feudalism, and Scott's popularity as a poet after *The Lay of the Last Minstrel* (1805) might have encouraged it. But he refused this simple view. His direct response to the *Lay*, *The White Doe of Rylstone*, is a narrative about a family split by politics and religion and is in any case, as I argue in Chapter 5 below, more concerned with other matters.

Wordsworth's Borderers are occupied with quite other (and quite anachronistic) ideas about moral conduct. The central predicament of the play, as is well known, is whether Marmaduke (Mortimer) will accept Oswald's (Rivers's) Godwinian conviction that action, in this case a murder that is presented as emotional parricide, should be based on

> the only law that sense
> Submits to recognize; the immediate law
> From the clear light of circumstances, flashed
> Upon an independent intellect.
> Henceforth new prospects open on your path;
> Your faculties should grow with the demand[.][28]

The importance of this passage is not just that it expresses Godwin's rationalism and his corresponding devaluation of family affections,[29] but that it twists his rational optimism into a crude progressivism that is *almost* biological, almost a matter of eugenics. In this respect it perhaps draws on Erasmus Darwin's *The Loves of the Plants* (1789), which was attacked in the Tory satiric magazine *The Anti-Jacobin*. In the pages of *The Anti-Jacobin*, especially in its satiric poem 'The Loves of the Triangles', Godwin and Darwin were indistinguishably fused as enemies of the social order. (The poem also attacked Southey and Coleridge.) The idea that Wordsworth used in *The Borderers* had, then, a distinctly scientific tinge. But it is a romanticised science, a heroic science in which the scientist feels his solitude as an intellectual leader. This stands out in the play as a correlative but also an opposite of the emotional and transcendent solitude of *The Prelude*. Oswald later comments on the murder he has committed in Palestine before the play began (Wordsworth's hero is Byronic fifteen years before the 'Turkish Tales') in similar terms:

> I seemed a being who had passed *alone*
> Into a region of *futurity*,
> Whose natural element was *freedom* . . .
>
> (IV, 1816ff; emphasis added)

The Borderers crucially sets these ideas in a narrative of family relations, actual in the case of Herbert and his daughter Idonea, and adoptive in the case of Marmaduke and Oswald (and Marmaduke and Herbert). At the centre of the action is the very question whether Idonea is really Herbert's daughter, and this leads into other questions about the way Wordsworth imagines fatherhood in the play, literal and metaphorical. At the end of the first Act Marmaduke, convinced by Oswald and a suborned peasant woman that Herbert has only usurped the role of father to Idonea, expresses a religious concept of fatherhood that is quite familiar but perhaps particularly questioned in Romantic writing:

> Father! – to God himself we cannot give
> A holier name; and, under such a mask
> To lead a Spirit, spotless as the blessed . . .
>
> (I, 543–5)

The idea that a father is above all a mirror of God, or vice versa, and that therefore loyalty and obedience to a father are religious duties, is the dramatic core of Shelley's *The Cenci*, another Romantic play about parricide. *The Borderers* is not strictly about parricide, but about a young man's not preventing the death of an old man whom he has long thought of with filial feelings – the parricide is virtual rather than real. In a strange variation of the wooing scene in *Othello*,

Marmaduke tells how Idonea's accounts of her father's adventure's led him to love him:

> I remember, when a Boy
> Of scarcely seven years' growth, beneath the Elm
> That cast its shade over our village school,
> 'Twas my delight to sit and hear Idonea
> Repeat her father's terrible adventures,
> Till all the band of playmates wept together;
> And that was the beginning of my love.
>
> (I, 89–95)

In another narrative, not fully told but alluded to a little later (180ff) we learn that Herbert was blinded saving his daughter from a fire in which his wife and infant son died. Marmaduke becomes a surrogate son through emotional sympathy, though (unlike *Othello*) the play avoids expressing sexual attraction between him and Idonea: he becomes, specifically, a surrogate son rather than a prospective son-in-law.

Against Marmaduke's and Idonea's emphasis on non-political meanings of fatherhood we can set Oswald's clear and tendentious politicisations. Trying to persuade Marmaduke to kill Herbert, he refers to the latter as a 'Parricide' (II, 895), meaning a usurper who, having murdered Idonea's true father, presents himself in that role – for the purpose, Oswald claims, of selling her to Clifford. This is a distinct extension of the meaning of the word, designed apparently, to show Oswald manipulating Marmaduke by invoking his sense of the sacredness of fatherhood. Marmaduke is too full of reverence not to be moved by this image of brutal usurpation and naked power; in fact Marmaduke is too reverential and politically naive generally, and it is this that makes him ineffectual in the play, drifting off into self-imposed exile at the end. Although Oswald is clearly the villain, his irreverence and independence are not presented as simply negative qualities.

The troubled political opposition of reverence and independence is echoed in the ethos of the play, partly through the casual remarks of the minor characters. Marmaduke passes on to his 'troop' Oswald's lie about Herbert, and their spokesman Lacy expresses his outrage in a pointed asseveration:

> Now by the head
> Of my own child, this Man must die; my hand,
> A worthier wanting, shall entwine
> In his grey hairs!
>
> (II, 1107–10)

A casual oath, in which Lacy typically reverts to simple sanctities, unthinking forms of words that become ironically significant in the play's emotionally charged emphasis on paternity. The historical context is the centralisation of power in the reign of Henry III, especially the re-establishment of authority in the Border region. Now, Wordsworth's Borderers are presented as a group ('band', 'troop') of 'friends' conscious of *sharing* decisions about their actions mutually and fairly, with no direct correspondence between age and authority. It is important that Marmaduke is apparently younger than Lacy and Wallace but not therefore subject to their authority. But when Lacy responds *as an individual* to Marmaduke's news he is ready, metaphorically, to sacrifice his son's life for his own end. This does not mean Lacy is either villainous or tyrannical, merely that his casual assertions in moments of passion unthinkingly reinforce the *power structure* of a stereotypical father–son relationship. His habits conflict with his politics.

But even when politics are not explicitly the issue, there are conflicts between different metaphorical uses of familial names, for example when emotional relations are named as legal ones. Just before the play's climax when Marmaduke tells Idonea he has helped murder her father, she claims him as her guardian ('an orphan, / Committed to thy guardianship by Heaven'). She assumes, hopes, that 'Heaven' can make human relationships, just as the law can institutionalise them. But both concepts lead in this case to delusion. It is not only that there is a possible conflict between Marmaduke's role as adopted guardian of Herbert's daughter and as adoptive son of Herbert. The two roles (elder brother, surrogate father) seem often to have coalesced in early nineteenth-century England and, as I shall argue below, the conjunction is important in Wordsworth's writing, and Dorothy's. It is that the impulse to *name* relationships in familial terms is natural but always leads to over-specific metaphors. In a personal context it makes confusion; when the metaphors are given a political dimension they can be uncontrollable simply because a nation, even a smaller community, is not in all respects like a family.

There is another context for the play that leads to similar

conclusions. Especially in its earlier versions *The Borderers* is distinctly Gothic in its treatment of landscape and emotion. Like Ann Radcliffe's Emily St Aubyn, Matilda (Idonea) is a Gothic heroine who finds herself in inhospitable country and runs from one male to another for protection, and is deceived about their integrity. It is a landscape of fear and disorientation. Yet something similar is true of Marmaduke, and it is *his* search for an effective political role *which can also be described in familial terms* that lies at the centre of the play. In terms of Gothic fiction Marmaduke is a feminine figure who nevertheless is expected to fulfil masculine roles. This is an area in which Wordsworth explores in the consciousness of a male character the meanings of the familial and the domestic, areas typically thought of as feminine,[30] just as in 'Vaudracour and Julia' he imagines a father as a surrogate mother.

I think the *idea* of family relations is unavoidable, and unavoidably political, in *The Borderers*, but not in the broad and often sentimental way of Scott, whose notes in the *Border Minstrelsy*, for example, are largely taken up with matters of lineage, family branches, and distinctions between different historical characters with the same name: an idea of family which makes it coterminous with an identifiable political group. This conception of family is a little like Burke's, though not identical. Burke is now read as having believed that family relations and political relations are microcosm and macrocosm: a very Victorian reading of Burke's insights into local and national allegiances. Scott's Border figures are much more simply feudal and self-righteous (in the name of family) than any figure of humankind in Burke, but it is easy to see how the two ideas relate. And it is worth linking them in order to show how Wordsworth's image differs. Dramatisation of family feeling in *The Borderers* has strikingly *little* to do with lineage, the idea of a collective or rather seminal identity persisting through history that is ubiquitous in Scott.

Lineage as a gendered image linking family and power has much more importance in 'Vaudracour and Julia', a poem and episode that is difficult to read satisfactorily. If we think of it chiefly as a piece of disguised autobiography concealing Wordsworth's affair with Annette Vallon and the birth of their daughter Caroline, the disguise seems remarkably feeble, even allowing for the fact that it was not published as part of *The Prelude* until 1926.[31] If we emphasise its clearly deliberate echoes of *Romeo and Juliet*, it simply suffers by comparison, and in any case the echoes lead us away from a number of issues that have less to do with Shakespeare's play than with Wordsworth's poem, especially religion and class. (Political partisanship is common to both.) Julia's 'stock' is 'Plebeian, though ingenuous', while Vaudracour's is noble, and such pastoral imagery as there is in the poem, especially that of vineyards and property, tends to reinforce the notion of 'stock' as nature rather than nurture. As to its relation to the rest of *The Prelude*, most readers' experience seems to be that it is a more or less alien interruption of the narrative of Wordsworth's experiences in France. But as Mary Jacobus argued, this is an important aspect of the poem, not an accidental one. She shows that patriarchal authority – paternal authority in a political context, with a feeling for lineage – is a correlative of the 'authority' of textual genre:[32] just as the patriarchal society of the poem rejects and devalues Vaudracour's attempt to live outside its laws, so the controlling conventions of autobiographical narrative, the unfolding of the heroic self, leaves no room for a disruptive fiction, and the story is excluded from the published version of *The Prelude*.

I find Jacobus's discussion stimulating but also limiting. In support of her feminist reading of the poem she goes too far, in my view, in claiming that 'all acts of naming in poetic making such as those lavished on Lucy might be said to involve the constitution of the speaking and writing subject at the expense of the silenced object'.[33] How does this help us to distinguish one poem from another? Nevertheless she is surely right to point to the 'feminising' of Vaudracour, not just in his inability to counter the patriarchal law embodied in his father, but also (though Jacobus does not discuss this) in the prominent image of Vaudracour's *mothering* Julia's infant child in her enforced absence. This contrasts with other images of the young *masculine* protagonist of *The Prelude*.

If we accept the generic difference of 'Vaudracour and Julia', we are free to look at it as a short verse novel or romance[34] on the common theme of thwarted inheritance, such as we find in, for example, Frances Burney's *The Wanderer*, set in the same period. Burney's novel is a powerful embodiment of the insight that for women in the middle and upper classes of society loss of social connection amounts to loss of identity. Juliet Granville, the heroine (her name recalls Rousseau's heroine in *Julie, ou la nouvelle Héloïse* as well as Shakespeare's Juliet, and I think the same is true of Wordsworth's heroine), is obliged to give up her name and accept an *alter ego* as 'Ellis', a name made up of arbitrarily chosen initials 'L.S.', and repeatedly adopts different social roles as the opportunity of earning a living presents itself – milliner, actress, music teacher – and and is repeatedly accused of deception. The truth is that she *does* deceive her acquaintances: she is a gentlewoman but prevented from acknowledging her lineage by political pressures in France and Britain in 1794. Comparison with Wordsworth's poem is interesting because Vaudracour has something of the same experience as Burney's Juliet, and in this way he is feminised, and marginalised, and deprived of his identity.

When Vaudracour at last recognises that his father is adamant in taking away his power of choice, symbolised by the operation of a *lettre de cachet* that has him imprisoned and, ironically, by a secret order releasing him, he plans to win his father back by exhibiting his son:

> Now, even now,
> I see him sporting on the sunny lawn;
> My father from the window sees him too;
> Startled, as if some new-created thing
> Enriched the earth, or Faery of the woods
> Bounded before him; – but the unweeting Child
> Shall by his beauty win his grandsire's heart,
> So that it shall be softened, and our loves
> End happily, as they began!

The image recalls *The Winter's Tale* in presenting the birth of the new generation as something at the same time magical (divine) and natural. But whereas Shakespeare's play stages renewal as a magical event (the 'statue' of Hermione coming alive) and persuades us it is natural, Wordsworth foregrounds the relation of the natural and the lineal. The child in the poem has to be male in order to emphasise the theme of lineage, legal inheritance, and perhaps also to suggest that grandpaternal affection may have a very particular element of self-love: seeking a vicarious rebirth in age. But at the same time Vaudracour wants the event to be or to seem 'natural', *unfathered*. The poem could not work if the child were a girl, yet the child has to be 'man' in both senses, male and human: specific and unspecific. In the figure of Vaudracour Wordsworth embodies a particular political idealisation of the family in which legitimacy and inheritance are combined with a deep, perhaps mystical, trust in biology. This is one of the meanings of 'nature'.

Although it is right to compare the poem with contemporary

novels involving inheritance and identity, the differences are just as important, and the Shakespearean influence is one of the differences. Yet Romantic fictions of 'natural' education like Bernardin de Saint-Pierre's *Paul et Virginie* (moral and emotional education at a distance from anything that can be called 'society') themselves differ from Shakespeare's romances because they try to dissolve the distinction between nature and nurture that animates *The Tempest* and *The Winter's Tale*. In fact both the Jacobean and Romantic periods had their versions of new-world fiction (Chateaubriand's *Atala* was an influential example), and the latter can look thin and sentimental beside the former. *Paul et Virginie* is a delightful fantasy of human moral self-sufficiency, but it ends with a necessary return to 'society' when there is a need to give a framework for the sexual attraction of the hero and heroine. 'Nature' can be a simple and successful metaphor for human life as long as human nature is thought of as essentially asexual or pre-sexual. Many readers of Wordsworth feel that his poems express this frame of mind. 'Vaudracour and Julia' is important because it questions the assumption. In spite of its simplifications and (from a biographical point of view) concealments, it has the strength of a work that is generically odd, testing certain thematic and formal conventions of its time, and it contains a passage of powerful but delicate sensuality:

> Through all her courts
> The vacant city slept; the busy winds,
> That keep no certain intervals of rest,
> Moved not; meanwhile the galaxy displayed
> Her fires, that like mysterious pulses beat
> Aloft; – momentous but uneasy bliss!
> To their full hearts the universe seem'd hung
> On that brief meeting's slender filament!   (94–101)

The poem also recalls another literary kind, the Gothic novel of pursuit, especially Godwin's *Caleb Williams*, with its scenes of imprisonment and legal dispute. Like Godwin's novel Wordsworth's poem takes a popular genre and gives it a political shape. The most powerful metaphors in *Caleb Williams* are those that give political meaning to the *domestic* reality of imprisonment and concealment, the physical construction of imprisoning devices like casements and bolts, and well as the deceptive familiarities of a thieves' den. And at the centre of the novel is a narrative in which Williams realises that the loved and familiar habitat is becoming a prison, and the admired employer, Falkland, a gaoler. It explores the nightmare moment, dramatised in so many horror films, when a familiar person or place suddenly becomes unfamiliar and threatening, a focus of many Gothic novels of the 1790s such as Ann Radcliffe's and, perhaps most strikingly, Charles Brockden Brown's *Wieland*, in which a familiar voice becomes a medium for supernatural ventriloquism. To invoke Brown's chilling novel is to move some distance from 'Vaudracour and Julia', but Wordsworth's poem forcefully conveys the idea that fathers are both most known and most unknown. This nexus of feelings is at the root of his writing about power, whether political, familial or sexual. He wrote that the latter was based on the perception of 'similarity in dissimilarity'. I suggest that paternal and political relations in Wordsworth have the same ambivalent base in familiarity and unfamiliarity, and that his discourse of the sexual, the political and the familial have much in common.

I would like to agree with Christopher Ricks's striking remark that Wordsworth is the most paternal of our major poets, because there is a peremptory fussing and an equally demanding self-denial in much of his work that suggest paternal certainties and anxieties. But this view diminishes his wider exploration of family roles, especially in relation to authority and sex. The actualities of family life are inescapable to readers of Wordsworth, and they do have symbolic and political values. But they are much more interesting than any *simple* idea that equates paternity and authority. (The idea has come to be accepted as part of what Jerome McGann called the 'Romantic Ideology'.) I don't claim that Wordsworth's metaphors of family relations are not sexist and paternalist in today's framework, but I do argue that his sexism and paternalism are not identical; nor can either be regarded as simply politically authoritarian.

Childhood and socialisation

Romantic paternity is the subject of much mythologising among readers – professional readers, at least – perhaps because Romantic writers did not on the whole deal with it directly. The opposite is true of childhood, which is the most striking scene of mythologisation in Wordsworth's writing – in *The Prelude* , the 'Immortality Ode' and in poems like 'We Are Seven' and 'Anecdote for Fathers' – and one of the effects of the process is to withdraw childhood from the complexities of family relations. The Romantic construction of the 'child of nature' denies familial relations and can be merely a rewriting of autogenesis in transferred or metaphorical terms. Coleridge's 'Frost at Midnight' superimposes an imagined future for his son that corrects his own recalled past and consoles him for its miseries. Wordsworth wrote little about his children, but much about his own childhood in *The Prelude* (in this sense the poem is a second self), and many of his other poems about childhood are associated with his sister rather than his children – which, again, seems to offer an opportunity to write about childhood and largely ignore parenthood. In this sense Wordsworth's concerns seem even more thoroughly autogenetic than Coleridge's: he scarcely imagined the specific otherness of his children.

That is only partly true. Though poems about Dora in her early years ('Address to My Infant Daughter Dora') are disappointingly thin in comparison with those about the fatherless 'Lucy', poems about her adulthood, particularly 'The Triad', have a quite different focus: women, marriage and authorship; topics which, by 1830, were more resonant than the child of nature. Wordsworth's later textualisation of Dora is sufficient evidence that he did not ignore social debate in his later years. In any case the earlier poems about childhood, those written in 1800–2, do show a concern with *socialisation*, the non-biological process by which a child turns into an adult, which are absent in 'Frost at Midnight'. The point can be illustrated by comparing Coleridge's poems about his son Hartley, especially 'Frost at Midnight' and the conclusion to the second part of 'Christabel', and Wordsworth's 'To H.C.'.

'Frost at Midnight' comprehensively remakes the narrator's past by subsuming all its details in a future life where social tensions are absent:

> For I was reared
> In the great city, pent 'mid cloisters dim,
> And saw nought lovely but the sky and stars.
> But *thou*, my babe! shalt wander like a breeze
>
> . . .
>
> so shalt thou see and hear
> The lovely shapes and sounds intelligible
> Of that eternal language, which thy God
> Utters . . .
>
> Therefore all seasons shall be sweet to thee . . .

Just as nature is in the place of the 'great city', so God's language supersedes human language. Human languages are associated with disharmony; more particularly with the opposition between familar and unfamiliar that is so prominent earlier in the poem in the image of the 'stranger' on the hearth. The hearth has a paradoxical role because it signifies both the narrator's own emotional focus at the present moment of the poem and, in memory, the hearth at his school that he gazed at longing for the 'stranger', who would in fact be a friend or perhaps a member of his family. This double / opposite meaning subverts human language, and the instability of the narrator's own experience is further thematised in images of the seasons. He is disquieted by the winter, which reminds him involuntarily of summer: whereas '*all* seasons shall be sweet' to his son.

If the 'Conclusion to Part II' of 'Christabel' (1801) is a sequel to 'Frost at Midnight', it is a sadly ironic one:

> A little child, a limber elf,
> Singing, dancing to itself,
> A fairy thing with red round cheeks,
> That always finds and never seeks,
> Makes such a vision to the sight
> As fills a father's eyes with light;
> And pleasures flow in so thick and fast
> Upon his heart, that he at last
> Must needs express his love's excess
> With words of unmeant bitterness. . . .
> And what if, in a world of sin
> (O sorrow and shame should this be true!)
> Such giddiness of heart and brain
> Comes seldom save from rage and pain,
> So talks, as it's most used to do.

Contemplating the child's words and actions, all self-absorbed and self-sufficient, the father is disoriented, not consoled. The terrible supposition that in adults only rage and pain could produce such 'giddiness', such extreme emotion in which self and action, self and language, are identical, is certainly a testimony to the power of association. Coleridge might also have used it to expose the power of social custom, that proscribes 'mindless' joy as madness, but he seems to shy away from that reading towards a religious scheme in which children are innocent and adults inhabit a 'world of sin'. That being so, we are left with a stark opposition: if Hartley in the earlier poem speaks only to God, he is beyond human (i.e. adult) conversation. (As a 'conversational poem', 'Frost at Midnight' is very one-sided, as indeed are the other poems often grouped under the heading.[35]) Writing to Southey, Coleridge described the poem as 'A very meta-physical account of Fathers calling their children rogues, rascals, & little varlets – etc –';[36] but, if it is not taking too seriously the common guilts fathers confess to fathers, I would say that it is not metaphysical enough.

Wordsworth wrote nothing quite like either of these poems. The nearest to the 'Christabel' conclusion is 'Anecdote for Fathers', in which the narrator accepts misunderstanding; more particularly, he accepts that adults use conventional habits of speech that mean nothing to children, even when put in the simplest terms. The question whether the child (not Wordsworth's child, but Basil Montagu's) prefers one place to another foists upon him concepts of taste, judgement and causation that lurk in the most ordinary ('innocent') speech.[37] He at first refuses to play the game, and though he subsequently gives in, the narrator realises that a meaningless question has resulted in a meaningless answer. It is a poem very easily politicised, and none the worse for that: a display of forcing someone else to argue in one's own terms – an indictment, too, of the *habit* of pedagogy.

I am arguing that Wordsworth's representation of childhood, in contrast with Coleridge's, includes awareness that distinctions between childhood and adult behaviour are a matter of social convention, and are therefore negotiable. This has two corollaries: first, that the idea of childhood can be the more readily used to challenge conventions of adult behaviour, and secondly, that child-hood is not a mystical state of innocence. The 'Immortality Ode' *examines* notions of innocence according to a Platonic hypothesis but considers socialisation as well: the child is represented as fantasising adult rituals, 'as if his whole vocation / Were endless imitation'.[38] It is too easy to read the 'Ode' as if these lines expressed simple regret: they take their place in a complex enquiry into what *becomes* of innocence in the social world. This is one of a number of areas where Wordsworth seems either not completely 'Romantic' (unlike Coleridge, and unlike Novalis, who invoked an image of youth and health which was also an image of death)[39] or else post-Romantic, a writer who understood what we would now call the constructions of Romanticism.

The language of socialisation in Wordsworth's poems is a medium in which aesthetics and ethics frequently overlap, and they can be creatively confused. The word 'wild' (with its derivatives) is a powerful example, and it is prominent in 'To H.C.'. It is a term highly charged with meaning in the discourse of the sublime and the picturesque, and it also denotes, as we have seen, behaviour for which some defence, apology or explanation is needed. In rhyming 'wild' with 'child'[40] Wordsworth invokes a large debate about the nature of polite or refined society as against more 'primitive' ways of life; an opposition explored implicitly and often explicitly in travel writing (a favourite genre with Wordsworth, if the sale catalogue of his library is a reliable guide) as well as in more abstract discussions about the nature of human society and progress. Metaphors that liken the progress of society to the stages of human growth and maturity abound in the latter; often, as when Shelley writes of 'the infancy of society', in contexts which speak of progress *and* the search for enduring value or original 'truth' in records of primitive societies.[41] Peter France has shown how the dominant cultures in eighteenth-century Europe were paradoxically both attracted to and repelled by *social* 'wildness', whether of Scottish Highlanders in Boswell's account or of Corsicans in Rousseau's.[42]

The question of language played a crucial part in these speculations. One measure of the sophistication of an individual or a society was its ability to use abstract language (the idea is not unfamiliar today), a measure that Coleridge used in criticising Wordsworth's theories in the Preface to *Lyrical Ballads* and which derives ultimately from the eighteenth-century concept of universal grammar: all languages in their perfection are images of reason.[43] This point of view generates notions of secondary languages: imperfect, childish or (in some discussions) feminine.[44] But if the language question is seen in the broader context of the contrary attractions of the wild and the sophisticated, the 'superiority' of abstract language is less evident than it might seem. I argued in Chapter 1 that Wordsworth's consciousness of regional and class difference in language challenged certain accepted hierarchies: so too, I think, does his language of youth and age. This is evident above all in 'To H.C.', a major contribution to the mythologising of Hartley Coleridge as a 'child of nature'.

The poem's central discovery, 'Thou art so exquisitely wild', could be described as a self-defeating statement. More accurately it is a statement that plays upon different points of view. Wildness is admired only from a distance – that distance that allows a judgement of *taste* ('exquisite') to come between the spectator and the object – but the condition of wildness in itself is beyond taste; it excludes taste by definition. Putting it the other way around, taste and judgement put the spectator outside the condition of wildness. In this poem intense pleasure in the object is met by the pain of recognising difference, and the result is not mere nostalgia because it includes the fear that H.C. is, after all, uncivilised and will remain so (a view Hartley's father came to share). The word 'wild' is the crux and turning point of the poem. Up to this point it celebrates H.C.'s non-human affiliations: he is a 'faery voyager', a 'blessed vision'; but then he becomes a 'happy child', and the rhyming word 'wild' in the following line leads the poem from celebration to anxious anticipation. It introduces a temporal dimension, and also a social one.

> . . . happy Child!
> That art so exquisitely wild,
> I think of thee with many fears
> For what may be thy lot in future years.

> I thought of times when Pain might be thy guest,
> Lord of thy house and hospitality:
> And grief, uneasy Lover! never rest
> But when she sate within the touch of thee.

Changes in the relation of speaker and object are signalled by the introduction of 'I', for the first time in the poem, and by a change of tense ('I think . . . I thought') where the past tense impinges almost as an explanation of the *unspoken* fears of the previous moment. The poem then moves into a mode of domestic allegory ('when Pain might be thy guest'), so that as the subject becomes humanised and separate from the speaker, he also becomes socialised. Hartley is host, guest, lover and beloved.

The poem envisages a *rite de passage* not just from childhood to adulthood, nor just (if at all) from 'Nature' to humanity, but also from social indefinition to guesses at definition. And this is also a matter of language use. Like the exemplary child in the 'Immortality Ode' who fashions 'a wedding or a funeral'

> As if his whole vocation
> Were endless imitation[,]

H.C. uses language as 'mock apparel'; but soon he will be unable to play (divinely, ironically) with language but become its victim, when 'Pain' and 'grief' are guest, host and lover. It is crucial to the poem that these specific personifications name social and familial relations and suggest that they are the beginnings of signification generally. The second half of the poem imagines a transition from solitude to society, from indefinition to definition – but regrets that the terms of definition are too gross to contain the essence of the boy as he seems at present: he will 'slip in a moment out of life', because life, as the poem presents it, defines temporality in terms of specific social roles, so that there can be no future, no sense of time at all, without them.

A simple response to Wordsworth's poems might dwell on the movement from solitude to society as a matter only of loss, but we should see that the feelings this poem expresses include regret that H.C. will not be able to cope with social actuality, however he might play with it, and that neither 'solitude' nor 'society' is an absolute term. Solitude is not a pure absence of relationship but a negation of particular possibilities or expectations.[45] Here the possibilities are specifically domestic, and as if domestic relationship were a half-way house between absence of relationship and complete social integration; a simplified image of 'society' in which a few formalised relationships do duty for all.

What is peculiar to this poem is that the relationships envisaged are extremely formalised and limited, domestic but not familial in a broad sense: lover and guest. Such a pared-down vision of H.C.'s *possible* future (the poem then denies even this possibility) brings a curious bleakness. Wordsworth is especially paternal at this point. The poem focuses on a male relationship in different guises (father and – almost – son; male adulthood and boyhood) threatened by a stranger or a (female) lover. Gendering is evident because H.C. is envisaged as *having* a 'hearth'; he is its owner and therefore male. The bringers of pain and grief might be of either sex. So the transition the poem envisages and rejects is from solitary childhood to essentially solitary (male) adulthood. But to say that is to measure its lack and its longing, the longing to leap over or put away (on H.C.'s behalf) any more complicated relationship. A reading that sees the poem as purely celebratory ignores these imprisoning implications. But to read the poem as simply reflecting the supposed peculiarites of the historical Hartley Coleridge (who later became aware that he had been a child-man and then a man-child, and who seems to have found it impossible to express emotion to an adult woman) is equally limiting: the poem is a critique of solitude in human terms, and counts precisely and specifically the pains that the 'bliss of solitude' masks.[46]

In the matter of gendering, 'To H.C.' should be compared with 'Characteristics of a Child three Years old', another poem that rhymes child and wild, if only in the title and first line. Here the image of a child's solitude is unlike that in the earlier poem: she is like a fawn, a breeze, in harmony with nature, but not an object of fear or pity. This is striking because the final lines

> as the stir
> Of the soft breeze ruffling the meadow flowers;
> Or from before it chasing wantonly
> The many-coloured images impressed
> Upon the bosom of a placid lake [–]

closely recall the vision of another dead boy:

> or the visible scene
> Would enter unawares into his mind
> With all its solemn imagery, its rocks,
> Its woods, and that uncertain Heaven, received
> Into the bosom of the steady Lake.

What protects the girl from dissolution (or rather, what protects the adult speaker from fear for her future) is a delicately balanced discourse of socialisation and 'innocence' at the beginning of the poem, in which adult society is safely charmed and teased by her:

> Loving she is, and tractable, though wild;
> And Innocence hath privilege in her
> To dignify arch looks and laughing eyes;
> And feats of cunning; and the pretty round
> Of trespasses, affected to provoke
> Mock-chastisement and partnership in play.

Moreover the first image of solitude applied to her is a domestic one:

as a faggot sparkles on the hearth,
Not less if unattended and alone
Than when both young and old sit gathered round
And take delight in its activity[.]

Without the assurance that her behaviour is 'innocent', it would look distinctly 'missish' (as Jane Austen's Mr Bennett would say): 'arch looks . . . cunning . . . pretty round of trespasses, affected . . .'. But it is not innocence as an inherent quality of the child that makes the scene so safe from misinterpretation, but rather the solid fact that she is 'tractable' and voluntarily participates in 'mock-chastisement'. This is a parent-oriented poem (a poem about authority) in which 'endless imitation' is approved, avoiding philosophical investigation of innocence. For this reason, I think, the child's solitude at the end of the poem doesn't communicate a crisis of identity and role as 'To H.C.' and the 'Immortality Ode' do. It is another case in which the Romantic image of solitude is seen to be gendered.

Female solitude: 'Louisa', 'To a Young Lady'

Discussing 'To a Highland Girl' in Chapter 1 I pointed to a momentary fusion of paternal, fraternal and sexual feeling. The latter is dominant when the poem builds desire on a foundation of difference – language difference, in particular, and the impossibility of verbal communication. The poems I now turn to differ in that their affective gestures are founded on familiarity as well as difference; or to put it another way the claims the speaker makes on his imaginary object conflict in different ways. One question that arises in relation to these poems is the nature of the familiarity projected – whether it has to do with familial structures.

It is worth remembering that both 'Louisa' and its companion piece[47] 'To a Young Lady who had been reproached for taking long walks in the couuntry' have been thought of as 'about' Dorothy. While that provides some justification for discussing them in this chapter, it is not an indispensable context, and in fact may raise more problems than it is supposed to solve. To anticipate, there are moments of clear sexual attraction in 'Louisa', but that need not lead us to imagine lurid scenes at Grasmere.

Dorothy Wordsworth has only recently emerged from the shadow of the men around her: not only her brother, Coleridge, and De Quincey, but also various later visitors to the Lake District have left records of their impressions, more or less fashioned in agreement or in contrast with her brother's mythologised image of her in poems like 'Tintern Abbey'. It is the 'more or less' that needs to be examined. John Barrell gave the title 'The Uses of Dorothy' to a discussion of that poem, in which he argues that Wordsworth attributes to Dorothy the 'language of sense' while reserving for himself a more analytic, intellectual language.[48] The division, he says, corresponds to eighteenth-century gender stereotypes. There is justice in the argument, but it does not isolate specifically familial qualities: a younger sister–elder brother relationship, which is subject to its own pressures from stereotypes. Such a relationship might find both more passionate and more hierarchical expression in an era when the extended family expected, more strongly than now, that he would become the head of the household and she its domestic manager, stepping into paternal and maternal roles. So much is evident in, for example, the family narratives recorded in Leonore Davidoff and Catherine Hall's *Family Fortunes*.[49] It is clear from these accounts that the relationship could be virtually a spousal one, a trial period in domestic economy. The Wordsworths' case was peculiar because they were orphaned, brought up separately and as young adults very dependent financially on their guardian aunts and uncles – who were displeased with William's expectation of independence and possibly with news about Annette and Caroline Vallon. In spite of these complications Dorothy's love and admiration of William led her to look forward in her early twenties to a *natural* progression from childhood to domestic intimacy, as her letters to Jane Pollard show.[50] Her ideals remained entirely bound up with setting up home with her brother, and they show a curiously intense confidence that the past can be recreated in the future. For Wordsworth it must have been different. It is hardly speculative to infer from *The Prelude* and the worldly tone of his letters in 1794 (while Dorothy was confiding in Jane) that his education and experience of sex and parenthood-in-absence had caused so decisive a break in the history of his affections that the past was not *simply* available. At the same time Dorothy could be seen from a distance as a powerful figure of continuity and re-enactment;[51] a malleable figure, sometimes evanescent, sometimes more solidly human, a means of contemplating life freed of social distinctions based on age, status and customs of behaviour.

That is the general pattern I'll be using in this discussion, but it is important to stress that the 'uses of Dorothy', to revert to Barrell's phrase, are various: 'Tintern Abbey' projects a quite different 'Sister' from the child in the poems of Spring 1802, where 'Emmeline' is clearly of a pre-sexual age (or an age which a pre-Freudian era saw as pre-sexual), and the narrator's role is both fraternal (in memory) and paternal in the way it guides and constructs memory. The fact that these two coalesce points to the ambivalences in the elder brother–younger sister relationship that I've suggested above. 'Louisa' is different again: so different, in fact, that we have to add to the role of father and brother in the other poems the role of lover.

Social structures aside, Jean Hagstrum is quite right in extending Empson's insight that 'sensation and imagination interlock' to encompass a sexual element in transcendent moments:

> If . . . physicality was an essential ingredient of Wordsworth's nature and entered almost every emotion that touched the poet's psyche – then we must expect that sexual attraction of some kind found a place here too, mostly natural and unaware but capable of coming to the surface of the poet's mind.[52]

Hagstrum properly relates this view to Wordsworth's discussion of 'similitude in dissimilitude' in the Preface to Lyrical Ballads (see Chapter 1 above) and notes that one of Coleridge's abstruser neologisms, 'coadunation', applies not only to the metaphoric structures of language but also to 'the union of "Feeling and Sensation" in "sexual Pleasure" '.[53] The question is how social and other conditions mediated the surfacing.

Louisa clearly represents an ideal of freedom in nature, that is, a condition in which the will is allowed free reign and discovered to be 'natural'. So far she is similar to Lucy, especially the Lucy of 'Three years she grew'; but there is a fundamental difference in the way freedom is conceived. Lucy is 'unknown' to all but 'few', and the only perspective we have on her life is the narrator's own. In 'Louisa', on the other hand, the narrator *defends* his view (and her habits) against the implicit censure of others, grappling with the fear that both he and she will be misunderstood:

> I met Louisa in the shade,
> And, having seen that lovely Maid,
> *Why should I fear to say*
> That she is ruddy, fleet, and strong . . .[54]

The poem celebrates both her behaviour and his feelings towards it.

But this is not a poem of shared confidence as erotic poems often are ('Busie old fool . . .'), because Louisa escapes the narrator's physical desire ('Oh might I kiss . . .') and he is forced to retire into spectatorship:

> Take all that's mine 'beneath the moon',
> If I with her but half a noon
> May sit beneath the walls
> Of some old cave or mossy nook,
> When up she winds along the brook
> To hunt the waterfalls.

The note of voyeurism, stronger in a manuscript version ('When she goes barefoot up the brook'),[55] hints at an unstated preference that desire remain unfulfilled: there is a protective barrier, supplied in this poem by the very vigour and self-absorption that arouses desire. Louisa slips away. There is a similar ambivalence in 'To a Highland Girl', as I suggested above, but in that case the barrier is partly linguistic.[56] Wordsworth's revision of 'Louisa' adjusts distances between the narrator and the girl, and between the narrator and audience ('Why should I fear to say / That nymph-like she is fleet and strong'), suggesting some unease at the self-contradictions of desire as it is figured here. The curious allusion to Gloucester's suicide in King Lear ('For all beneath the moon / Would I not leap upright') is a piece of lover's hyperbole, but if it also suggests the self-destructiveness of passion, it is a further mark of protective inhibition.[57]

I've dwelt on physical desire because it is inescapable in the poem, despite Wordsworth's diminishing it in revision (changing 'ruddy' into 'nymph-like' – clothing physicality in a familiar, respectable fiction) and by publishing in 1842 a note that the poem was 'designed to make one piece' with a far less erotic poem, 'To a Young Lady who had been reproached for taking long walks in the country'.[58] These merely draw attention to his difficulty. But Louisa's wilfulness, part of her freedom, is equally prominent, and it has particular social meanings in a poem concerned with defiant explanation and protection. In that respect it is like 'To a Young Lady', because both defend wilfulness in a female figure whose behaviour is distinctly at odds with social customs and expectations.

If 'Louisa' has anything to do with Dorothy, it must suggest that Wordsworth recognised a sexual element in Dorothy's vehement affections and felt the need to surround her with a protective (explanatory) barrier in figuring her energy and desire in his poems – barriers designed to discourage interpretative distinctions between sister, wife, daughter, lover, chiefly by dissolving conventional associations between behaviour and age. It isn't simply that poems 'representing' Dorothy don't correspond consistently to her present age or a specific remembered time (why should they?), but that *within* individual poems her age and social status are presented as indeterminate.

In a way the historical Dorothy simply confuses readings of the poems. (They never use her name.) Invoking her as a figure behind 'Louisa' and 'Three years she grew' has made readers hesitate to dwell on sexual desire in these poems because there is a risk of seeming to talk about incest, pederasty, and childhood sexuality. Yet there is no reason why a 'Lucy' poem cannot be read as engaging sexual taboos – as Coleridge's 'Christabel' does, and Goethe's 'Erlking' and any number of literary ballads of supernatural seduction – without reflecting directly on Dorothy. Alternatively we can see both 'Louisa' and 'Three years she grew' as poems which foreground an absence of 'narrative' information about her age and social status and refuse to specify her relationship with the narrator. In my experience many readers assume that the speaker in 'Three years she grew' is Lucy's father, and the assumption cannot be *disproved* by arguing that another relationship is specified (brother, sister, mother, lover). Yet Nature's peremptory demands of her ('She shall be mine, and I will make / A Lady of my own') and its assumed authority ('Myself will to my darling be / Both law and impulse') unavoidably suggest male dominance – whether that of elder brother, father or lover – and therefore bring to mind conventions of behaviour that we categorise under those headings. (In other cultures the categories would be different: in medieval Icelandic literature, for example, maternal uncles had carefully defined authority and responsibility.)

Determination to read poems like 'Louisa', the 'Lucy' poems and contemporary ballads of supernatural seduction in a transcendental way leads to transcendental criticism, which always stresses the self-reflexive element in Wordsworth's poems and therefore ignores its engagement with social frameworks. Exploring the latter is not a denial of transcendental impulses but an attempt to do what (ironically, but in the end obviously) Wordsworth himself was famously accused by Coleridge of doing: risking bathos by being too literal.[59]

'To a Young Lady' engages even more explicitly with the language of socialisation.

TO A YOUNG LADY
WHO HAD BEEN REPROACHED FOR TAKING
LONG WALKS IN THE COUNTRY

Dear Child of Nature, let them rail!
– There is a nest in a green dale,
A harbour and a hold:
Where thou, a Wife and Friend, shalt see
Thy own heart-stirring days, and be
A light to young and old.

There, healthy as a shepherd boy,
And treading among flowers of joy
Which at no season fade,
Thou, while thy babes around thee cling,
Shalt show us how divine a thing
A Woman may be made.

Thy thoughts and feelings shall not die,
Nor leave thee, when grey hairs are nigh,
A melancholy slave;
But an old age serene and bright,
And lovely as a Lapland night,
Shall lead thee to thy grave.

It is a synoptic life history that emphasises the persistence of youthful experience into old age. It uses the terminology of ageing (child, lady, woman, old age) but in fact denies the changes and transitions these terms mark. The 'Young Lady' of the title remains a 'Child of Nature'; the 'mother' of stanza two is 'healthy as a shepherd boy'. The poem also invokes and dismisses (or bridges) social distinctions. The 'Lady' indulges in unladylike behaviour, which 'they' (l. 1) rail at. (Wordsworth's 'they' is like Edward Lear's in his limericks, with the difference that 'they' are here opposed by 'we': Louisa is not one of Lear's solitary victims.) But, the title asserts, she is still a lady, as though vigour *were* decorum if read correctly, or as though nature could inculcate decorum as well as vigour and beauty – as 'Nature' does in 'Three years she grew': 'She shall be mine, and I will *make* / A Lady of my own.' The assumption that only socially approved custom can turn a female into a lady is invoked and denied. There is a similar movement in the second stanza when the mother is described as 'healthy as a shepherd boy'. Two stereotypes are invoked here, one endorsed and one denied: rural vigour against metropolitan refinement, and male vigour against female delicacy. A further transition develops the poem, one that combines the languages of age, gender and social status:

> Thou, while thy babes around thee cling,
> Shalt show us how divine a thing
> A Woman may be made.

> Thy thoughts and feelings shall not die,
> Nor leave thee, when grey hairs are nigh,
> A melancholy slave.

'Babes' grow up and leave; thoughts and feelings persist. Both are presented as natural occurrences, and the equation glosses over the institutionalised, social, marker of procreation, marriage. Husbands and fathers are absent. (In this sense the poem is a *contrastive* companion piece to 'Louisa'.)

Broadly speaking the poem embodies an opposition between nature and society, but because it uses the language of social distinctions and stereotypes the other opposition I've mentioned (between 'we' and 'they') opens up the question who is to judge, or rightly perceive, the lives of other people. The lady will 'show *us* how divine a thing / A Woman may be *made*'. 'Made' by whom? Surely the implication is that 'we' to some extent make the woman a divine thing: the formative, protective circle of admirers who vindicate her actions and who now name her 'woman' in a direct challenge to society's preference for ladies. Moreover, though the phrase 'how divine a thing' reminds us of Lucy ('She seemed a thing that could not feel / The touch of earthly years'), it also plays with the polite, denaturing slang of socially approved Romantic lovers or would-be lovers that Jane Austen satirised in the language of Isabella Thorpe: 'I never saw anything half so divine.'

Wordsworth's poetry of relationship engages deeply with social distinctions and assumptions implicit in acts of naming and categorising other people, even when its aim is to define more 'permanent' values. Distinctions of this kind are generally more explicit in novels, but that is no reason for ignoring them in poetry. It is surely relevant when reading 'Louisa' to remember Henry Tilney's dismissive allusion to popular novels: 'Do not imagine that you can cope with me in a knowledge of Julias and Louisas.'[60] Dismissive – but it suggests that even people with intellectual interests (Tilney reads history) may also read popular novels. Wordsworth challenges readers familiar with one kind of Louisa to think again. For that matter, 'Emmeline', a name he used for his sister in two poems about childhood, was also a common name for heroines in popular novels.[61]

Daughters and writers: 'The Triad'

I am not trying to make a case that Wordsworth's writings are free of gender bias, simply that he explores gender bias in particular kinds of socialisation. His poems about children are well known, but even here, as I have been arguing, neither gender nor sex is irrelevant. In his few poems about his children as adults there is a different negotiation of gender and authority, and it also has to do with writing but in a quite different way. In 'The Triad' and related poems there is a deep connection between the freedom of sexual and emotional choice and the freedom to write – and these things are clearly and powerfully gendered.

'The Triad', written in 1828, is a triple portrait of Dora Wordsworth, Sara Coleridge and Edith Southey as young women, and it inevitably brings to mind the trio of poets thirty years earlier. These are in some sense their representatives, though female (interestingly Wordsworth never attempted a poem grouping either of his surviving sons with either of Coleridge's and Cuthbert Southey), and the poem has an extremely gendered approach to its subject. Its framing fiction is of a man offering a vision of three women to a young suitor – adopting one of the traditional roles, that is, of fatherhood: the role of marriage broker. The fiction is supported by references to the three Graces and to the judgement of Paris, references that work in contrasting ways. Though the Graces have physical beauty in common with the goddesses Paris judged, the two sets of figures are in other ways opposite, because the Graces symbolise harmony (they are often represented in a linked dance), while the goddesses embody discord in this mythic scene.[62] The poem emphasises the former in descriptions of the three girls and the latter in the fictional frame, which is about choice, judgement and differences. The end of the poem is focused on the unnamed suitor's choice, but before that the emphasis is on the narrator's own show of power as he summons and dismisses a vision of the three in a Prospero-like gesture ('The Charm is over; the mute Phantoms gone . . .' [l. 212]) and tells the suitor that one of the figures may become his bride though not by his act of choice. In this sense the poem teases the surrogate (male) reader with an ambivalent possibility of possessing what he has seen. Both offering and choosing are masculine activities, and the females are passive.

The three women represented in the poem were all daughters of famous writers, and two of them, Sara Coleridge and Dora Wordsworth, were themselves to become authors. Nothing in the poem does justice to their intellectual interests, even though Sara had already published two lengthy translations.[63] (Oddly, only the Edith Southey figure, the third in the poem, is associated with literature in the image of a solitary reader, and she did not become an author.[64]) There may in fact be a veiled joke in the first section of the poem where Sara is named 'Lucida' and her beauty is likened to 'heavenly day', because she was nicknamed 'Celestial Blue' in the Wordsworth circle, an apparent reference to her blue-stocking tendencies (which she herself mocked) as well as the colour of her eyes.[65] But that hardly amounts to serious consideration of her authorship, and the poem does not challenge the prejudice that 'intellectual' women make unattractive marriage prospects. Sara Coleridge was well aware of the prejudice (she applied it ironically to her own case),[66] and it may have contributed to her opinion that there was no truth in the poem as a whole.[67]

Sara's experience gave her a special perspective on the family problems that arose when Dora became an author, an episode that sheds some light on the issues raised in the poem. Dora's *Journal of a Few Months' Residence in Portugal* was published anonymously (as Sara's translations had been) in 1847. The only positive comment Wordsworth made on it was that 'Women observe many particularities of manners and opinions which are apt to escape the notice of the Lords of Creation'.[68] Though his irony about male mastery is refreshing, the comment confines Dora's work to a gendered category appropriate to journalistic or novelistic detail but not to historical or philosophical insight. Within these restrictions Dora might write, but she must not publish except for money, and then it must be done anonymously.[69] She must not 'appear before the public' as an author.

In all of this Wordsworth is a very heavy father indeed, but the language in which he represented the episode is worth exploring a little. He insisted that Dora 'was induced at Moxon's request' to publish the journal,[70] as though there were an element of indecency in her offering the work on her own behalf. Sara Coleridge's comment provides an interesting perspective:

> Mrs Wordsworth insists so [sic] that the only motive for publishing the tour was pecuniary gain. . . . Mrs Wordsworth has all her life wished her daughter to be above both marriage and authorship, & finds it hard to submit to these vulgarities on her behalf at this stage of her life career.[71]

Marriage and authorship are equally 'vulgarities'. The view Sara attributes to Mary Wordsworth implies more, I think, than that Mary felt Dora's need of either resulted from her own failure to provide security and fulfilment. Either is a breach of decorum. I'm not concerned with whether Sara's remark is fair to Mary, nor with whether Wordsworth shared or conceived this view, but with what this conjunction of marriage and authorship implies. Authorship is often thought of as the opposite of marriage in that it provides a way of being independent of male support, but since the publishing industry was and to some extent is male-dominated, the female author was still at the mercy of economic forces controlled by men, and her behaviour towards a publisher might still be regulated by customary (gendered) rules of decorum. The two options could generate the same sort of rhetoric of female modesty, which denies female choice or will. Dora was '*induced*' to publish. (Similarly, when Wordsworth included three of Dorothy's poems in his 1815 collected edition, he assured his readers that he had '*extorted* them from the Authoress'.[72])

What I have said about Dora's relationship with her publisher (as her parents saw it) may be too specific, because the same rhetoric of modesty might apply to the relationship between a female author and the reading public at large. Addresses to 'the reader' in prefaces tend to have built into them the assumption that the reader is male, and the assumption was correct in 1847 to the extent that reviewers (vocal, influential readers) *were* mostly male. That would suggest that disapproval like Mary Wordsworth's arose from fear of a kind of exhibitionism. Either way, women should be reticent in addressing men whether in person or in print: they should not solicit publication, or, failing that, not put their name to the work. On this view publication *is* like marriage: a woman loses her name.

Looking over these biographical matters helps us see clearly the real strength of the poem: the way it particularises and in some ways questions the social rituals of the *appearance* of young women before the public in person (as potential wife) or as an author. A girl's rites of passage are accepted here as different from a boy's (as imagined in the 'Immortality Ode'), and becoming an author is another passage with other rites. The fascinating thing – of much more than biographical interest – is that Wordsworth brings the two together in a poem that has as much to say about the anxieties of authorship as about the social restrictions of young women. Wordsworth could himself be coy, reserved and falsely passive in his dealings with publishers, as I shall argue in relation to *The White Doe of Rylstone*.

The central and longest passage of 'The Triad' is about Dora and imagines female solitude, associating it with both maidenhood and 'primal truth' (l. 139). The implication is that she cannot be married without losing her nature. Yet her association with nature is complicated by specific and limited human relationships with the family circle ('Encircled by familiar faces' [l. 153]), which is both the scene of her life and its audience. She behaves with the 'self-forgetfulness' (l. 160) and absence of shame allowed to children and animals, and in fact her 'sportive wit' (l. 168) is the only attribute that distinguishes her from a pet animal, allowed to move entirely at her own will between 'nature' and home. The family circle, on its side, shows indulgent understanding that would be impossible with 'strangers', that is, society at large. There is a private language of look and gesture between them. Gesture is foregrounded in dance, when she is likened to Euphrosyne (l. 106).

That brings us back to the kind of barrier between the circle with a shared language and the world at large that Wordsworth explored in some of the 'Poems on the Naming of Places', where the role of the poet is to define, explain and translate. The speaker claims a special understanding of the girl, and in the context of the poem's framing fiction there is the further implication that this understanding, this ability to 'translate' a private language, is part of a father's role. Though the girl is a figure of freedom, she is also imagined as *needing* explanation, and to explain is to protect.

In one sense Wordsworth is projecting his own fear of being misunderstood in his young female solitaries, and perhaps the reason why 'Louisa' and 'The Triad' exude confidence is that Wordsworth is doubly present in the poems: as innocence and as its protective interpreter, guaranteeing that it loses neither its pre-social ('primal') integrity nor its ability to communicate. One implication is that being female and growing up is like being an author and being published. In another sense the separateness of the speaker and his daughter persists and is the site of attraction that is in part physical. Through an image of daughterhood Wordsworth is able to construct a double image of the writer, the summoner and the summoned. The poems oscillates between emphasis on his control and on her tantalising freedom,[73] and the writer is both.

Notes and references

1. Few if any other British writers have occasioned a journal whose title uses the word 'circle'. The irregular volumes of *Shelley and his Circle*, edited by Donald Reiman, are a partial exception.

2. *PW*, II, p. 507.

3. *The Feminist Reader*, ed. Catherine Belsey and Jane Moore (London, Macmillan, 1989), p. 30.

4. Though the term 'Lake Poets' gained currency long before the publication of *The Prelude*, in which Coleridge is most conspicuously Wordsworth's 'brother'.

5. See Chapter 3 above.

6. See Ben Ross Schneider, *Wordsworth's Cambridge Education* (Cambridge, CUP, 1957); Z.S. Fink, 'Wordsworth and the Republican Tradition', *JEGP*, 47 (1948), pp. 107–26; and Duncan Wu, *Wordsworth's Reading, 1770–1799* (Cambridge, CUP, 1993).

7. See Richard E. Brantley, *Wordsworth's 'Natural Methodism'* (New Haven, Yale UP, 1975).

8. Lawrence Lipking, *Abandoned Women and the Poetic Tradition* (Chicago, University of Chicago Press, 1988), p. 137.

9. 'Memorial Verses', *Selected Poems and Prose*, ed. M. Allott (London, Dent, 1978), p. 87.

10. For a recent summary of the biographical background see Richard Holmes, *Coleridge. Early Visions* (Harmondsworth, Penguin, 1990), ch. 12.

11. This poem is often 'placed' by critics and biographers as one of merely anecdotal interest; a poem about 'the sofa incident at Gallow Hill', as Richard Holmes puts it in *Coleridge. Early Visions*, p. 309.

12. See J. Beer, *Wordsworth and the Human Heart* (Cambridge, CUP, 1978) for a discussion of the centrality of the fountain image.

13. Perhaps the most conspicuously relevant entry is for December 1803 (*Notebooks*, I, 1718), in which Sara's breast is punningly related to both shipwreck and haven: '. . . what visions I have had, what dreams – the Bark, the Sea, all the shapes & sounds & adventures made up of the Stuff of Sleep & Dreams, & yet my Reason at the Rudder: O what visions, (μαστι) as if my Cheek & Temple were lying on me gale o' mast high [μεγαλωμαστοι = large breasts] – Seele meines Lebens! – & and I sink down the waters, thro Seas & Seas – yet warm, yet a Spirit –.' Holmes has a brief discussion of this passage (*Coleridge. Early Visions*, pp. 316–17).

14. Coleridge, *Notebooks*, II, 2938 and 2998 (discussed by Gill in *Wordsworth*, pp. 256–7).

15. F.R. Leavis, *Revaluation* (London, Chatto and Windus, 1937), ch. 5, note 2.

16. Michael Mason notes that it is the only poem in *Lyrical Ballads* that deals with sexual morality (*Lyrical Ballads*, ed. M. Mason [London and New York, Longman, 1992], p. 276).

17. 'Guilt and Sorrow', a late version of 'Salisbury Plain' was published in 1842.

18. Mason, *Lyrical Ballads*, p. 387.

19. The subject has been widely discussed recently. I recommend Mary Louise Pratt's *Imperial Eyes: Travel Writing and Transculturation* (London, Routledge, 1992).

20. Mason, *Lyrical Ballads*, p. 280.

21. In, for example, 'To a Butterfly' ('Stay near me'; Gill, p. 244).

22. The fact is central to the whole enterprise of 'Poems on the Naming of Places'. See Chapter 2 above.

23. As David Punter does in *The Romantic Unconscious* (London, Harvester Wheatsheaf, 1989).

24. Juliet Flower MacCannell, *The Regime of the Brother: After the Patriarchy* (London, Routledge, 1991), p. 87.

25. Jonathan Bate makes a similar point in *Romantic Ecology: Wordsworth and the Environmental Tradition* (London, Routledge, 1991), but he is concerned specifically with 'green' politics.

26. Coleridge's *Biographia Literaria*, ch. 22, is the *locus classicus* of this view.

27. *PW*, I, pp. 341–2.

28. *The Borderers*, III, 1493ff (*PW*, I, p. 187). I give the names in the first edition of 1842 followed by the names in the holograph MS B.

Wordsworth changed his mind more than once about the names: see *PW*, I, pp. 343ff for details.

29. Famously Godwin argued in the first edition of *An Enquiry concerning the Principles of Political Justice* (1793) that if you had the choice of saving your mother or a great philosopher from a domestic fire, you should save the philosopher first. He dropped the passage in later editions.

30. See, for example, Anne K. Mellor's *Romanticism and Gender* (London, Routledge, 1993), ch. 4.

31. 'Vaudracour and Julia' (written in 1804) was first published in 1820 as a separate poem and restored to its place in *The Prelude* when the 1805 version was first published by de Selincourt in 1926.

32. Mary Jacobus, *Romanticism, Writing and Sexual Difference* (Oxford, Clarendon, 1989).

33. Jacobus, pp. 251–2.

34. 'Verse novel' is a term that has been applied to a number of long Victorian narrative poems. It clearly reflects an idea that verse fiction is simply a branch of prose fiction, just as a century earlier Fielding made a case for the seriousness of the novel by describing *Joseph Andrews* as a 'comic epic poem in prose'. The novel began by imitating epic and romance, but in the early nineteenth century the romance was distinguished as less serious than the novel. Recent research has shown how these distinctions are gendered (romance as feminine; the novel as masculine). Jacobus follows this scheme in her analysis of 'Vaudracour and Julia'.

35. Coleridge applied the phrase only to 'The Nightingale', but both 'Frost at Midnight' and 'This Lime-Tree Bower My Prison' are usually considered to be conversation poems. On Wordsworth's 'The Fountain', subtitled 'A Conversation', see Chapter 1 above.

36. Coleridge, *Collected Letters*, ed. E.L. Griggs (Oxford, Clarendon Press, 1956) vol II, p. 398.

37. Compare the judgemental compulsion Wordsworth describes as a bar to imagination in the narrative of his early adult years (*The Prelude*, XI, 130ff).

38. On socialisation, see J.P. Ward, 'Wordsworth and the Sociological Idea', *Critical Quarterly*, 16 (1974), pp. 331–55.

39. Der Jüngling bist du, der seit langer Zeit
     Auf unsern Gräbern steht in tiefen Sinnen . . .
     Im Tode ward das ewge Leben kund –
     Du bist der Tod und machst uns erst gesund.

('Hymnen an die Nacht', quoted from *Werke*, ed. Uwe Lassen, [Hamburg, 1966], p. 25.)

40. The words occur as rhymes or in near conjunction over a dozen times in 'Poems Referring to the Period of Childhood' and 'Poems Founded on the Affections'. 'Wild' occurs five times in 'Tintern Abbey'.

41. Shelley, *A Defence of Poetry*, quoted from Donald H. Reiman and Sharon B. Powers (eds), *Shelley's Poetry and Prose* (New York, Norton, 1977), pp. 481–2.

42. Peter France, *Politeness and its Discontents* (Cambridge, CUP, 1992), ch. 11. See also Chapter 6 below, for a discussion of Wordsworth's attitudes to Italy in this context.

43. Hans Aarslef, *The Study of Language in England, 1780–1860* (Princeton, N.J., Princeton UP, 1967), ch. 1.

44. This is the framework of John Barrell's discussion of 'Tintern Abbey' in *Poetry, Language and Politics*, ch. 5.

45. The opposition 'solitude/society' was borrowed by the Romantics from Milton, as Coleridge's 'The Nightingale' shows.

46. It is worth remembering that the phrase 'the bliss of solitude', familiar to thousands of visitors to Grasmere, is Mary Wordsworth's, and that Wordsworth distrusted 'the *self-sufficing* power of solitude' (*The Prelude*, II, 78).

47. *PW*, II, p. 521.

48. Barrell, *Poetry, Language and Politics*, ch. 5.

49. Leonore Davidoff and Catherine Hall, *Family Fortunes* (London, Hutchinson, 1987).

50. See, for example, Dorothy Wordsworth to Jane Pollard, 10–12.7.1793; 30.8.1793 (*Letters*, I, pp. 97ff, 109ff).

51. Perhaps the reason why 'Home at Grasmere', a vehement celebration of their return to the Lakes late in 1799, is repetitious, full of circular structures and distinctly lacking in a sense of the future is that Wordsworth attempted to write it from the perspective I have associated with Dorothy. It is a poem with nowhere to go. Oddly, Dorothy never quoted or referred to it in her journals at that period, though she mentions many others: a telling silence? See Chapter 6 below.

52. Jean Hagstrum, *The Romantic Body* (Knoxville, University of Tennessee Press, 1985), p. 97.

53. Hagstrum, p. 76; quoting Coleridge's *Notebooks*, 3605 f. 118.

54. My emphasis. I quote the original version, which Wordsworth retained until 1832 (*PW*, II, p. 28).

55. *PW*, II, p. 28. Compare the voyeuristic interest in peasant women's feet recorded by Donna Landry in *The Muses of Resistance*; see above, Chapter 1.

56. See above, Chapter 1.

57. *King Lear*, IV, 5, 26–7. I am not entirely convinced the allusion *is* to *Lear*, though that view has de Selincourt's authority (*PW*, II, p. 472).

58. *PW*, II, p. 471.

59. *Biographia Literaria*, ch. 22.

60. *Northanger Abbey*, ch. 14.

61. See Janet Todd (ed.) *A Dictionary of British and American Women Writers 1660–1800* (London, Methuen, 1987).

62. In accounts and images of the Judgement of Paris (such as Rubens' painting) the action is overseen by the shadowy figure of Discord.

63. *An Account of the Abipones*, by Martin Dobrizhofer, appeared in Sara's translation in 1822, and *Memoirs of the Chevalier Bayard* in 1825.

64. Many years after her death her husband J.W. Warter published '*Wise saws and modern instances*', *or*, *pithy sentences in many languages* under his own name, though the collection was begun by Edith.

65. *Letters of Sara Hutchinson*, ed. K. Coburn (London, Routledge and Kegan Paul, 1954), pp. 332, 448.

66. *Letters of Sara Hutchinson*, p. 233.

67. Her comment is quoted in *PW*, II, p. 522.

68. To Moxon, 1.10.1846. *Letters*, VII, pp. 803–4.

69. To Moxon 12.10.1846; to Christopher Wordsworth 27.2.1847. *Letters*, VII, pp. 805, 836.

70. *Ibid.*, p. 836.

71. Quoted by Norma Clarke, *Ambitious Heights* (London, Routledge, 1990), p. 63, from *Letters of Dora Wordsworth*, ed. H.P. Vincent (Chicago, Packard, 1944), Introduction, p. 10.

72. 1815 Preface, *PW*, II, p. 444. The italics are Wordsworth's. The passage was dropped in editions after 1832.

73. I think it is a misreading of this kind of oscillation to collapse it into the simple paradox of wish-fulfilment or narcissism that David Punter discusses (*The Romantic Unconscious*).

CHAPTER 5

Vision and time: a critique of reading

In any account of Wordsworth's career as a poet, 1815 must be a crucial year. It saw the publication of the first collected edition of his poems, together with its Preface and supplementary Essay in which he developed ideas about power and authority in writing, and about a mutual relationship between writer and reader. I have dealt above with the constructive power of these ideas, but the biographical circumstances in which they arose are also important to Wordsworth's themes. The Essay, a highly critical analysis of contemporary reading habits, was no doubt partly a response to the *relative* failure of *The Excursion* (1814) with the reviewers, but 1815 brought a much more complete critical (and financial) failure when *The White Doe of Rylstone* appeared in an expensive quarto edition. Posterity, it must be admitted, has largely endorsed their negative response, but that should not obscure the particular shape of the crisis of readership that Wordsworth was undergoing in these years and the ways in which *The White Doe* can be read as part of it. He was by no means a 'popular' poet (like Scott or Campbell), and he had not enjoyed much critical esteem either. Five years later he achieved both popular and critical success, but for the moment these must have seemed a long way off.

With hindsight we can see the poem as an *example* of Wordsworth's failure with his readers, but we should also see it as a text that addresses the very issue of sympathetic readership. It is, among other things, a critique of reading, just as the Essay is. But there are differences of emphasis that link the poem with Wordsworth's earlier critical concerns, particularly the critique of figurative language in the Preface to *Lyrical Ballads*. *The White Doe* is an extended meditation on ways of reading metaphors (or ways of 'seeing' them or 'understanding' them: each term implies a different conceptualisation of reading).

Wordsworth's thinking about metaphor was always more directed towards the psychological and the social (in broad terms) than the epistemological. We're accustomed to thinking about Romantic

185

metaphor in Coleridgean and Shelleyan terms: metaphor as a means towards new knowledge. Discussion of the implications of metaphor in the 1960s and 1970s – in Hartman's work particularly – follows this view, and deconstructions of Romantic metaphor, notably Paul De Man's, have been concerned basically with epistemology. In De Man's case it is perhaps because he approaches Wordsworth through an interest in the self-destroying metaphors of Rousseau, whose writings are a fascinatingly continual, obsessive, search for the grounds of authenticity in expression. Wordsworth's interest in psychology is evident in his persistent and various comparisons between the processes of reading and the processes of writing, and his derivation of knowledge of taste from observed or imagined habits of reading, rather than from established *aesthetic* canons. He had a habit of fussing over his readers that focuses some of the *social* issues involved in poetic figuration. This is particularly true of the texts he published around 1815, when he made his greatest claims on his readers, but it has much earlier roots.

Wordsworth's exploratory analysis of figuration used to be thought of as something that ended after the so-called 'great decade'. John Jones's discussion of *The White Doe of Rylstone*, which still has something to offer readers of Wordsworth, is premised on the idea that the poem is an expression of 'the Baptised Imagination', as if the Anglican church offered all that he needed in the way of 'justified' (that is, codified, accepted) metaphor. But the 'great decade' is Arnold's invention (though to some extent founded on Wordsworth's own narratives of imaginative growth and decay in 'Tintern Abbey', the 'Immortality Ode' and 'Peele Castle'), and the issue became more, not less, important after that decade ended.

In a letter to Catherine Clarkson, Wordsworth defended himself at length against the charge that he had used 'little imagery' in *The Excursion* (1814). The complexity of his argument is a measure of its importance. He has avoided, he says, the kind of imagery Thomas Campbell used in 'Gertrude of Wyoming' and 'The Pleasures of Hope', by which he apparently means the personifications of hope near the beginning of the latter:

> Angel of life! thy glittering wings explore
> Earth's loneliest bounds, and Ocean's wildest shore.
> Lo! To the wintry winds the pilot yields
> His bark careering o'er unfathom'd fields;

Now on Atlantic waves he rides afar,
Where Andes, giant of the western star,
With meteor-standard to the winds unfurl'd,
Looks from his throne of clouds o'er half the world!   (53–60)

Wordsworth told Crabb Robinson the last three lines were 'a mere jumble of discordant images, meaning, in fact, nothing'.[1] His dislike of personification is evident in the criticism of Gray's sonnet on the death of Richard West in the Preface to Lyrical Ballads. But The Excursion, he goes on to say, has much imagery

> either collateral in the way of metaphor coloring the style; illustrative in the way of simile; or directly under the shape of description or incident[.][2]

These are interesting distinctions, but they are submerged in a later passage that replaces analytic terminology with a single metaphor: nature is 'the Bible of the Universe' which 'speaks to the ear of the intelligent, as it lies open to the eyes of the humble-minded'. (There is a similarity here with the ambitious but misleading analysis of the metaphors in 'Resolution and Independence' in the 1815 Preface.)[3] But, Wordsworth goes on to say, nature cannot be read by 'a Soul that has been dwarfed by a course of bad culture'.[4] The argument is contiguous with that in the 'Essay, Supplementary to the Preface', which traces bad taste (the neglect of good writing) back to bad education, bad habits of both living and reading. In the letter he asks, 'Do you not perceive that my conversations almost all take place out of Doors, and all with the grand objects of nature surrounding the speakers for the express purpose of their being alluded to in illustration of the subjects treated of?'[5] The implication is that meaning accrues in the mind by a kind of osmosis, provided that the mind has not become furnished with 'monstrous' ideas. Less fancifully, the argument proposes that shared experience leads to shared figuration. What links the two is Wordsworth's constant preoccupation with habit.

Figuration and habit

The relation of habit to figurative language is problematic, and it is pervasive in Wordsworth's criticism from his earliest writings. In the Preface to Lyrical Ballads much of Wordsworth's language is associationist, although the argument is often not. I suggest that here, as in later texts, his *chief* interest is not in epistemology but in psychology, not with the philosophical status of figurative language but with the supposed processes that generate it. The advantages of this approach to language are that it can be conceived as empirical and as providing a way of describing figuration as 'natural': observation suggests that there are circumstances in which 'men' will naturally use metaphor. The disadvantage is that it shifts the grounds of understanding and judgement of figurative language from language itself to the moral condition of language users, whether speakers, readers or writers, implying that only certain people, those with 'healthful associations', can write or judge correctly.

Basing an aesthetic on habit has other implications for a writer in Wordsworth's time. It engages with the pedagogic commonplace that example teaches more effectually than precept and therefore with the language of books of instruction for children. Mary Wollstonecraft prefaced her *Original Stories from Real Life* (1788), a book about habits implanted by exemplary narratives, with the comment that 'Good habits, imperceptibly fixed, are far preferable to the precepts of reason,' and went on to say that this is particularly, though not exclusively, true in the education of children.[6] There was another commonplace about rational and figurative language, namely that books addressed to readers not formally educated (including women) should make use of concrete or figurative rather than abstract language.[7] In instructional language the issue of example against precept converges with the issue of figuration against abstraction. In placing habit at the centre of his aesthetic Wordsworth adapts the strategies of instructional writing to poetry.

Both issues are reflected in Wordsworth's earliest analysis of habit and figuration in the fragmentary 'Essay on Morals', written in Germany in December 1798. It is particularly interesting because it has inner conflicts that are embedded in the more considered prose of the later Prefaces. One strand of argument is that no book of systematised moral philosophy, like Godwin's and Paley's, is (and the implication is, *can be*)

> written with sufficient power to melt into our affections, to incorporate itself with the blood and vital juices of our minds, and thence to have an influence worth our notice in forming those habits of which I am speaking. [Such books,] presenting no

image to the mind can convey no feeling which has any
connection with the supposed archetype or fountain of the
proposition existing in human life.[8]

This view occurs in many passages of The Prelude concerning
Wordsworth's own 'restoration'[9] to moral health and can be linked to
the political opposition of affection against reason in Godwin and
Burke.[10] It became a commonplace in post-Romantic writing that (as
Whitman put it) 'Logic and sermons never convince, the damp of the
night drives deeper into my soul'. But it has other interests. It implies
(which The Prelude passages do not) faith in books of a different kind,
though the kind is not specified. In particular, imagery ('presenting
. . . image to the mind') will effect what 'a series of propositions' will
not. Figuration is necessary to alter habit. Now Wordsworth's
argument is about inducing or strengthening good habits, but why
shouldn't bad habits be induced or strengthened in the same way?
Wordsworth fends off that objection by implying, contradictorily, that
systematic philosophies, though 'impotent to all their intended good
purposes', may not be 'equally impotent to all bad ones'; recognising
the contradiction, perhaps, when he adds 'This sentence will, I am
afraid be unintelligible'. A way out of the impasse would be to say
that the processes of habit formation are different in the case of good
and bad (as the strait gate differs from the wide gate in the Sermon on
the Mount), but Wordsworth chooses two other ways, which are not
easily reconciled: first, he configures reasoning as a 'juggler's trick'
that 'strip[s] the mind of all its old clothing' when it 'ought to . . . .
furnish it with new';[11] and secondly, he defines certain acts as
'accidental and indefinite' rather than habitual. So, for example, a
public act of benevolence ('in a mixed company') might be accidental
in 'the vain man, the proud man, the avaricious man', and all their
motives on the occasion will differ.

Habit, then, is a two-edged sword, especially when it is redefined as
an element of taste, that is, brought from an ethical into an aesthetic
framework. But I think it is crucial to Wordsworth's writing, not just
in the associationist terminology of the Preface to Lyrical Ballads, but
more importantly in his analysis of bad reading habits in the 1815
'Essay, Supplementary to the Preface', where the link between habit
and taste (the moral and the aesthetic) is most clear and becomes a
basis for artistic communication.[12]

Wordsworth and Scott: *The White Doe of Rylstone*

Readers' habits, or Wordsworth's conception of them, bulk very large in the whole project of writing and publishing *The White Doe of Rylstone*, his one attempt at a full-scale verse romance. It is a poem about which the author's intentions are so completely documented that they have hardly been evaluated; a poem that neo-formalist criticism had no way of rescuing from its initial neglect *because* it makes a conscious attack on those 'pre-established codes of decision' that Wordsworth inferred (in this case) had become naturalised in readers of Scott's verse romances. The year of its publication, 1815, also saw the first collective edition of Wordsworth's poems with its idiosyncratic arrangement of poems according to the mental faculty they were thought most to engage and its rebarbative 'Essay', a denunciation of public taste through the centuries. Both are authoritarian gestures. Facing the fact of Scott's popularity, and more recently Byron's, Wordsworth defiantly implied they were pandering to a pre-existent taste by claiming that a 'genius' must 'create the taste by which he is appreciated'. But in the same essay he declared that 'taste' is a misnomer when applied to critical judgement because it is the word used to name what he considers mere mechanical (sensuous) discrimination, like judging wines (another assumption with which there is room to quarrel). The concept of 'taste' becomes very problematic: we could argue that Scott and Byron had precisely created the taste by which they were appreciated.

In this context *The White Doe* is crucial.

> Unread his works – his 'Milk-white Doe'
> With dust is dark and dim;
> It's still in Longman's shop, and oh!
> The difference to him.[13]

The poem remained in Longman's shop for a very long time indeed. The first edition of 750 copies was still not exhausted in 1831, sixteen years after publication.[14] By then the poem had been reprinted in cheaper collective editions from 1820 onwards, so that further sales of the original quarto volume were hardly to be expected; in that respect Hartley Coleridge's squib is unfair. But it accurately reflects Wordsworth's valuation of the poem and his extreme disappointment with its unpopularity. *The White Doe* is still hardly more often read than Hartley's poem[15] and deserves reconsideration in terms of our own presuppositions as well as those of Wordsworth's contemporaries. For his first readers – and reviewers – there were, I believe, specific challenges, as there were also in the 1815 edition, its Preface and the supplementary Essay, especially the questions of generic expectation and the nature of the reading public. It is clear that after the critical failure of *The Excursion* ('This will never do')[16] Wordsworth's views about the readership of poetry, the taste of the consumer, became sharper, more polarised, more defensive but also more searching than they had been. For us there is the question of Wordsworth's misunderstanding his readers (if he did); the question how he came to write such a 'dull' poem (I do not find it dull); and broader considerations of cultural value.

'This, we think, has the merit of being the very worst poem we ever saw imprinted in a quarto volume.'[17] Jeffrey's opening remark in the *Edinburgh's* review of *The White Doe* stands worthily next to that on *The Excursion*, but it differs importantly in drawing attention to the *format* in which *The White Doe* appeared. (*The Excursion* had also been produced expensively on heavy paper in a sparsely lineated folio: Wordsworth's financial demands on his publisher were heavy.) 'Quarto' meant the format in which Byron had achieved spectacular sales with 'Lara' (printed with Rogers's 'Jacqueline') in 1814 and in which Scott's *The Lay of the Last Minstrel*, an earlier best seller, had appeared in 1805. But Wordsworth insisted *his* quarto must be sold at a guinea a copy, roughly three times the going rate, to 'show the world my opinion of it'.[18] The history of its preparation for the press, its publication and reception is complex, bitter and sometimes farcical. The facts are given in Kristine Dugas's edition for the Cornell Wordsworth[19] and don't need to be repeated in detail, but some of them are worth reconsidering because they suggest contexts in which we can see the writing and publishing of the poem as a complete venture.

It is evident that Wordsworth published *The White Doe of Rylstone* as a challenge to Scott's and Byron's readers.[20] The poem is in a verse form popularized by Scott (though Coleridge touchily claimed to have invented it),[21] and the quarto format, a choice Wordsworth made in 1808 though the poem did not appear until 1815, invoked *The Lay of the Last Minstrel*. In the seven years that elapsed between the completion of the poem and its publication in revised form[22] there is little to suggest that his attitude towards it had changed, except perhaps that he became more consciously defiant of expectations. By

1815 the popularity of Scott's poems had been exceeded by that of Byron's, but Scott still sold enormously. A few pages after the entry for *The White Doe* the Longman's impression book shows *The Lord of the Isles* going into a fourth edition of 6000 copies.[23] As Coleridge and Lamb had predicted, reviewers compared Wordsworth's poem unfavourably with Scott's and Byron's – Scott's especially, because of the similarity of subject matter. Wordsworth raised the expectations of a tale of adventure and the supernatural but then spent the whole of the first canto of the poem criticising the matter of such tales: stories of (respectively) pious legend, bloody deeds and revenge, and the supernatural. *The Lay of the Last Minstrel* has its shape-changing dwarf and its harp of inspiration, and Wordsworth's transformation of the latter is particularly interesting: he replaces Scott's picturesque harpist with an invisible Spirit whose influence is felt in 'soft and breeze-like visitings'. There is another similarity, probably fortuitous, in the first lines of the two poems: 'The feast was over in Branksome Tower' and 'From Bolton's old monastic tower'.

Matters of sales, price, format and reception, even the Romance machinery, should not be dismissed as historical curiosities because they are congruent with issues that are foregrounded in the text: the psychology of reading; the processes of habit, in relation to both moral judgement and aesthetic taste; and the ways in which figuration is culturally used and valued. We can begin with a glance at the fashion for stories of shape-changing, a narrative equivalent of metaphor. The story of Thomas Rhymer, half-poet, half-legend, anthologised by Percy and elaborated by Scott, is an archetype of spiritual possession in which change in the poet stands for access of inspiration and the ability to make similar inspirational, spiritualising changes in perception through figurative narrative. Keats's 'La Belle Dame sans Merci' gives a vampiric equivalent where possession leads to spiritual death. The ambivalence of narratives of possession in the Romantic period corresponds to an ambivalence in discussion of figuration: they both go beyond rhetoric, even beyond morality, to questions of spiritual health or disease. The discourse of health and disease is clearly present in the Preface to *Lyrical Ballads* when Wordsworth discusses the moral effect of poetry on readers. He argues that, provided the poet himself is 'possessed of much sensibility', he will produce work from which 'the understanding of the being to whom we address ourselves, *if he be in a healthful state of association*, must necessarily in some degree be enlightened . . .'.[24] But the poet must be a true poet, not one who feeds his readers badly and thereby produces bad health (a bad 'state of association') in them. He deprecates

> Poets, who think they are conferring honour upon themselves and their art, in proportion as they separate themselves from the sympathies of men, and indulge in arbitrary and capricious habits of expression, *in order to furnish food for fickle tastes, and fickle appetites, of their own creation.*[25]

So the grounds for distinguishing among different examples of figurative language become moral rather than aesthetic: critical judgement is based on the *health* or unhealthiness of different rhetorical strategies.

These canons of taste in the Preface to *Lyrical Ballads* are echoed in the critical texts of 1815, and provide a useful background for the different but no less compelling analysis of faulty taste in *The White Doe*. This poem is both less and more prescriptive: less, because, like 'The Thorn', it does not simply condemn the apparently unhealthy state of communal association that produces local legend and superstition. More prescriptive, because, as I shall argue, there are certain kinds of individual response to (symbolic) objects that are judged to be unthinking, divisive and politically dangerous. There is a sense that *shared* legend is, if not sacred, at least valued, provided that it is shared among geographically contiguous individuals, people who – like the speakers in *The Excursion* – can invoke a shared landscape as if that were a guarantee of shared experience. Wordsworth's poem protects this kind of communal figuration. Comparison with *The Excursion*, however, points to a major difference between the poems. In the latter, where the central image is the churchyard among the mountains, religious communion (shared faith in the figurations of Anglicanism) coincides with geographical community. The poem is at once *essentially* universalising and *essentially* local. But at each edge, as it were, of its range of figuration there is an excluded extreme. The aetiology of legend in Book IV, often read, as it was by Keats, as licensing the use of Greek myth, includes a warning against the dangers of animism, an extreme form of attachment to locality. At the same time the implied claim to a universally valid figuration is limited by antagonism to Roman Catholicism, which is presented as foreign and given to illusion and mystery. It is the disillusioned Solitary who links Pagan animism with 'The weeds of Romish phantasy' (IV, 908), but Wordsworth's spokesman, the Wanderer, also speaks of 'bewildered Pagans' (IV, 934) and says nothing in defence of 'phantasy'. Faith may be built on nature but it will not tolerate weeds.

In *The White Doe* Wordsworth develops a more explicit critique of figuration that touches on the religious concerns of *The Excursion* but focuses on individual acts of 'reading' objects. The prefatory 'Dedication' addressed to Mary Wordsworth makes a specific comparison between reading poetry and 'reading' objects. The emphasis is on *shared* experience of reading and on the fact (for it's stated as a fact) that a poem will itself gather significance – signify in different ways – over a period of time. Wordsworth's strategy here is to recommend his poem to the reader with a warning that it may not work at once but with the guarantee, as it were, that it *has* worked with its first audience (the fact that it did not work for Coleridge or Lamb or Longman's partner Rees is naturally ignored). There is a further warning that the poem is both like and unlike the Una episode in *The Fairie Queene*, alike in meaning but different in figuration because there will be no 'magic spell' or 'specious miracle' in 'This tragic Story'.[26]

The poem itself reflects upon its means of expression, chiefly by distinguishing different processes of figuration associated with the two main images in the poem, the doe and the banner. Broadly, the latter functions emblematically[27] as a political rallying point, but it is also an object with a particular history and particular human associations, and these things generate a 'meaning' quite different from its emblematic significance. The conflict between the two is at the heart of the story. So, too, with the doe: much of the poem is taken up with speculation about its appearance, its actions and its significance (too much for some tastes: a contemporary reviewer complained that 'the reader is forced to stand in Rylstone Churchyard [*sic*: it's actually Bolton Abbey] and look all the while at a White Doe, and listen all the while to a rhapsody, the import of which he is not led to perceive, upon its whiteness, and brightness, and famousness, and holiness').[28] What, in the end, we are led to perceive is that Wordsworth goes to great lengths to make us consider the various relations of object and meaning, and the processes of the mind by which objects are given significance.

The narrative of the doe and the banner is prefaced by a series of synoptic narratives of supernatural transformations that evoke the world of *The Lay of the Last Minstrel*. Through these Wordsworth begins to question the communal psychology of readers of such tales and to suggest means of distinguishing different kinds of transformation. The analysis seems to be based on the view that all figuration is transformation (not substitution but interpretation); that is, that transformation is unavoidable as soon as an object (the doe, the banner) is put into a narrative context.

The stories are those of, respectively, the 'bearded, staff-supported, Sire' who tells of the Lady Aäliza and her son (Wordsworth wrote the tale in 'The Force of Prayer'), and of her transformation into a doe; that of the 'Dame of haughty air', who thinks the doe is in some way associated with the ignominious death of her ancestor; and that of the 'scholar pale, from Oxford', who thinks the doe to be a transformation of the fairy which attended the reclusive Lord Clifford (Wordsworth uses this legend too, in 'Song at the Feast of Brougham Castle'). What these stories share is a supernatural element, and it's for this reason that they are rejected at the end of the first Canto; the true story of the doe will be a 'mortal story'. Yet Wordsworth's rejection of the supernatural is not blind: in fact he distinguishes among the stories in terms of both the kind of supernatural event involved and, more important, the attitude and motive of the teller. The first (217–41) is in the nature of a pious local legend about the founding of the priory, which was built as a memorial to the Lady Aäliza's drowned son, and which she revisits centuries later in the form of a doe. What Wordsworth emphasises is, first, that the teller's motives are reverential, and secondly, that his story doesn't do complete injustice to the appearance of the doe:

> Which, though seemingly doomed in its breast to sustain
>
> A softened remembrance of sorrow and pain,
> Is spotless, and holy, and gentle, and bright, –
> And glides o'er the earth like an angel of light. (241–4)

The words 'spotless', 'holy', 'gentle', 'bright' are all adjectives which the narrator of the true story will apply to the doe elsewhere in the poem. (In fact the first three are prominent in the seventh canto, when the doe, its story having been told, comes into its full symbolic significance.) This is important because the narrator subsequently makes a point of asserting that the true story about a being such as the doe cannot belie its appearance. His response to the third of the tales in Canto I makes this explicit:

> Ah, pensive Scholar! think not so,
> But look again at the radiant Doe!
> What quiet watch she seems to keep,
> Alone, beside that grassy heap!
> Why mention other thoughts unmeet
> For vision so composed and sweet?   (309–14)

'Look again': the point of the imperative is that the mere looking – the precise looking, the full act of attention – would show that to associate the doe with a story of magic *must* be wrong because it belies an appearance of purity and holiness.

There is more to it than this. The story that engrosses the scholar is a story of transmutation. He is fascinated by Clifford's alchemical and astrological researches; and alchemy may be taken as an archetype of the process of turning an object into something else. Wordsworth's attitude to it may be indicated by the cautionary note at the end of the tale:

> through strong desire
> Searching the earth with chemic fire:
> But they and their good works are fled –
> And all is now disquieted –
> And peace is none, for living or dead!   (304–8)

Material transmutation is an *ignis fatuus*. A revision dating from 1832–6 describes

> transmutations
> Rich as the mine's most bright creations.
> But they and their good works are fled,

emphasising a contrast between the protean nature of mind and the stubborn materiality of things by a word-play: it is difficult to read of 'the mine's . . . creations' without thinking of the *mind's* creations, since 'creation' might more easily be applied to the mind's work than to the products of mines. The scholar who remembers the tale is clearly attracted to it, and he too (an Arnold figure to a kind of Scholar-Gipsy) indulges in transmutations of his own in fancying that the doe might be the fairy who befriended Clifford. It is true that the scholar is apparently taking over, with approval, a popular legend (the tag in line 277 – ''Twas said' – suggests this), but in appropriating the legend he has added his own contribution. Again, we are faced with the imperative: 'Look again': the equation of the doe with a fairy is simply not 'true' to the object.

At the heart of the matter is a more fundamental transformation, one which takes us closer to Wordsworth's direct concern with figuration:

> It is, thinks he, the gracious Fairy,
> Who loved the Shepherd Lord to meet
> In his wanderings solitary:
> Wild notes she in his hearing sang,
> A song of Nature's hidden powers;
> That whistled like the wind, and rang
> Among the rocks and holly bowers.
> 'Twas said that she all shapes could wear;
> And oftentimes before him stood,
> Amid the trees of some thick wood,
> In semblance of a Lady fair;
> And taught him signs, and shewed him sights,
> In Craven's dens, on Cumbrian heights;   (270–82)

The evocation of nature's powers rests momentarily (273–6) on a familiar Wordsworthian strain reminiscent of both the 'Lucy' poems and of Lucy Gray's 'solitary song / That whistles in the wind'; but it slides into something different, because Clifford's access to hidden powers is through the agency of a fully hypostatised supernatural figure; an elusive figure, moreover, whose function is to lead or to tempt. The potent naturalism of lines 273–6 remains, in the end, embedded in a broader context of supernaturalism.

It is this initial transformation that makes the tale supernatural in essence. There is no suggestion, of course, that Clifford created the fairy out of natural mysteries; rather it is the popular imagination that has done so: this is the process that Wordsworth isolates and evaluates. Again he is not interested in the rights and wrongs of what the popular imagination does (just as he doesn't criticise the 'bearded Sire' who tells the story of Lady Aäliza). Speculation has arisen among the attendant crowd 'spite of sober truth, that sees / A world of fixed remembrances / Which to this mystery belong' (211–13). Their superstition is part of their reverent response to a creature 'more bright' than dreams (195–6). The criticism he does offer is directed towards the scholar, towards the sophisticated mind which takes over and romances upon the reverent though superstitious product of the collective imagination of a rural community. One implication is that if local superstition (local legend) is properly valued, its value lies in the collective consciousness of the community whose 'history' is the legend, not in any transferred, merely *aesthetic* value the scholarly mind may give it – nor in the piquant exoticism it represents to the culturally distant reader. How then can a local legend have any real significance to readers who don't share the specific local pieties (love of place and object) it embodies? How in fact can the poet be *of* the interpreting community and at the same time write about it? Another question: if *these* transformations are judged to be unworthy of the object, what kind of transformation (figuration) has any deeper claim to validity? In what sense can interpretation be 'true' to the object?

The narrator's own act of attention to the doe amplifies the injunction 'look again' because it is sustained over a period of time:

> What harmonious pensive changes
> Wait upon her as she ranges
> Round and through this Pile of state
> Overthrown and desolate!
> Now a step or two her way
> Is through space of open day,
> Where the enamoured sunny light
> Brightens her that was so bright;
> Now doth a delicate shadow fall,
> Falls upon her like a breath,
> From some lofty arch or wall,
> As she passes underneath:
> Now some gloomy nook partakes
> Of the glory that she makes, – . . .
>
> The presence of this wandering Doe
> Fills many a damp obscure recess
> With lustre of a saintly show;
> And, re-appearing, she no less
> To the open day gives blessedness.   (81–94; 102–6)

It is the sense of movement (conveyed rhythmically as well as semantically) and the subtle change of appearances that make these lines so remarkable; and these are the qualities that distinguish the narrator's vision of the doe from the scholar's. The latter begins with a static image and immediately grasps at a meaning the narrator judges not to be inherent in the image. By contrast the narrator's series of images seems always about to yield a fixed meaning, which however is withheld in the movement from one image to the next. Language internalises the changes: 'pensive' refers to the way the mind perceives the change. Further, the changes are mutual: the doe and the landscape change each other.[29] What the passage emphasises is that object and context interact so that the significance of each is dependent on the other.

In this way the narrator's perception contrasts deeply with the scholar's, but what is not so clear is how it relates to the superstitions of the local community. My feeling is that the poem projects an ideology in which personal experience of time and change is congruent with that sense of history as collective memory that gives validity to local legend. The two are not logically connected, and it is the purpose of the whole poem to give the doe a significance *different* from its communal meanings, a significance generated on the one hand by the suffering of the individual heroine Emily and on the other by broader historical processes. Yet at the same time the narrator's story remains in competition with the prefatory narratives, which are dismissed at the end of the first canto as 'busy dreams and fancies wild'.

Figuration and narrative

Narrative, with its temporal dimension, affords Wordsworth a medium for exploring acts of figuration. It has long been argued that Romantic metaphor generally includes a temporal element,[30] but the implications for Romantic *narrative* verse have not been fully explored precisely because Byron's and Scott's tales have been taken as typical. In many of Wordsworth's poems he is concerned to show how certain significations come about *through time*, whether personal time in memory or habit, or historical or legendary time. Narrative forms become media for evaluating changes of signification in objects and subjects.

'Hartleap Well', a poem with obvious affinities to *The White Doe*, is an experiment in narration, a twice-told tale in which the first and second tellings generate quite different figurative meanings. Each is a conscious act of commemoration: Walter, the knight who hunts the hart, celebrates its leap in a frankly anthropomorphic, self-magnifying spirit of 'gallantry' and commemorates it with a piece of landscape architecture designed to last

> Till the foundations of the mountain fail[.]

The shepherd who retells the tale points to a blighted landscape where even the trees have lost their distinctive identity ('You see these lifeless stumps of aspin wood, / Some say that they are beeches, others elms'), and the story is a denaturing parable. The place will remain denatured

> Till trees, and stones, and fountains all are gone[,]

until, that is, all trace of previous figuration has disappeared; as if the first figuration must last its course before a truer image can emerge. The two prophecies correspond to the two acts of interpretation. That, I think, is a deep reflection on the power of *use*, of communal habit. But Wordsworth typically does not let the matter rest there; he gives us the interpretive processes of his narrator / shepherd, which, though the result differs from the superstitions of his neighbours, are nevertheless designed to stand for the growing and developing processes by which objects gather meaning for specific localities:

> Some say that here a murder has been done,
> And blood cries out for blood: but, for my part
> I've guess'd, when I've been sitting in the sun,
> That it was all for that unhappy Hart.

'I've guessed': an act of figuration that's both tentative and repeated, imitating what is assumed to be a communal process. Wordsworth's shepherd embodies the problems of figuration because he functions as both a critic of unthinking possession and an independent interpreter: as though the two could be different, as though personal habit guaranteed the truth of figuration *in the same way* that communal knowledge does. Other experiments in the *Lyrical Ballads* involve *potentially* redoubled narration and prompt similar questions. 'The Thorn' and 'The Danish Boy' are both presented as fragmentary, the first lacking 'an introductory Poem' and the second being 'a prelude to a ballad poem never written'.[31] These statements are complementary but converge on the single problem, generated by Wordsworth's interest in habit, that figuration can lose its validity by being merely idiosyncratic. In both cases Wordsworth's note seems to suggest a need for a psychology of figuration as well as a controlling, impersonal, legend. It has been the custom to set aside Wordsworth's comments and argue that the poems are complete in themselves, like other Romantic fragments. In an influential discussion of 'The Danish Boy' – but let us restore its original title, 'A Fragment' – Hartman argued that the boy's ghost is an emanation of the poetic spirit, a centrally important case of unmediated vision or, as I would prefer to call it, free-floating figuration.[32] That argument makes Wordsworth look like Coleridge ('A Fragment' is Wordsworth's 'Kubla Khan': both poets made a public show of the respective poem's inadequacies), but it does not help us to grasp the problems of figuration I've outlined above: an area in which Wordsworth's assumptions and judgements differ widely from Coleridge's.

It would be quite easy to give 'Hartleap Well' a simple political meaning if we ignored this problem: Sir Walter single-handedly appropriates nature for his own purpose, while the shepherd merely reports a consensus of understanding: one is an aristocratic act – an unquestioning act of possession – while the other reflects a communal will. But that would not take into account the difference posited here between persistence and possession.

To return to *The White Doe*: Wordsworth suspends our interest in the doe over the whole poem. In fact when the narrative gets under way in Canto II, he turns to the other principal symbol, the banner. I propose to follow Wordsworth's example and consider it now, because the juxtaposition is, in my view, part of his strategy. In the synoptic introduction of this canto he indicates promptly what the issue is:

> For She it was, – 'twas She who wrought
> Meekly, with foreboding thought,
> In vermeil colours and in gold
> An *unblessed* work; which, standing by,
> Her Father did with joy behold, –
> Exulting in the imagery;
> A Banner, one that did fulfil
> *Too perfectly* his headstrong will:
> For on this Banner had her hand
> Embroidered (such was *the* command)
> The Sacred Cross; and figured there
> The five dear wounds our Lord did bear;
> Full soon to be uplifted high,
> And float in rueful company!
>
> (347–60; emphasis added)

Though sacred, the banner is unblessed; this is not only because of the

company it will keep – a band of rebellious earls – but also because its
maker has no faith in it. Emily's (Anglican) faith 'leans another way'.
To Norton, on the other hand, the banner is an object of emblematic
power, which demands an automatic response. When Norton carries it
to the earls he expects it to produce the same kind of automatic
response that it does in him; but the event proves him slightly but
importantly wrong. When he unfurls the banner, asserting, not quite
correctly, that it was made by

> A Maid o'er whom the blessed Dove
> Vouchsafed in gentleness to brood
> While she the holy work pursued   (673–5)

there is a significant pause:

> 'Uplift the Standard!' was the cry
> From all the Listeners that stood round,
> 'Plant it, – by this we live or die' –
> The Norton ceased not for that sound,
> But said, 'The prayer which ye have heard,
> Much injured Earls! by these preferred,
> Is offered to the Saints, the sigh
> Of tens of thousands, secretly.' –
> 'Uplift it,' cried once more the Band,
> And then a thoughtful pause ensued.
> 'Uplift it!' said Northumberland –   (676–86)

The 'thoughtful pause' plainly expresses Northumberland's political
thinking: the banner has no mesmerising effect on him, but he realises
that it is a powerful, politically useful, rallying point. Wordsworth has
previously made clear that the earls' motives in beginning the uprising
is purely political. The two are 'fast leagued in discontent' but ready
to use, if necessary, their subjects' loyalty to the Catholic faith: they
'boldly urge a general plea / The rites of ancient piety / To be
triumphantly restored'. And the subsequent action of the poem
confirms them in political expediency: against the superior forces of
loyalty to the crown they simply melt away leaving Norton to be
captured, still holding the banner. It is worth noting, incidentally,
that Wordsworth's account of these matters – the earls' motives and
the fate of the Nortons – differs from fact (as Scott pointed out)[33] and
from both the old ballad of 'The Rising of the North' and, more

surprising, Wordsworth's own prose version appended to the first edition of the poem.[34] So much for the earls. The more pertinent matter is Wordsworth's characterisation of iconic responses generally. The crowd reacts *as* a crowd and carries its religious fervour to the extreme of tearing the book of prayer and treading the bible beneath their feet. Norton is caught between the untrustworthy politicking of the earls and the undisciplined enthusiasm of the crowd. Again, as with responses to the doe in Canto I, Wordsworth is not interested in ascribing guilt to the unreflective mind; what he does emphasise, and that most vividly, is the kind of spiritual dilemma Norton's faith has led him into. Having attempted to rally the army unsuccessfully Norton looks again at the banner:

But the familiar prospect shed
Despondency unfelt before:
A shock of intimations vain,
Blank fear, and superstitious pain,
Fell on him, with the sudden thought
Of her by whom the work was wrought: –
Oh wherefore was her countenance bright
With love divine and gentle light?
She did in passiveness obey,
But her Faith leaned another way.
Ill tears she wept, – I saw them fall,
I overhead her as she spake
Sad words to that mute Animal,
The White Doe, in the hawthorn brake;
She steeped, but not for Jesu's sake,
This Cross in tears: – by her, and One
Unworthier far, are we undone –
Her Brother was it who assailed
Her tender spirit and prevailed.
Her other Parent, too, whose head
In the cold grave hath long been laid,
From reason's earliest dawn beguiled
The docile, unsuspecting Child:
Far back – far back my mind must go
To reach the well-spring of this woe! –   (868–92)

Norton's pain is 'superstitious' because he regards it precisely as a *bad omen* that the banner was not sanctified by an appropriate faith in

Emily; moreover he is suspicious, though in an unspecified way, of Emily's relationship with the doe. But another point of view emerges from the passage, a different analysis of Norton's shock: the banner is a 'natural' symbol of Emily's filial piety but not of her faith, and it symbolises too her relation with her mother. The banner, that is, has a real history of having caused Emily pain, since it divides her loyalties. Wordsworth contrasts Norton's perception of the banner as a pure sign and Emily's perception of it as a cause of sorrow in her own personal history. Perhaps Norton does momentarily see it from Emily's point of view, but if so he instantly rejects these dawning paternal and spousal sympathies when he is approached by his 'Enemy', his son Francis (926ff).

Norton's faith is unquestioning. It is shaken by these events but he immediately reaffirms it. He cannot seize the chance to analyse it because he is committed to a course of action which would be fundamentally disabled by the kind of reflection this incident prompts. Wordsworth has begun an analysis of faith which, explicitly and implicitly, is touched on several times in the poem. Norton's 'pain' is superstitious: so is his inability to name Emily and his wife: he names neither in the poem – as if names, too, had an iconic power. (The iconic power of names plays a role in the 'Lucy' poems.) Neither can Norton deal with his 'recreant' son Francis, except by calling him names: he denies his existence when first presenting himself to the earls, and subsequently repudiates him to his face. These things are at the heart of Wordsworth's idea: superstition, the trust in or fear of signs (whether names or icons) is the result of the mind's being possessed by the purpose the icon serves. The contrasting state of mind is Emily's, in which the object gathers meaning from its human associations as an object. Norton attends to the object's signification only: Emily to its lineaments as a particular object with a particular history. The iconic response is generalising, timeless; the symbolic grows (in time) from particularities.

In these paragraphs I have brought together two issues which are logically separate; one of them illustrated (at this point in the poem) by the doe and the other by banner. On the one hand there is a movement from object to story; and on the other a movement from object to figure. That Wordsworth brings these together seems to me the point; his argument, I take it, is that the activity of making or embroidering stories about things is analogous to, or in some sense the same thing as, giving objects significations: each is a way of making something into that which, in itself, it is not. That is why both narrative and figurative interest are in suspense until the last canto of the poem, by which time Wordsworth has shown, through the banner, ways of symbol- and story-making that are *not* appropriate to the doe. We shall not know its true significance until we have heard the true story. This conjunction of interests is common in Wordsworth's narrative poems, though the meditative, analytical element is seldom so pronounced.[35]

One of the most far-reaching revisions Wordsworth made to the poem after its first publication was to explore the role of Emily's eldest brother Francis and give it a force in the general argument about figuration that it did not previously have. Francis had always been a problem: Wordsworth had initially made him betray his family, an action that Coleridge found incomprehensible.[36] In all published versions Francis is a victim of the religious and political differences within his family, but the question of his motivation remained problematic. In order to make his sacrifice worth while, Wordsworth had to present a powerful (dominating) narrative of choice. In the 1815 version he has Francis simply amazed by his action of seizing that banner (thus implicating himself in the Northern rebellion). Revising the passage, Wordsworth particularised his amazement by having him act unconsciously under the influence of a memory that is hypostatised in a 'spectre' of his previous self. The revision blunts the contrast between automatic and considered (iconic and lived) response that the 1815 version has been at pains to construct, but it makes the poem more subtly self-reflective because Emily's dilemma with the banner is repeated in different terms in Francis's. The revised version deals with more explicitly semi-conscious processes than the earlier.

In both texts Francis's story is one of haunting or possession. Geoffrey Durrant[37] noticed that in his pursuit and death there is an implicit image of a stag hunt:

> At this he from the beaten road
> Retreated towards a brake of thorn,
> Which like a place of 'vantage shewed:
> And there stood bravely, though forlorn.
> In self-defence with a Warrior's brow
> He stood, . . .
> But, from behind, a treacherous wound
> Unfeeling, brought him to the ground.   (1492–1509)

Durrant argued that the implied image is a kind of Ovidian metamorphosis, and that it is typical of Wordsworth's dislike of mythological figuration that the image should be implied and not stated. This is an important observation in view of the prominence of metamorphosis in the first canto of the poem (Wordsworth's lifelong admiration for Ovid has still not been properly studied). It's clear that the idea of possession can be related to the idea of self-transformation: the outcome of Francis's being possessed or haunted by a spectral memory is that he too becomes a spectral figure; or, more precisely, his identity is displaced by an image. There is a symmetrical relation between an iconic response to objects and creating the self in a single static image.

Figuration and memory

In Francis, then, memory has become a power not for joining but for dividing past and present: it has an iconic power in the revised version when it is formally objectified in a 'spectre'. There are two ways in which the poem places this process and forces us to judge it. First, its legacy is a kind of despair which the action of the poem proves simply inadequate: Francis tells Emily to 'hope nothing', but the long seventh canto of the poem is the story of Emily's victory over despair.[38] Secondly, the disruptive quality of memory in Francis is set against a less tangible but more creative view of memory in Emily. In Francis, memory simplifies consciousness at the expense of blotting out parts of it and sets up a barrier between past and present; whereas in Emily it is a power by which the fragmented mind is gradually reassembled into wholeness. Francis's experience of memory is static and disjunctive; Emily's is dynamic, moving through time and establishing that relationship between time and meaning which is adumbrated in the first canto of the poem.

The termini of Emily's narrative are set out explicitly in the seventh canto. After Francis's death her mind initially comes to rest in 'subjection' to

> a holy,
> Though stern and rigorous, melancholy! (1615–16)

This gives place to a condition in which her soul is

> blest
> With a soft spring-day of holy,
> Mild, delicious melancholy: (1775–7)

The terms are religious, but the contrast marked here is not between two dogmas but between two attitudes towards faith. There is no change in her belief but there is a change in her ability to accommodate it emotionally and intellectually. It is a change in the sense of self. Wordsworth undoubtedly represents the change as a triumph (a 'victory in the world of the spirit'),[39] and it is this that has caused some of his critics to become impatient with the poem: a story, it can be said, that moves resolutely towards a transcendental view of the significance of human action. But this is true only as a general impression. Wordsworth devotes his attention to the nature of the change, a process involving precisely those acts of memory and imagination that have been brought into question earlier in the poem: in particular, the act of self-definition through changing figuration.

The canto opens with the narrator's asking that 'Spirit' which is his muse where Emily may be; and the locations he guesses at seem to have metaphoric significance:

> What mighty forest in its gloom
> Enfolds her? – is a rifted tomb
> Within the wilderness her seat?
> Some island which the wild waves beat,
> Is that the Sufferer's last retreat?
> Or some aspiring rock, that shrouds
> Its perilous front in mists and clouds?
> High-climbing rock – deep sunless dale –
> Sea – desart – what do these avail?
> Oh take her anguish and her fears
> Into a calm recess of years!   (1575–85)

'What do these avail?': these things, places, avail neither Emily nor the narrator. Each of the images, in fact, both 'finds' Emily and loses sight of her: she may be on 'an aspiring rock' but she is shrouded in mist, invisible; and the tomb image is both a specific location and a sign of her absence. Images do not 'avail' because the visual is too specific, it too easily becomes a static metaphor. Wordsworth abandons the visual in the final phrase: 'a calm recess of years'. Here 'recess' is no longer potentially both literal and metaphorical but metaphorical only; or we might say that the temporal dimension of 'years' empties 'recess' of its spatial (visual) dimension and emphasises the connection with 'recession' – a going backwards.[40]

However one worries over these lines, two things seem to be clear: first, that Wordsworth's use of imagery specifying place is ambivalent (the metaphoric relation of place and state of mind is continually suggested and abandoned – as in the description of the doe in Canto I); and, secondly, that the visualising tendency in spatial imagery can be controlled or repressed by temporal associations. These things are important because they suggest a deep relationship between the narrator's poetic and narrative strategy on the one hand and the substance of the narrative – Emily's self-definition – on the other.

Emily's state of mind at this point presents an extreme contrast to Francis's and Norton's: absorbed not by an image but by the total rejection of imagery, even those images available to her in her immediate surroundings. And there is a corresponding constraint in her appearance: her face shows an 'awfulness' which unnaturally 'overshadows . . . the tender gleams of gentleness and meek delight'. This is an act of self-transformation which indeed *resembles* Francis's in that it insufficiently represents the whole being, but is the opposite because of its psychological origin: what is imposed is an idea (and a negation) and not an image.

The process of redefinition begins through the agency of the doe; and here too the poem is concerned with the ways in which objects acquire significance over time. Emily's initial response to her surroundings is troubled because she sees in them images of her former misery ('all now was trouble-haunted ground'); and so she wanders further in flight from memory. But a contrary impulse arises from the doe's presence. Its steadfastness and companionship – its actions, that is to say, not its mere appearance – awaken in Emily a sense of the continuousness of the present, a sense that time and change are still occurring; and this knowledge frees her from the static images of the past. Her gradual awakening involves the return of a temporal dimension in her idea of self.

> For she hath ventured now to read
> Of time, and place, and thought, and deed,
> Endless history that lies
> In her silent Follower's eyes!
> Who with a power like human Reason

Discerns the favourable season,
Skilled to approach or to retire, –
From looks conceiving her desire,
From look, deportment, voice, or mien,
That vary to the heart within.
If she too passionately writhed
Her arms, or over-deeply breathed,
Walked quick or slowly, every mood
In its degree was understood; (1733–46)

The metaphor of reading suggests an act of comprehension going beyond the visual though making use of it: not a passive response but an active seeking; and in the doe's movements there is that emphasis on time and change – external change expressing inner fluctuations – that we saw of the narrator's description of it in Canto I (it is only *now* that the doe's movement finds its metaphoric equivalent). It remains only for Emily to 'read' also her surroundings and find a new relationship with them:

With her Companion, in such frame
Of mind, to Rylstone back she came, –
And, wandering through the wasted groves,
Received the memory of old Loves,
Undisturbed and undistrest,
Into a soul which now was blest
With a soft spring-day of holy,
Mild, delicious, melancholy:
Not sunless gloom or unenlightened,
But by tender fancies brightened. (1770–9)

The contrast between these lines and the earlier ones ('a stern and rigorous melancholy') is rhetorical as well as substantial: metaphor is now available ('spring-day') because the narrator now has access to Emily's mind through landscape. The poem draws out the implications of metaphor and finds it justifiable when it becomes explicable metamorphosis. In that way it is a critique of the shape-changing trope of romance.

Erasing the visual

'Reading' is opposed to 'seeing'. In Wordsworth's critical texts, including the 'Dedication' to *The White Doe*, reading books is likened to reading nature. In this part of the poem, as in many passages of *The Prelude*, reading nature is likened to reading books. Nature is to be read sequentially as if it had a temporal dimension corresponding to human memory and anticipation, while, inversely, texts can claim the authority of nature. The tropes converge in a paradoxical concept of mutability and universal validity; life has the solidity of art, and art has the plasticity of life.

One inference to be drawn from that is that there is a specific *ordering* of the arts. I shall return to that below. Wordsworth's doctrine is in general terms anti-visual, sharing with Burke's concept of the sublime an emphasis on visual obscurity and affective clarity. The visual *as visual* is erased in the characteristic terms 'Vision' and 'Presence', both used in this section of *The White Doe* (1757, 1763) and in an earlier passage defining the formative influence of Emily's mother:

> An Image faint –
> And yet not faint – a presence bright
> Returns to her, – 'tis that bless'd Saint
> Who with mild looks and language mild
> Instructed here her darling Child,
> While yet a prattler on the knee,
> To worship in simplicity
> The invisible God, and take for guide
> The faith reformed and purified.

>   'Tis flown – the Vision, and the sense
> Of that beguiling influence!
> 'But oh! thou Angel from above,
> Thou Spirit of maternal love,
> That stood'st before my eyes, more clear
> Than Ghosts are fabled to appear
> Sent upon embassies of fear;
> As thou thy presence hast to me
> Vouchsafed – in radiant ministry
> Descend on Francis: – through the air
> Of this sad earth to him repair,
> Speak to him with a voice, and say,
> 'That he must cast despair away!'[41] (1036–57)

In this passage the link between seeing and 'vision' is attenuated by the succeeding formulations: 'the *sense* / Of that beguiling *influence*'. And again, though the vision has clarity – 'more clear / Than ghosts'

– yet the negation within the phrase ('fabled') complicates the assertion of clarity, which is further attenuated in the word 'presence'. What happens in the paragraph as a whole is that the mother's presence modulates from the visual to the aural: we are left, finally, with a voice.

Like many of Wordsworth's oppositions (poetic language as opposed to the real language of men), the opposition of the eye and the ear is complex in analysis and construction. Among other recurrent constructions there is one, especially prevalent in passages critical of political enthusiasm, that links sight and reason (the 'light of circumstances, flash'd / Upon an independent intellect'),[42] as opposed to another sense (hearing, touch) and insight or imagination. In some passages that opposition is presented in the language of proximity and remoteness ('no need of a *remoter* charm, / By thought supplied, nor any interest / Unborrowed from the eye') or surface and depth. The habit of 'comparing scene with scene / Bent overmuch on superficial things' is paraphrased as 'the love / Of sitting . . . in judgement' which interrupts 'deeper feelings' and colludes with a state in which

> the eye . . .
> The most despotic of our senses gain'd
> Such strength in me as often held my mind
> In absolute dominion.[44]

It is not difficult to find the image of light used in an opposite way in *The Prelude*, and occasionally 'eye' can denote uncriticised understanding, especially in the early books,[45] but where eyesight is a metaphor of analytic thinking it is usually represented as partial, arbitrary or misleading.

Substituting voice for visual image is a common way of invoking power and authority in sublime poetry. In Shelley's poem Mont Blanc has 'a voice . . . to repeal / Large codes of fraud and woe'): like many unidentifiable spectral voices in the poetry of the period, it seems to offer a fiction of orphic, undeniable figuration. But if voice is imagined as that of an identifiable individual it is just as potentially idiosyncratic and incomplete as the visual image it erases. Saying is irreducibly individual, whereas seeing is thought of as universal. (Thus, 'say' is the colloquial signal of hypothesis, whereas 'see' is the signal of the obvious. Compare 'anyone can say that' with 'anyone can see that'.) Hartman showed that disembodied voices are never given unqualified authority in Wordsworth's poetry, ascribing the fact to a fear of unmediated vision.[46] I suggest rather that it reflects Wordsworth's concern with time and communality in figuration and a consequent ambivalence about the status of his aural imagery: breezes, streams, and birdsong are *questionable* revelations, teasing and evanescent. In a poem about a 'silent poet' the eye's independence is completely erased in a phrase which, paradoxically, praises it: 'an eye practised like a blind man's touch'. And the central text of epiphany in Wordsworth is the 'spots of time' passage in *The Prelude*, which also, again paradoxically, concerns the place of time and memory in figuration and the relation of individual fears to communal reverences.[47]

It is worth bearing these things in mind because they refine and modify Walter J. Ong's seductive discussion of the visual and the aural that I referred to in a previous chapter. In *The Interface of the Word* he argues that oral / aural communication is the appropriate model of art that is concerned with relationship, and that an art of visual imagery turns the audience into mere spectators, witnesses from a distance.[48] This analysis would suit the purpose of my reading of Wordsworth if it did not ignore the exigencies of publishing and profit-making that Wordsworth himself seldom ignored, much as he wished them away, and the conviction, which I share, that there is no use in making a metaphysical opposition between the oral and the literary in discussions of poems that work (like this) in print. It also needs historicising.

Historically Wordsworth's mistrust of the visual has a correlative in his anti-Catholicism, which I touched on in comparing *The White Doe* with *The Excursion*. During the years when these poems were written and published it was largely a *political* conviction, a response to the threat, as he saw it, of Catholic Emancipation, but it is intimately connected with his critique of figuration. The facts are fairly well documented. In a group of letters written between 1808 and 1811 to his friend Wrangham, an Anglican minister who favoured emancipation, Wordsworth expressed his fear that any degree of emancipation would lead eventually to Catholic establishment in Ireland, which would be constitutionally dangerous. He supposed the issue to be 'a mere pretext of ambitious and discontented men'.[49] Wordsworth was not alone in this attitude. A few months before he began to write the poem the Whig government (the 'Ministry of All

Talents') had resigned because it could not give George III an assurance that it would not again raise the issue of opening higher army appointments to Catholics. 'No Popery' had been a popular slogan in the general election of the previous year. The matter was prominent again in 1813 when Grattan, having obtained the approval of the Secretary of Propaganda in Rome, presented a bill in favour of some degree of emancipation: the bill failed because it was not radical enough for the Irish Catholics. During 1814 and 1815 it was referred back to Rome and presented again in parliament, again unsuccessfully.

Wordsworth's fear that the emancipation movement was a pretext for the discontented is perhaps expressed in his presentation of the northern earls in the poem. They are opportunists who banded together to 'disturb' the crown of Elizabeth and who, it is implied, made use of honest zeal as a pretext. (This is emphasised in Wordsworth's reworking of his sources, as I noted above.) In this they contrast with Norton, whose faith is genuine though mistaken. That Wordsworth saw how powerful a political pretext religion might be is shown in the section of the poem dealing with the actions of the crowd, which degenerates into a violent mob, tearing the Prayer-Book and trampling on the bible. He emphasises the heterogeneous composition of the mob and the way mob-action gathers momentum when it is set in motion (ll. 707–21).[50] In these ways he distinguishes 'zealous Band[s]' from the truly communal groupings present in Canto I.

The chief target of Wordsworth's criticism of Catholicism is its political misuse: that is what motivates the martial action of the poem. But at bottom there is a critique of Norton's faith. If his response to the banner is iconic, it is also at odds with his human-kindness, as we see in his denying his daughter a name; whereas Emily's faith grows out of her human nature, her emotional experience and relations. Her faith is a fulfilment of her nature; his, a denial. Many of the issues Wordsworth raises in this analysis of two kinds of faith are easily restated in sectarian terms because he uses similar terms in such polemical writings as *Ecclesiastical Sonnets*, which were written because the Catholic question had suggested to him the subject of an 'Ecclesiastical History of our Country'.[51] Though they show certain kinds of toleration of the Roman Church, it is clear that he was sharply critical of its symbols and forms of worship. He goes to the heart of the matter in the sonnet on transubstantiation (II, xi), in which the Host is said to breed 'awe and supernatural horror', and he contrasts approvingly the faith of the Waldenses who 'adore the

Invisible, and Him alone'. A subsequent poem, entitled 'The Point at Issue' (II, xxx) puts the matter plainly:

> For what contend the wise? – for nothing less
> Than that the Soul, freed from the bond of Sense,
> And to her God restored by evidence
> Of things not seen, drawn forth from their recess,
> Root there, and not in forms, her holiness

(Emily is advised to 'worship in simplicity the invisible God'.) Elsewhere in the sequence Wordsworth scorns 'the old idolatry', 'gods of wood and stone', 'sorceries of talent misapplied' (St Dunstan's contests with the devil), 'ghostly tenants of the wind' and the 'superstition' that aided the spread of the 'Magic wand of Papal power'.[52] It is, of course, true that these are standard criticisms of Roman forms of religion (Southey, for example, concludes his *Book of the Church* (1824) with a spirited denunciation of 'superstition and idolatry'); and it is true, too, that Wordsworth's criticism of Catholicism has other targets, such as the abuse of papal and monastic power and the 'bigotry' which opposed the translation of the bible into the vernacular. The latter is the subject of a sonnet that distinctly echoes *The White Doe*:

> and thousands wild
> With bigotry shall tread the Offering
> Beneath their feet, detested and defiled . . .
>
> (II, xxix)

There is in fact a deep fear of mob action in the recurrent image of trampling, literal or metaphorical, that links idolatry and lawlessness (the Waldenses 'seek defence . . . From rites that trample upon soul and sense' [II, xi]).

Wordsworth's criticisms of Catholicism converge on the issue of idolatry in Norton's faith: the separation of form from feeling and dazzlement by the visual. In responding to the banner as he does he is not 'free from the bonds of sense'. It is evident that Norton represents for Wordsworth spiritual errors which he felt to be peculiarly Catholic, and to that extent the poem is anti-Catholic. It takes its place in the collected poems next to the *Ecclesiastical Sonnets*.

Art and the visual

Wordsworth's scepticism about visual experience is easily seen as a limitation, a literal blindness, when it comes to the question of response to visual art. He lacks, it seems, the enthusiasm for the visual arts that is so attractive in Keats, and this is one of the axes on which they are so often contrasted, another being 'negative capability' and the 'egotistical sublime'. But in fact Wordsworth's interest in painting and sculpture is quite enough for a monograph on its own, even if we leave aside landscape painting and gardening.[53] The years 1815–16 are particularly interesting in this respect. They saw the beginning of an extensive correspondence with Haydon, whose devotion to historical figural painting, as well as his sheer ambition and the sense of his own worth, were to lead to his artistic isolation and in some measure to his suicide thirty years later. The two shared an interest in the representation of human action and the relation between the artist and the public, and in these years Haydon was engaged on a typically huge painting, 'Christ's Entry into Jerusalem', in which he used Wordsworth's and Keats's features for two of the witnesses. This was the occasion of his life mask of Wordsworth.

Ambition; artist–public relations; the difference between historical and landscape painting; the nature of figuration: these are among the subjects that arise from Wordsworth's dealings with Haydon, and if what I have said above is valid, they relate particularly to Wordsworth's experiment on the public taste in The White Doe.[54] The challenge to Scott and Byron coincided with the most damning reviews he ever got (for The Excursion and The White Doe itself), to which he replied in the intemperate 'Essay, Supplementary to the Preface' (1815) and the bilious 'Letter to a Friend of Burns' (1816). Association with Haydon and, through him, Keats, brought him in contact with two obsessively ambitious artists who celebrated human action as distinct from nature. The fate of Haydon is generally linked with a declining fashion for historical painting in Britain[55] (though one wonders how the argument would differ if Britain had had a Delacroix; Byron, Shelley and Hemans were among poets who wrote on contemporary history in the early 1820s, and Byron and Hemans were not ignored by the public); and it is easy to see how Wordsworth's later commercial success reflected a general movement from history to landscape. The River Duddon, published in 1820, was by far his most successful volume yet, and from that moment his reputation climbed rapidly. But the struggle for significant ways of representing human action went on in the art of those who were ambivalent about mythology (as I've suggested, Wordsworth was in his representation of the springs of Greek and other myths in *The Excursion*). The issue was whether to work with the freedoms and constraints of classical mythology or to go on asserting that there was such a thing as communal legend endorsed by individual exploration, whether an artist could make or reach a community of image makers and readers who could see 'history' as contemporary and contiguous with their own lives.[56]

For this reason it is worth pausing to consider the sonnets Wordsworth sent to Haydon and to compare them with Keats's. It is important to remember that Wordsworth's were published, with Haydon's assistance, in Hunt's *Examiner* and John Scott's *The Champion*, the former a journal reviled by Wordsworth's critics in the *Edinburgh* and *Blackwood's*. 'High is our calling, Friend!', written to Haydon in response to a letter in which Haydon typically 'proclaimed Wordsworth's genius and his own determination to persevere in his vocation',[57] locates 'glory', the artist's true reward, somewhere beyond the 'obscure distress' of actuality: a high-minded poem that borders on the patronising. But Haydon was touched 'to my heart strings'[58] by lines attributing to his art both heroism and sensitivity:

> a mind and heart
> Though sensitive, yet in their weakest part
> Heroically fashioned – to infuse
> Faith in the whisper of the lonely muse,
> Though the whole world seems adverse to desert.

Keats clearly had these lines in mind when he wrote his sonnets to Haydon, 'Highmindedness, a jealousy for good' and 'Great spirits now on earth are sojourning'. In the first Keats emphasises 'glory', and his 'steadfast genius, toiling gallantly' is reminiscent of Wordsworth's 'Heroically fashioned'. In the second his conviction that Haydon's

> stedfastness would never take
> A meaner sound than Raphael's whispering

– a comparison sneered at in *Blackwood's* notorious review of *Endymion* titled 'The Cockney School of Poetry' – recalls Wordsworth's formulation of art's imperative:

> to infuse
> Faith in the whispers of the lonely Muse.

In both cases inspiration whispers, whereas (by implication) the critics shout. Keats was overwhelmed when Haydon showed the second poem to Wordsworth.[59]

Yet Wordsworth was less enthusiastic about Haydon than Keats was, and this may be why his sonnet offers only a *general* defence of artistic endeavour. He never compared Haydon in verse with a Renaissance artist as Keats did, and as Lamb did in a punning comparison of Palma Vecchio with the artist of 'Christ's Entry into Jerusalem', with its arcade of *palms* ('thy palms put every other down').[60] He clearly took Haydon seriously enough to solicit his opinion of Winckelmann's *Reflections on the Painting and Sculpture of the Greeks*, which Wordsworth himself found 'very erroneous' on the question of allegorical painting (Haydon agreed: a 'useless rhapsodist'), and, in a later letter (January 1816) on 'Christ's Entry', to praise the theme as 'more than heroic' (explaining the reference to Milton) and advise Haydon to follow Raphael in cultivating sublimity and avoiding 'dramatic diversities' that would spoil the unity of effect.[61] But whereas Keats's poem invokes Raphael to praise Haydon's achievement, Wordsworth's letter names him as an ideal to strive for and fears that Haydon's tendency to visual diversity will lead him astray. And there are other ambiguities in this exchange of approval. Wordsworth wanted his poem to Haydon published in *The Champion* as 'a private communication of friendship' rather than a public, disinterested tribute, and he also wanted it printed next to his sonnet to Beaumont ('Praised be the Art'), 'a favourite of mine'.[62] Had they appeared together they would have made a striking contrast, because the latter is specifically about landscape painting; it praises Beaumont's 'ambition *modest*' as against Haydon's 'heroic' ambition; and it speaks of artistic *achievement* as against struggle. There is ambiguity, too, in the fact that the two other sonnets Wordsworth sent to Haydon, 'September, 1815' and 'November 1', both published in *The Examiner*,[63] unmistakably recommend landscape images, though they *can* be read as explorations of the enforced solitude of an unrewarded artist.

On the issue of artist–public relations, comparison of Wordsworth and Haydon finally reveals important differences. Haydon thought in terms of a national community attuned to heroic art, whereas

Wordsworth was less insistent on the national than the local. For that reason the interface in Wordsworth's poems between figural and landscape art is much more complex, and so are his negotiations with readers, whom in 1815 he variously divided between 'The Public' and 'The People' and into a wider range of groups corresponding to varying kinds of miseducation. After *The White Doe* came another experiment in historical figuration, both grander and more minute: the *Ecclesiastical Sonnets*. National in aim, the series is also what the original title (*Ecclesiastical Sketches*) suggests, a series of sketches of religious communities in which Wordsworth finds more intimate models of shared signification than in the story of Emily Norton's spiritual heroism. I suggest there is a strong correlation between the dispersed images of society in *Ecclesiastical Sonnets* and the dispersed readership Wordsworth described in the 1815 'Essay.'

Though most of Wordsworth's significant later poems about paintings are about landscape art and are addressed to Beaumont in a spirit of collaboration,[64] there are a number that, like the *Ecclesiastical Sonnets*, look for models of communication in religious images. One of the more interesting is the 1820 sonnet on Leonardo's 'Last Supper':

> Tho' searching damps and many an envious flaw
> Have marred this Work; the calm ethereal grace,
> The love deep-seated in the Saviour's face,
> The mercy, goodness, have not failed to awe
> The Elements; as they do melt and thaw
> The heart of the Beholder – and erase
> (At least for one rapt moment) every trace
> Of disobedience to the primal law.
> The annunciation of the dreadful truth
> Made to the Twelve, survives: lip, forehead, cheek,
> And hand reposing on the board in ruth
> Of what it utters, while the unguilty seek
> Unquestionable meanings – still bespeak
> A labour worthy of eternal youth!

Here the language of surface and depth is combined with an analogy between artist–spectator relations and the image of communication (complete or incomplete?) among the figures represented; a metaphor (metonym?) in which words and gesture replace each other; and a suggestion that nature collaborates with the human hand to produce an art that is eternally young. As Christ's face 'awes' the 'Elements', so it awes the 'Beholder' – spectator and disciple – and as the undecayed face is not covered by flaws, so the beholder's self is divested of its 'traces' of disobedience. As the hand 'utters',[65] so the painting communicates what the spectator / reader would like to translate into 'unquestionable meaning'. The poem seems to arrive at the paradox that though *unquestionable* meaning' is still hidden in the whole conception, there is yet a significance that will not age. But meaning could not arise without the effects of time because they are the metaphorical equivalent of the frailty of human understanding. Wordsworth's note interestingly dismisses any distinction between nature's and man's agency in the painting's deterioration ('These niceties may be left to the connoisseurs – I speak of it as I felt'),[66] which is, I take it, a way of generalising time's constructive role in giving meaning to an example of the 'static' art of painting. Even though the painting is of a scene of instruction ('the primal law'), its meaning is made by the chance actions of time. It is a power *like* one of nature's because its human origin is the hand of a known genius *and* of a multitude of unknown others.

I choose this poem as an example of Wordsworth's meditation on paintings of human figures rather than landscapes, and one that raises the question of how meaning is negotiated between the work and generations of spectators in succeeding times. Where Wordsworth imagines the posterity of his *own* art he is apt to figure poetry as *inscription* on nature and be less content that time should take its course:

> why hath not the mind
> Some element to stamp her image on
> In nature somewhat nearer to her own?
> Why, gifted with such powers to send abroad
> Her spirit, must it lodge in shrines so frail?
>
> (*The Prelude*, V, 44–8)

The aesthetic of developing and negotiated figuration that I have suggested he explores in *The White Doe*, for all its power, provides no answer to these questions. It offers a model of negotiation between reader and writer but no mortgage on the future.

Notes and references

1. *Henry Crabb Robinson on Books and Their Writers*, ed. E.J. Morley (London, Dent, 1938), vol. 1, p. 90. Reprinted in Markham L. Peacock, *The Critical Opinions of William Wordsworth* (Baltimore, John S. Hopkins UP, 1950), p. 207.

2. Letter to Catherine Clarkson, January 1815; *Letters*, III, pp. 187–8.

3. See Chapter 1 above.

4. *Letters*, III, p. 188.

5. *Ibid.*, p. 191.

6. Mary Wollstonecraft, *Original Stories from Real Life* (second edn, 1796; repr. Woodstock Books, Oxford, 1990), p. iii.

7. John Barrell, *Poetry, Language and Politics*, p. 161; Olivia Smith, *The Politics of Language 1791–1819* (Oxford, Clarendon, 1984).

8. *Prose Works*, I, p. 103

9. It is interesting that Wordsworth uses both 'revolution' and 'restoration' as terms naming *inner* changes in *The Prelude*; which does not mean, of course, that they do not have political significance.

10. *Prose Works*, I, pp. 99–107; Gill, *Wordsworth*, p. 160.

11. Compare the argument in *The Prelude*, X, 693ff: '. . . Reason seem'd the most to assert her rights / When most intent on making of herself / A prime Enchanter . . .'.

12. See my discussion of 'power' in Chapter 3 above.

13. Text from E.L. Griggs (ed.), *New Poems* (London, OUP, 1942). The poem was first published in *Notes and Queries*, 24 July 1869, twenty years after Hartley Coleridge's death and nineteen years after Wordsworth's.

14. *The Archives of the House of Longman*, 'Impression Book', No. 5, p. 201 (Microfilm edn [Cambridge, Chadwyck-Healey, c. 1980], reel 38).

15. Theresa M. Kelley's pages on the poem in *Wordsworth's Revisionary Aesthetics* (1988) are among the most rewarding recent discussions. Her general context is a discussion of the concepts of the sublime and the beautiful.

16. The opening of Jeffrey's review of *The Excursion*, *Edinburgh Review*, November 1814, partially reprinted in *Romantic Criticism 1800–1825*, ed. Peter Kitson (London, Batsford, 1989), pp. 180ff.

17. *Edinburgh Quarterly*, 25 October 1815. Quoted in Elsie Smith, *An Estimate of William Wordsworth by his Contemporaries* (Oxford, Basil Blackwell, 1932), p. 226.

18. Quoted in Moorman, II, p. 285.

19. *The White Doe of Rylstone*, ed. Kristine Dugas (Ithaca, Cornell UP, 1988), Introduction.

20. Peter Manning, 'Tales and Politics: *The Corsair*, Lara, and *The White Doe of Rylstone*' in *Seventh International Byron Symposium: Byron's Poetry and Politics* (Salzburg, 1981).

21. Coleridge wrote to Byron (22.10.1815) saying that Wordsworth had intended to prefix to the poem an 'advertisement' noting that 'the peculiar metre and mode of narration he had imitated from the Christabel' and recollecting that Scott had read 'Christabel' with admiration in 1802 (Coleridge, *Letters*, III, pp. 601, 603).

22. The text discussed below is Dugas's reprint of the first published edition of 1815. Her edition includes a conjectural reconstruction of the original text (1807–8) sent to Longman. Coleridge's comments on the poem before publication refer to this earlier version, which differed considerably, especially in the portrayal of Emily and her brother Francis and consequently in the balance of political and spiritual action in the poem as a whole. For this reason there is little evidence to support Theresa M. Kelley's remark that the published version 'still exhibited the "faults" which Coleridge had summarized in 1808' (*Wordsworth's Revisionary Aesthetics*, p. 150), but nevertheless the published poem still attracted adverse comparisons with Scott on the grounds of obscurity and ethereality.

23. *The Archives of the House of Longman* (Microfilm edn, reel 38). See also W.J.B. Owen, 'Costs, Sales and Profits of Longman's Editions of Wordsworth', *The Library*, NS, XII (1957).

24. Gill, p. 598 (my emphasis).

25. Gill, p. 597 (my emphasis).

26. Dugas seems to me to miss the point in claiming that Wordsworth asks his readers to 'yield to his fictiveness . . . in the same way that they yield to the fictiveness of Spenser' (p. 59). Kelley shares Dugas's view (*Wordsworth's Revisionary Aesthetics*, p. 152).

27. Kelley follows James Heffernan (*Wordsworth's Theory of Poetry* [Ithaca, Cornell UP, 1969]) in using the word 'emblematic' of both the banner and the doe. She notes that the doe is 'couchant' (1. 203), as heraldic animals sometimes are. Whether this is a formative means of figuration in the poem is precisely the point at issue.

28. *Eclectic Review*, 5 (January 1816); quoted by Elsie Smith in *An Estimate of William Wordsworth by his Contemporaries*, p. 237.

29. Cf. Kelley's remark: 'Her singularity is the aesthetic measure of her power to compose landscape and feeling' (*Wordsworth's Revisionary Aesthetics*, p. 153).

30. See Paul De Man, 'The Rhetoric of Temporality' in *Blindness and Insight* (rev edn, London, Routledge, 1983) and W.K. Wimsatt, 'The Temporality of Romantic Metaphor' in *The Verbal Icon* (Lexington, University of Kentucky Press, 1954).

31. *PW*, II, pp. 512, 493.

32. Geoffrey Hartman, *The Fate of Reading* (Chicago, University of Chicago Press, 1975), p. 184.

33. This is evident from Wordsworth's reply (*PW*, III, p. 542).

34. *Ibid.*, pp. 536ff.

35. Interest in 'The Thorn' is notoriously divided between narrative curiosity ('But *what's* the thorn . . .?) and the symbolic power of objects. In the later itinerary poems objects are repeatedly explained by – given meaning by – stories associated with them, and Wordsworth is at pains to understand and evaluate the communal processes by which stories are generated.

36. Dugas, pp. 32ff.

37. 'Wordsworth's Metamorphoses', *English Studies in Africa*, 7 (1964), pp. 13ff. Durrant uses the revised text of 1836, but the point is as well illustrated by the text of 1815.

38. For a discussion of the Stoic philosophy implied in these lines, see J. Worthington, *Wordsworth's Reading of Roman Prose* (New Haven, Yale UP, 1946; repr. 1970), pp. 70–1.

39. Wordsworth to Coleridge, 19.4.1808 (*Letters*, II, pp. 222–3).

40. Kelley offers an interestingly complementary example of Wordsworth's 'emptying [figures] of meaning' in the description of the Norton mansion (*Wordsworth's Revisionary Aesthetics*, p. 155).

41. Punctuation is as in 1815 (Dugas). The muddled quotation marks neatly (but fortuitously) indicate the ambiguous nature of the 'voice'.

42. *The Prelude*, X, 829–30; originally *The Borderers*, 11. 1495–6. Compare *The Prelude*, X, 844–6: '[I] sacrificed / The exactness of a comprehensive mind / To scrupulous and microscopic views.'

43. See Kelley's exploration of the metaphor of surface and depth in relation to the sublime and the beautiful: *Wordsworth's Revisionary Aesthetics*, Introduction and ch. 1.

44. *The Prelude*, XI, 149–77.

45. For example, 'Yes, I had something of another eye . . .' (IV, 200); 'my trust is . . . in the eye of him that passes me' (IV, 494–5).

46. Hartman, *The Fate of Reading*, pp. 179ff.

47. The gibbet episode (*The Prelude*, XI, 279–345) relates a personal experience built on a neighbourhood 'superstition'.

48. Walter J. Ong, *The Interface of the Word* (Ithaca, Cornell UP, 1977), ch. 5.

49. *Letters*, II, p. 742.

50. Lamb's friend Manning praised the 'manly (implied) interpretation of (bad) party-actions' in this passage. Lamb, *Letters of Charles Lamb* (London, Dent, 1909), I, p. 387.

51. *PW*, III, pp. 556–7.

52. This list gives a distinctly stronger impression of Wordsworth's attitudes than those that Moorman gives (Moorman, II, p. 395). For a brief discussion emphasising Wordsworth's ecumenism in the sonnets about Christianity in America, see Alan G. Hill, 'Wordsworth and His American Friends', *Bulletin of Research in the Humanities*, 81 (1978), pp. 146–60.

53. Martha H. Shackford's *Wordsworth's Interest in Painters and Pictures* (Wellesley, 1945) is little more than a catalogue.

54. For the purpose of this argument I am considering *The White Doe* as an historical poem, although, regarded as a competitor with Scott's and Byron's narratives, it is traditionally called a romance. Marilyn Butler's essay on 'The Giaour' ('The Orientalism of "The Giaour" ' in *Byron and the Limits of Fiction*, ed. B. Beatty and V. Newey [Liverpool, Liverpool UP, 1982]) makes a good case for considering it a historical poem, though that is not her main purpose. What it is *not* is a mythological poem like *Endymion* or *Prometheus Unbound*.

55. For example, see J. Barrell, *The Political Theory of Painting from Reynolds to Hazlitt* (New Haven and London, Yale UP, 1986). Haydon himself published in 1829 *Some Enquiry into the Causes which have obstructed the Course of Historical Painting for the last seventy years in England*.

56. My term 'communal legend' is intended to mean the kind of agreed significance that John Barrell, in more overtly political terms, calls 'civic discourse' (*The Political Theory of Painting from Reynolds to Hazlitt, passim*).

57. Moorman, II, p. 286.

58. B.R. Haydon, *Correspondence and Table Talk*, ed. F.W. Haydon (London, 1876), II, p. 21.

59. Keats to Haydon, 21.11.1816 (*Letters*, ed. M.B. Forman [third edn, Oxford, OUP, 1947], p. 11).

60   *The Works in Prose and Verse of Charles and Mary Lamb*, ed. T. Hutchinson (London, OUP, 1908), II, p. 624.

61. Wordsworth, *Letters*, III, pp. 258, 274; Haydon, *Correspondence*, II, pp. 21–2. In October 1816 they corresponded about the heroic stature of Napoleon (Wordsworth, *Letters*, III, pp. 335–7).

62. *Letters*, III, p. 274.

63. 'November 1' also appeared in *The Champion*, 28.1.1816.

64. There are, however, two late sonnets about Haydon's representations of Napoleon (one of the nineteen Haydon executed) and Wellington.

65. Wordsworth justified the analogy by reference to Milton's *Paradise Regained* (*PW*, III, p. 481). That he felt it *needed* justification is a further sign of his care with metaphor.

66. *PW*, III, p. 481.

CHAPTER 6

The collaborative imagination: place, time and textuality in some later poems

Collaboration? Wordsworth figures in the general imagination as an egoist who dominates the contexts we put him in, domestic, aesthetic or political. Though the first edition of *Lyrical Ballads* was a genuine case of collaboration with Coleridge, collaboration is remote from our usual image of Wordsworth, and we remember that Mary's and Dorothy's verses were variously annexed as his own. But the image distorts Wordsworth's poems, as I read them, and ignores his critical thinking about tradition and ambition, and about propriety and property.

If propriety means writing to some extent like every one else, making poems that, whatever they have of vigour or invention, don't break certain conventions of taste, then perhaps 'originality' – to an age that prized this quality – is a sense of difference that overlaps with the idea of intellectual property in the written or published text. I wrote above that Wordsworth's response to Scott and Byron had a lot to do with fame, and even money. His letters, especially the later letters about the copyright laws, leave us in no doubt about his interest in the matter.[1] It can seem trivialising or even invidious to think that great writers were concerned with the sale of their books, but Wordsworth was very clearly concerned about it, and the nature of his concern is interesting: he came to think the sale of his books was no less than an index of the moral health of the nation. Why should this concern the reader? It does so because in a broader cultural context it tells us something about his writing.

Designs and intentions

'Shall I ever have a name?' The question appearing in a note among the earliest drafts of *The Prelude* seems to invite an existential conception of fame, which is equated with identity; to succeed in poetry is to achieve an identity. In a way common in Romantic poetry the distinction between life and work is collapsed, and the particularly

Wordsworthian nature of *his* question is that it points to the process of exploration as well as the goal, the coherent self, the unified ego. For Wordsworth coherence of the life and the work becomes a coherence of process, a continual construction. Recent studies in deconstruction have appropriately sought to uncover the means by which *continuity* replaces a static notion of wholeness in Wordsworth's work.[2] One thing that emerges from these studies is that continuity can be achieved only at the cost of perpetual revision, so that the significance of a Wordsworth poem is not only its 'own' isolated meanings but also its revisionary force. In this sense Wordsworth is always collaborating with a former self, and the archetypal text is the autobiography, *The Prelude*. Such studies, that is, are a way of examining Wordsworth's perpetual presence on the page.

In previous chapters I have been arguing that Wordsworth's poetry is a poetry of relationship that establishes and explores images of community in a general sense, moving away from the insistent feeling that the only relationship worth talking about is the one with himself. The way he categorised his poems and constructed an *oeuvre* is, on the one hand, an extreme example of his authoritarianism towards his readers, and, on the other, a recognition that there are other relationships to be established than that with the former self. We write of the 'design' of a particular volume or of a 'complete works'; in doing so we must recognise the double meaning of the word: construction and intention – Keats's 'palpable design'. Again, an authoritarian position. But for Wordsworth design means recognising that there is new ground to be fought over, that a relationship with readers is *not* taken for granted but an integral part of artistic endeavour, part of the question, 'shall I ever have a name?' It is a central part of his writing. Evidence for this lies in its indeterminacies: not just the syntactical ones I have discussed above, but the multiplicity of allusions we find in his poems, which become problematic as soon as the question of readership is addressed. I want to explore a few cases, but first it is useful to ask whether the ways he described his whole output has a bearing on authority and relationship.

Wordsworth meditated an arrangement of his poems on the basis of mental faculties as early as 1809, but it was not until 1815 that it became public in the first collected edition. We find 'Poems of the Imagination', 'Poems of the Fancy', 'Poems of Sentiment and Reflection' among others. He stuck to these terms, although many poems were subsequently transferred from one section to another and

many of the later poems – the tour poems, for example – did not fit
into to any of these psychologised categories. The whole project shows
an unusual confidence about the *effect* of each of his poems and is a
clear challenge to traditional generic divisions: the organising principles
are 'powers of mind' rather than 'various moulds and diverse forms'
(1815 Preface). And they provide a further example of his habitual
supposition that reading and writing are psychologically very similar
activities. But it is easy to make too much of this – as Arnold surely
did – because less than a third of the poems are categorised by a
faculty or an age group in the 1849–50 edition. (I am leaving out both
The Prelude and *The Excursion*. The proportion would be diminished
even further if they were included.) Properly the categories belong to
the 1815 edition, but even here only half the poems are so categorised
(124 out of 247, by my count). Most of the rest are sonnets,
categorised by form rather than power of mind.

   There are clear ideological reasons for deconstructing the
categories.[3] As signs of Wordsworth's intentions they can be thought
of as trespassing even further than authors usually do – even
Romantic poets – on the reader's freedom: they represent an extra-
textual site of authorial intervention (power), a *radical* denial of the
conventionality of language and publishing, as well of the mutability
of poetic texts. Granted that they challenge the notion of textual
integrity (as his textual revisions do also) and therefore suggest an
openness of discourse between reader and writer which is at odds with
the grounds of neo-formalist, iconic, criticism, they put in its place a
notion of authorial integrity. It is no accident, I imagine, that the
group 'Poems Referring to the Period of Childhood' was placed next
to 'Juvenile Pieces' in 1815, and 'Poems Referring to the Period of
Old Age' next to 'Epitaphs and Elegiac Poems'; each juxtaposition
suggesting that Wordsworth's own (public) life was representative.[4]
The suggestion is that when you buy this book, you buy more than a
collection of poems: you buy an *author*. 'As he is, so he writes.' The
1815 edition is quite astonishing because the contents pages don't
give the page numbers of the poems in the usual place. The right-
hand edge shows two columns of figures, the dates of composition and
dates of publication. Neither column is accurate. All of this is an
extension of the poet's claims on his readers, an unparalleled
intrusion, and *therefore* it has to be understood rather than ignored.
Each act designed to bridge the gap between reader and writer is
answerable. The question it must answer is, above all, why?

Wordsworth's thinking about reader–writer relations was in crisis in 1815, and the arrangement of the poems seems to me a symptom of it. Wordsworth had always fretted about the order of his poems, page design, book design and pricing, the habits and tastes of his readers and the attacks of reviewers.[5] But what is new is the sense that his work is his monument, the book, in all its minute organisation, is an image of the constructed self. 'Self-building',[6] self-creation, has long been seen as a central Romantic project. Kenneth R. Johnston's recent version of this argument shows that 'The Recluse' project is of crucial importance, not just because of its size, but because the very concept was an organising principle for shorter poems.[7] It was to be symbolic as well as actual, *standing for*, not just adding to, his other work. Wordsworth named the poem after the figure he intended to make of himself, standing apart from life and organising his experiences of it. However grateful we may be that he never achieved such a degree of detachment, the importance of the idea is obvious. And it raises interesting questions. If he had finished 'The Recluse', would there have been other worlds to conquer? Johnston speculates plausibly that Wordsworth gave up the idea after the failure of *The Excursion* in 1814 – certainly his relations with the reviewers and the public reached a crisis in that and the following years – and that the 1815 *Collected Poems* became a substitute for it, an alternative organising principle.

To return to 'The Recluse' project: Wordsworth's metaphor of coherence in the preface to *The Excursion* has its own tensions and ambiguities. *The Prelude* would be found, he wrote, to be an 'ante-chapel' to 'the body of a gothic church' (i.e. 'The Recluse') and the 'minor Pieces, . . . when they shall be properly arranged' would be 'the little cells, oratories, and sepulchral recesses, ordinarily included in those edifices'. The architectural image might suggest a visually formal structure, but it is more fluid and adaptable than that. 'Gothic' (without the 'k'), as applied to architecture in 1814, meant, as Coleridge put it, an art where unity is *felt*, not seen.[8] Coleridge also described it in images that suggest naturalness ('all its many Chapels, its pillared stem and leaf-work roof, as if some sacred grove of Hertha, the mysterious deity of their pagan Ancestors, had been awed into stone at the approach of the true divinity');[9] profusion; variety; and its effect on the spectator: 'the Gothic architecture impresses the beholder with a sense of self-annihilation; he becomes, as it were, a part of the work contemplated. An endless complexity and variety are united into one whole, the plan of which is not distinct from the execution.'[10]

Clearly this thinking reflects the pervasive distinction between the beautiful and the sublime, particularly the emphasis on indistinctness and self-annihilation. As applied to the relation between a reader and a book, however, it has the radical implication that the reader both finds himself in and is silenced by the text. To put it another way, Wordsworth's metaphor of the gothic church typically insists on the reader's cooperation and asserts his freedom. Typically, again, what looks like a *visual* metaphor of wholeness points in fact to wholeness *beyond* the visual; and the elaborations of the central metaphor bear this out. Why 'cells and oratories'? Why not chapels? Cells are for solitary existence; 'oratories' means something smaller than a chapel, a place for the 'conversation of prayer' in Dylan Thomas's phrase: it is an image that also emphasises solitary prayer and, crucially, voice and speech rather than visual perception. The emphasis on non-visual qualities in this series of metaphors is quite in keeping with the 1809–15 arrangement of the poems according to different mental faculties and phases of life. Both projects are part of a lifelong critique of visual definition of thinking.[11]

The dispersal of the self

It is a truism of modern theory that the self-conscious poet can never write himself out of his poetry. The wish to do so is itself paradoxical because it depends on the writer's recognising his own unavoidable presence. In fact much Romantic and post-Romantic writing is suffused with a longing for two opposing impossibilities: one, to make the author *present* on the page, and the other, to make the text anonymous and the author absent, not a source of authority. In Schiller's terms the *sentimental* poet envies the *naiv*, but if the *naiv* poet is known and a contemporary (Goethe was Schiller's great example) he embodies a paradox. Both longings are utopian, but the latter has recently been more fashionable than the former. Roland Barthes, a modern Romantic in this respect, fantasised over the death of the author and the rebirth of the reader (a transfer of authority, a rewriting of the accepted balance of power between reader and writer) and wished to 'desituate' writing, to mix different kinds of writing freely so that the text appears to be 'without a site of origin'.[12] His idea is both an optimistic avant-garde manifesto and a nostalgic dream of a pure void, as radical as any Romantic dream. This is so not only because all desituating strategies can themselves be situated,[13] but because for Barthes 'desituate' also means 'dis-alienate': *any* identification of voice with place is also an alienation from other places, other voices. 'Writing' is multi-vocal, or rather avocal, pure space. In this respect Barthes is so diametrically opposed to Wordsworth that they seem to speak the same language, though what is conscious metaphor in one is implicit ideology in the other. Barthes's term 'situate', which has become a cliché of recent criticism, uses the metaphor of physical place to suggest points on an imaginary graph, the coordinates of which are social identifiers: education, age, colour, gender, etc. But for Wordsworth place – physical, geographical location – could seem an origin of power and a site in which the author disappears, being at one with nature. So situation is not alienation but freedom.

The opposition between the two writers is illuminating because it is complete. It reminds us that Wordsworth's fiction of 'pure' place (and therefore pure voice) is as utopian as Barthes's void, where voice is erased, and it suggests ways of reading Wordsworth that are *precisely* perverse. Barthes's theory of desituated writing, like Bakhtin's dialogic mode, is a way of undermining the idea of writing as the expression of the individual imagination or genius, and both are implicitly about the relation of writer to writer and text to text. In this respect they complement Harold Bloom's *psychologised* fantasy of writers' relations with their predecessors, an explicit theory of 'influence'. For all three of them, though in different ways, the topic of a writer's relations with other writers is central, in fact formative, and they prevent us as readers from being satisfied with the idea that influence is measured chiefly by verbal echoes. ('Source' hunting has its value, but its significance is not always self-evident: the word 'source', meaning an earlier occurrence of the same phrase, is itself very tendentious. Wordsworth undoubtedly used lines and phrases by other writers, sometimes acknowledging the fact, sometimes not.[14]) I suggest we take a broader view and think of an *ideology of the book* in his work, which runs parallel to post-structuralist thinking about language and freedom. Wordsworth's arrangements and rearrangements can be seen as experiments with different sites of origin.[15]

From this point of view we can reconsider Keats's famous phrase 'the Wordsworthian or egotistical sublime' and the opposing notion of the 'chameleon poet'. Both writers strongly thematise ambition as something proper to the poet, though in quite different ways. The truth of Keats's remark seems to be that he and Wordsworth are *definitive* opposites, definitive in the sense that they share the same tensions between self-assertion and self-annihilation, though they expressed it differently and are generally seen to have come down on opposite sides. One thing is clear from Marjorie Levinson's *Keats's Life of Allegory* (amidst much that seems to me unclear), that both self-assertion and self-annihilation are acts in which writing runs a special risk of offending against rules of good taste: Keats's susceptibilities ('sucking at the sugar-stick of his mind', in Yeats's words, or 'frigging his imagination' in Byron's) can be as embarrassing a kind of self-absorption as Wordsworth's sometimes repellent certainties. Christopher Ricks is right in seeing embarrassment as part of Keats's art;[16] correspondingly a tetchy assertiveness is part of Wordsworth's. Both are parts of constructed identities, means of exploring poetic ambition.

Language and the local

I am suggesting a number of ways in which the Romantic ego can be dispersed – and perhaps *ought* to be dispersed – if we read Wordsworth openly. Tradition and ambition are interdependent. I return now to the question of language-choice in a different context, because there is, I believe, a decentralising impulse in his writing about language that is deeply related to these issues.

Now Wordsworth's overtly political thinking – about Reform, Catholic Emancipation, for example – shows a strong sense of the national and a fear of faction and disintegration; and for that reason it is often argued that his attachment to rural customs and economic structures *as a model* for a stable and conscientious civil society is backward-looking. But there is a counter-emphasis on the local in his writings, which in the context of the 1820s and 1830s could be said to work in the other direction. Evidence for this is suggested by the way the word 'provincial' and its derivatives were used at the time. Briefly, around the turn of the century 'provincialism' retained its earlier meaning, 'the manner of speech characteristic of a particular province; a local word, phrase, or peculiarity of pronunciation which is not part of the standard language of a country' (OED). Its primary application is to linguistic forms, and although there is implicit in the second part of the definition a contrast between 'standard' and non-standard, it is not explicitly politicised. The word meant broadly what we now mean by 'dialect'. By 1820, however, the word had a far greater and more obviously political range, including 'attachment to one's own province, its institutions, etc., *before those of the nation or state of which it is a part*; provincial patriotism; desire for the autonomy of the province or provinces rather than national unity' (*OED*). The *Annual Register* for 1820 noted 'the prevalence of a spirit of provincialism – and the factions into which the capital was split'.[17] Moreover usage began to emphasise the pejorative connotations the word still carries. 'Provincialism' impinges definitively on discussions of Wordsworth's poetry in Coleridge's *Biographia Literaria* (1817), where he paraphrases the Preface to *Lyrical Ballads*: he replaces Wordsworth's two formulations ('purified indeed from . . . all lasting and rational cause of dislike or disgust'; '. . . from the vulgarity and meanness of ordinary life') with the simpler phrase, 'freed from provincialisms'. In the light of contemporary usage, we must ask how accurate Coleridge's paraphrase really is. For there is a strong leaning towards linguistic centralising in *Biographia*, which suggests that in this text 'provincialism' has its political as well as its 'purely' linguistic meaning: a far more politically contextualised term than Wordsworth's own formulations, which have reference merely to a generalised standard of reason and taste.

It is true that both reason and taste – especially the latter – have *their* political contextualisations as well, and I suggested above (in Chapter 2) that some discussions of taste (Jeffrey's, for example) blur distinctions between education and class on the one hand and geography on the other: 'metropolitan' is a word that can be used both in praise of taste and in deprecation. In fact some uses of 'provincialism' make precisely the same elision: I think *Biographia* does, because the paraphrase of Wordsworth is in the context of an argument that rural language is partly the *residue* of learned language: it is enriched by words that used to be 'the exclusive property of the universities and schools'.[18] The implication is that linguistic innovation belongs to centres of learning. That view is not surprising because Coleridge thought the 'best part' of the language is that by which it reflects on its own powers of distinction and connection. Wordsworth's notions about language, on the other hand, challenge the assumption that abstractions are the best part of language.[19] Set against *Biographia*, the Preface can be seen as a decentralising text; its illogicality and utopianism are functional because they refuse to identify standards of taste with linguistic sophistication at a time when taste, learning and centralism were assumed to march together. What has this to do with Wordsworth as collaborator? Broadly, I am suggesting that there is a difference between the local and the central in Wordsworth's later writings that brings into question matters of taste and also the assumptions a writer might make when (for example) alluding to other writers. Twentieth-century readers of Jane Austen's *Mansfield Park* may recognise allusions to Cowper and Scott (or recognise their names in footnotes) but not to William Whitehead, whose name is now unknown even though he was Poet Laureate. Like other writers Wordsworth makes his own public construction of literary tradition (Chaucer, Spenser, Shakespeare, Milton, Wordsworth), but clearly this does not correspond in any simple way to the 'influences' on his poems, nor to the more obvious allusions in them. A list of the latter includes Daniel, Young, Akenside, Langhorne, Beattie and a host of other more or less contemporary writers. What does the discrepancy mean? Possibly very little in itself, but perhaps it points to implied assumptions about readers that have a bearing on the question of cultural centrality and marginality. The politics of allusion is doubtless complex. The particular point I am making here is that allusions make assumptions about readership, including assumptions about how a readership distinguished between major and minor and (a different matter?) between familiar and unfamiliar. As an academic I might make silent allusion to Milton and assume most of my readers would realise it, but I would not do the same with Akenside or Beattie. It is likely that Wordsworth's first readers would have recognised allusions to all of them without footnotes. Or is it? It is a matter for speculation, and an important matter if we want to know what Wordsworth's engagement with his readers amounted to in practical terms. Source studies – literary history of a traditional kind – have much to contribute to this question, but individual allusions remain problematic. Wordsworth's most famous footnote is teasing. The phrase in 'Tintern Abbey', 'both what they half-create, / And what perceive' has a footnote reading: 'This line has a close resemblance to an admirable line of Young, the exact expression of which I cannot recollect.' It could have any of the following implications:

(a)   I do not, at the moment of writing, have the resources to check the allusion because I am writing extempore. (This glosses over the period of time – about four months – between writing and publication.)

(b) Readers will know the line I have forgotten. (An index of Young's continuing popularity.)

(c) I don't suppose you recollect Young any more accurately than I do. (The footnote is an index of Young's demise.)

(d) Young is not as important to you or me as, say, Milton. You would expect me to quote Milton accurately and would not need a footnote, but we can afford to be impressionistic with Young.

Of (b) and (c), the latter is less likely, since *Night Thoughts* was still in print in the 1790s (the Edwards edition with Blake's illustrations appeared in 1797, but it was an expensive volume, not in itself evidence of a wide readership). The other two possible implications are more interesting. The first is easily recognised by New Historicist readers as a typical Romantic strategy aimed at conveying immediacy and presence, a denial of the material and social circumstances of literary production. The last is more doubtful. I think it could be supported by comparison with quotations (unnoted) from Milton's 'Lycidas' in 'Simon Lee' and from *Paradise Lost* in the 'prospectus' to *The Excursion*. On the other hand there are unnoted quotations from Spenser in the 'Dedication' to *The White Doe of Rylstone* and from Samuel Daniel in a late 'inscription' written for Wordsworth's patron Sir George Beaumont.[20] What inferences can we draw? Daniel was better known then than now (though Coleridge thought him 'most unjustly neglected' in 1817),[21] but better known to whom? Again, statistics about literacy and the circulation of different kinds of publication are helpful, but particular texts seem to imply particular familiarities. There is a hierarchy of known and unknown, which is easily thought of as a hierarchy of central and marginal. The reader of Wordsworth's poems could construct an *apparent* hierarchy, but whether this is an accurate reflection of public taste at the time would still be an open question.

If all these things were less indeterminate, a sociology of 'Wordsworth-reading' might be achievable. My arguments in this chapter will involve speculations about readership which are not always provable, but I shall be looking at texts which seem to me to engage with a sense of marginality and centrality that can partly be linked with 'tradition' – a word which is shorthand for a *chosen* difference between major and minor – and partly with geography:

'metropolitan' taste is both central and vicious; regional taste is both true and marginal.

The Yarrow poems

Among the poems that most clearly thematise these issues are those in which Wordsworth confronts the myth of a Border culture, not only, as I've suggested above, in direct relation to the ballads, but as a response to the modern poet most closely associated with the promotion of the subject, Walter Scott. For the sake of providing the discussion with a geographical coherence I shall focus on Wordsworth's poems about the river Yarrow. They deal with a scene already textualised and re-textualised before either Scott or Wordsworth wrote about them, and the interplay of different texts is a chief source of interest.[22]

The cult of the Yarrow grew quite remarkably during the ballad revival of the eighteenth century. Earlier it had had apparently little cultural significance: Drayton does not mention either it or the Ettrick (a tributary now famous because of James Hogg, the 'Ettrick Shepherd') in his politicised survey of British topography, Poly-Olbion (1612–22), though he makes much of the Tees, the Tweed, the Tyne, the Lyne, the Blyth and Wansbeck.[23] The reason is clearly that they were of no historical significance in the general context of this part of Drayton's work, war between the two kingdoms of England and Scotland. Yet two centuries later the Yarrow had its own literary tradition, which repays examination.

Wordsworth's poems reflect the difference in political significance between the Tweed and its tributary the Yarrow: 'Yarrow Unvisited' and 'Yarrow Visited' are both built on a power relationship in which a male speaker prefers the Tweed to its tributary the Yarrow and obliges his female companion to acquiesce in his choice. The hierarchy in the very word 'tributary' is suggestive. And a stretch of the Tweed forms part of the border between England and Scotland, a fact that may be relevant when we consider poems in which Wordsworth confronts cultural otherness.

'Yarrow Unvisited' and 'Yarrow Visited' are not merely loco-descriptive poems; they are explorations of the difference between textualised and untextualised space. I am aware of no poet in the English language who was so assiduous in examining the relations between language and geography. I use the word 'geography', not the more generalised term 'place': it is well known since Hartman's studies that the interaction of word and place in inscriptions is characteristic of Wordsworth's Romanticism, but what Hartman (and other more recent critics) do not take into account is locality – in the sense that different regions of the kingdom had different literary traditions as well, of course, as different political orientations. Although it is clear that in the most general sense 'nature' is never seen in and for itself, that broadly speaking 'nature' is always already textualised, there are reasons to be dissatisfied with the mere generalisation: for if it is always true, it has no power to distinguish particular strategies and historical circumstances, nor to deal discriminatingly with different kinds and levels of consciousness of textuality in different poems. One distinction that seems to me inescapable is between the dynamics of literary allusion and the aesthetics of landscape. Another, more tenuous but more challenging, is between centrality and locality. The whole 'Border' culture of the ballads, as I've argued above, is a case where a dominant central culture met its opposite and made it tractable. Wordsworth's Yarrow poems reflect this acculturation, but we can study in them ways in which it happened. They thematise borrowings and sharings in a way that involves human relations, the aesthetics of landscape, the opportunities as well as the anxieties of influence, and the question the centrality or locality of tradition.

'Yarrow Unvisited' suggests at first that *not* visiting a place leaves thought free, vision unconstrained –

> We have a vision of our own;
> Ah! why should we undo it?

But the sense in which the vision is 'our own' (that of the speaker and his travelling companion) needs questioning because it turns out to be very literary. All Wordsworth's Yarrow poems are highly allusive, not only to each other (even the first, 'Yarrow Unvisited', points prospectively to a companion-piece)[24] but also to a series of earlier poems that might themselves be said to constitute a tradition: numerous version of the ballads 'The Braes of Yarrow', 'Rare Willy Drowned in Yarrow' and 'Clyde's Waters'; poems by Nicol Burne, William Hamilton, John Logan and probably others. But if we were to construct a 'tradition' of Yarrow poems, it would quite clearly be a heterogeneous tradition which would raise the questions of how we distinguish between 'major' and 'minor' poems and between central and local popularity. National traditions function differently from local ones, being more obviously selective, evaluative and expressive of centralised power. Many of the poems that lie behind Wordsworth's are popular in the sense that they were frequently reprinted by provincial publishers in cheap pamphlets as well as in the famous ballad anthologies (Hamilton's 'The Braes of Yarrow' was reprinted in Percy's *Reliques*). Versions of the anonymous ballad 'The Braes of Yarrow' appeared in Herd's *Ancient and Modern Scottish Songs* (1776), Scott's *Minstrelsy* (1803) and Cromek's *Select Scotish Songs* (1810), but also in more ephemeral printings. The Herd version, for example, became popular as 'Convey a Kiss', reprinted in a pamphlet entitled *John Highlandman's Remarks on the City of Glasgow* (Glasgow, J & M Robertson, 1807).[25] A year later the same publisher issued *The Recruit's Farewell to his Wife and Three Children*, which contains another version of the ballad.

These are all narratives of love and murder. The basic story of the ballads is typical enough: in a 'dowie' (dismal) place a young man is ambushed by the nine (or sometimes three) brothers of his sweetheart; all are killed and the girl dies of grief. The cause of the conflict is usually not explicit, though some versions have the young man eloping with the girl against her family's wishes, a common feudal motif.

But there is another kind of Yarrow poem, descriptive, celebratory or elegiac, which seems to have achieved equal popularity, in some cases without explicit reference to the narrative of the ballads. The earliest example I know is Nicol Burne's 'Leader Haughs and Yarrow', published in various editions of Allan Ramsay's *Tea-Table Miscellany* from 1729 onwards.[26] Robert Crawford, Ramsay's assistant, contributed a song, 'The Rose of Yarrow', which may have provided a source for Scott's phrase 'the Flower of Yarrow' in *Marmion* (1808); and in the same collection appears another song, 'Mary Scott, the Flower of Yarrow'.[27] Scott himself refers to the Yarrow in elegiac mood in *The Lay of the Last Minstrel* (1805), where the river is particularly associated with poetic inspiration:

And Yarrow, as he roll'd along
Bore burden to the Minstrel's song.[28]

In this respect Scott follows Robert Fergusson's satire 'Hame Content', which, like Wordsworth's 'Yarrow Revisited' (addressed to Scott),

compares the 'dowie pools' of Arno and Tiber unfavourably with
familiar rivers, in this case the Leader and the Yarrow:

> On Leader haughs an' Yarrow braes
> ARCADIAN herds wad tyne their lays,
> To hear the mair melodious sounds,
> That live on our POETIC grounds.
> Our Scottish lads . . .
> Sae pleas'd, they'll never fash again
> To court you [the muse] on Italian plain[.][29]

Behind Wordsworth's poems, then, there are two kinds of tradition,
one lyrical and the other narrative. The two had been brought
together earlier in John Logan's 'The Braes of Yarrow', an elegy
written as if spoken by the bereaved maiden, with explicit reference
to the ballad story.[30] Wordsworth's line in 'Yarrow Visited', 'The
Water-wraith ascended thrice' refers to Logan's poem (the incident
occurs in no other version); and Coleridge reprinted the poem in *The
Watchman*, remarking that it was 'Simple, deeply pathetic, and even
sublime . . . the most exquisite performance in our language'.[31]

Wordsworth's poems allude to all of these and possibly more, and
the allusions work in different ways. The central lines of 'Yarrow
Unvisited' ('We have a vision of our own; / Ah! why should we undo
it?') seem merely to propose a contrast between individual vision on
the one hand and actuality on the other, whether historical or
geographical. But the explicit reference to William Hamilton's 'The
Braes of Yarrow' at the beginning ('the exquisite ballad of Hamilton,
beginning "Busk ye, busk ye my bonny, bonny Bride, / Busk ye, busk
ye, my winsome Marrow!" ')[32] suggests otherwise. The 'vision of our
own' is already textualised in terms of the tragic events narrated in
the traditional ballads and in Hamilton's reworking of them, and the
poem reflects them in a bizarre way. Hamilton's poem is a dialogue
between the murderer and the bereaved girl. The opening lines, to
which Wordsworth refers, are spoken by the murderer, who also seeks
to entice the girl away from the Yarrow, the scene of the murder,
towards his own lands on the Tweed. The girl answers with proper
force:

> How can I busk a bonny bonny bride?
>   How can I busk a winsome marrow?
> How luve him upon the banks of Tweed,
>   That slew my luve on the Braes of Yarrow?[33]

So when Wordsworth's speaker tells *his* 'winsome Marrow'

> . . . we will downwards with the Tweed,
> Nor turn aside to Yarrow[,]

there is a distinct echo of the murderer's words, as though his denying his companion's wish were like murdering her lover and then attempting to seduce her. And unlike the heroine of the ballad, Wordsworth's 'True-love' is given no words of reply; she merely 'sigh[s] for sorrow'.

But the other allusions in the poem are to descriptive poems and elegies and therefore seem to work against the tragic intent of Hamilton's. Wordsworth follows Nicol Burne, whose poem has nothing to do with ambush, murder and seduction, in referring in the last line to the 'bonny Holms of Yarrow', whereas Hamilton and all versions of the traditional ballad refer to the '*dowie* holms of Yarrow'. This and other echoes of Burne ('Leader Haughs' [l. 17]; 'The Lintwhites' [l. 20]; 'The sweets of Burn-Mill meadow' [l. 42]) suggest Wordsworth's poem evokes but then erases the tragic associations of the narratives and restores to the place its aesthetic and domestic meanings.

Read biographically, the poem could be set beside 'Tintern Abbey' as a text that erases the resolution and independence of Wordsworth's 'winsome marrow', his sister Dorothy.[34] Read another way, it problematises two kinds of sharing: first, the sharing of vision between individuals (a question often put in an erotic context, as in Coleridge's 'Letter to Sara Hutchinson' and 'The Daydream', as well as, later, in Yeats's 'Towards Break of Day'); and, secondly, the relationship between literature and the personal experience of nature. Wordsworth runs together personal and literary relations in a way that might seem indiscriminate, but can also be seen, more interestingly, as part of his programmatic blurring of the distinction between the literary and the actual. Not visiting the Yarrow, he re-enacts its story in comic terms.

Playful invocation of tragedy may seem both trivialising and un-Wordsworthian. I've suggested above that in many ways Wordsworth embraced the trivial programmatically in order to rescue it from artistic oblivion, indeed to question the category, which has often been a disguise for what a particular writer, school or age prefers not to bother with. But comic *allusion* perhaps presents a different problem because it makes assumptions about the relations of one age to another, or more precisely, about the orientation of a particular readership to earlier literature. If we cannot imagine Wordsworth joking about, say, Milton, why not? The situation can hardly be dealt with on the Bloomian hypothesis of suppressed father figures.[35] The 1832 revision of 'Simon Lee', in which Wordsworth restructured the poem around a comic allusion to 'Lycidas' ('But Oh the heavy change . . .') is often thought of as a particularly inept case of his making earlier texts more 'literary' in revision. The truth, as I see it, is that Wordsworth's thinking about genre and generic expectations became more subtle, not less, and that this *might* involve a sense of their social and possibly political implications. In the middle of an anti-pastoral poem he inserts a joking reference to *the* pastoral elegy which had notoriously combined topical satire, classical fiction and Christian consolation: a recipe for critical disaster. Johnson's feeling that the poem's fictions made it uneven, untrue to grief, can be paralleled in comments about Wordsworth's poems. This does not mean that Wordsworth and Milton were using the same strategies, but that at any time there are expectations – which it is easiest for us to describe as generic – that become invisible to later generations. Revising 'Simon Lee' in 1832, Wordsworth may have felt surer than he could have felt at any earlier period that those who read the 'classics' also read his poems. Wordsworth was himself becoming a classic writer. Allusion depends on familiarity, but because this is so it can be used as a defamiliarising device in particular contexts: a change of 'voice', a disturbing piece of indecorum. It is especially potent in the Yarrow poems, not just because they are crammed with allusions but because they project familiar relations between speaker and addressee, which are *made up*, in part, of textual familiarities. Allusiveness is thematised, and familiarity allows the tragic to be converted into the comic.

Returning to 'Yarrow Unvisited', the comedy of familiarity must be important because otherwise the reference to Hamilton could be bleakly ironic. When Wordsworth writes

> Let Yarrow Folk, *frae* Selkirk Town,
> Who have been buying, selling,
> Go back to Yarrow, 'tis their own,
> Each Maiden to her Dwelling!

we should remember that the *point* of the ballads is that the maiden has no home, because she is at odds with her father for setting her brothers to murder her lover. In Hamilton's poem the question of her 'dwelling' is a potent ambiguity. A Gothic element is introduced when the primary speaker (the murderer) apparently persuades the maiden to accept him as her bridegroom, but she turns and invites the bleeding spectre of her lover to 'lye all night between my breists'.

The last lines –

> Return return, O mournful, mournful bride,
> Return, and dry thy useless sorrow:
> Thy luver heeds none of thy sighs,
> He lies a corpse in the Braes of Yarrow –

leave it unclear whether her erotic fantasy leads her to drown. Wordsworth's poem is as much an 'experiment on public taste' as almost any in the *Lyrical Ballads*. It questions the word 'public' as much as the word 'taste' by not excluding violence from a companionable fiction of sharing literary knowledge and by asking whether those readers who recognise the Border culture it refers to are prepared to have it, as it were, in the drawing room. It is a poem easily dehistoricised since it seems to value imagination unimpeded by fact – Arnold included it in his influential selection of Wordsworth's poems in 1879, but omitted the initial reference to Hamilton's Gothic excesses – and since it ends with a withdrawal into the world of possibility:

> Should life be dull, and spirits low,
> 'Twill soothe us in our sorrow
> That earth has something yet to show,
> The bonny Holms of Yarrow!

This stanza is interestingly reminiscent of the vision of another river in the sonnet 'Composed upon Westminster Bridge':

> Earth has not anything to shew more fair:
> Dull would he be of soul who could pass by
> A sight so touching in its majesty[.]

The Thames is an aestheticised image of power ('The river glideth at his own sweet will') unencumbered with the traffic of the working day. Similarly the holms of Yarrow are 'bonny', not 'dowie' (as in the ballads): bonny in *prospect*, unseen. But this final gesture does not erase the heterogeneous traditions the poem evokes, which give it a power to disturb.

In a broader perspective, the poem is part of Wordsworth's first collection of travel poems, published in the 1807 edition, *Poems in Two Volumes*, among other 'Poems Written During a Tour of Scotland'. Others in the collection, 'Glen Almain', for example, are sceptical, querulous indeed, about the relationship of landscape and literary tradition.[36] 'Yarrow Unvisited', with its problematics of textualisation, is an introduction to the later volumes of travel volumes that were to become the staple of Wordsworth's new poetic publishing after *The River Duddon* appeared (1820), and I shall be arguing that its companion pieces, 'Yarrow Visited' and 'Yarrow Revisited' develop these problematics in different circumstances.

Like 'Glen Almain', 'Yarrow Visited' (1814) expresses disappointment that landscape is not 'visibly' textualised and in fact begins with the wish that 'some Minstrel's harp' (like Scott's, presumably) could be found to suppress actuality. Yet this poem has its literary antecedents, and like the earlier one, it includes a partial re-enactment of the ballad situation – this time at a greater emotional and, as it happens, geographical distance. The poem narrates a tour from St Mary's Lake, near the headwaters of the Yarrow, to the point where it joins the Tweed near Newark Castle ('Renowned in Border story'), the scene of *The Lay of the Last Minstrel*. At this point the speaker imagines decorating his 'True-love's forehead' with heather, in a gesture reminiscent of the maiden's prophetic dream in the ballad:

> Yestreen I dreamd a doleful dream;
> I kend there wad be sorrow;
> I dreamed I pu'd the heather green,
> On the dowy banks o Yarrow.[37]

Like the comic rewriting of seduction in 'Yarrow Unvisited', this gesture displaces the ballad event – literally displaces it by moving it downstream from the indeterminate point further upstream where the ballad is apparently set. (One version [Child 214 L] locates the scene at Dryhope, where the Yarrow emerges from St Mary's Loch.) Wordsworth's poem makes a point of asking where precisely it happened:

Where was it that the famous Flower
Of Yarrow vale lay bleeding?
His bed perchance was yon smooth mound
On which the herd is feeding:
And haply from this crystal pool,
Now peaceful as the morning,
The Water-wraith ascended thrice –
And gave his doleful warning.

The stanza compounds geographical indeterminacy with emotional loss of focus on the event, or rather, with the 'distance' proper to elegy. And in fact the poem Wordsworth invokes in the reference to the 'Water-wraith' (which I cannot find in any version of the ballads or its narrative offspring[38]) is Logan's 'The Braes of Yarrow', a lament spoken by the bereaved girl who is entirely given to sorrow and who never lets us know there has been a killing, only that her lover is dead:

Scarce was he gone, I saw his ghost;
It vanish'd with a shriek of sorrow;
Thrice did the water-wraith ascend,
And gave a doleful groan through Yarrow.[39]

Both Logan and Wordsworth invoke the ballads in the phrase 'the flower of Yarrow' (though, confusingly, one version of the ballad applies the phrase to both lovers),[40] but each in a different way distances his poem from them.

In Wordsworth's poem there is the sense of personal 'distance' supplied by consciousness of passing time – the poem is less concerned with the present than with the past and the future – but my point here is that he characteristically uses the spatial (geographical) distances of the tour poem to establish relations of familiarity with and alienation from previous textualisations of landscape. 'Yarrow Visited' curiously both appropriates and disowns the scene:

I see – but not by sight alone,
Loved Yarrow, have I won thee
A ray of Fancy still survives –
Her sunshine plays upon thee!

Wordsworth has in fact 'won' the place by separating himself from its traditional narrative but re-enacting the story in a disguised way.

Similarly the 'ray of Fancy' is double-edged, appearing to suggest the speaker's *own* fancy but at the same time acknowledging the fancy of earlier textualisations. Perhaps it would be portentous to describe the poem as a specimen of cultural colonialism, but it is about *winning* a landscape on a progress through it, and this runs parallel with a barely suppressed narrative of loss and gain in a human relationship. Geographical distance becomes a metaphor for literary engagement.

Between 1814, when 'Yarrow Visited' was published, and the writing of 'Yarrow Revisited' in 1831 much had changed in the cultural relations of England and Scotland. Essentially the royal family readopted Scotland when George IV visited it in 1822, an occasion on which Scott played an important role. The visit coincided with the building of a war memorial, imitating the Parthenon, to the Scottish dead at Waterloo, near a monument to Nelson completed in 1815. Wordsworth marked the event with a satirical sonnet, 'The Modern Athens', criticising it not simply as an example of pretention (Edinburgh had long encouraged comparison with Athens) but also as a mark of discontinuity, of historical revisionism.[41] *Yarrow Revisited and Other Poems* (1835) was Wordsworth's most successful volume in financial terms,[42] and that fact probably owes something to the general move towards accommodating or colonising Scottish culture. The book certainly reflects issues arising from these circumstances.

There is another historical factor: these poems were written during the agitations that accompanied the Reform Bill, which Wordsworth alludes to as a 'rash change, ominous for the public weal' in the final poem of the collection, 'Apology'. Potential political discontinuity is now imagined in England, and not chiefly on the border. The altered political circumstances have a curious effect on the volume: whereas in 1807, when Wordsworth wrote the first version of *The White Doe of Rylstone*, he could assert a national and Protestant tradition to which Scott was in part an outsider, Scott now becomes almost a symbol of fading power and fading political unity. The revaluation of Scott in this volume goes far beyond what we would expect from natural grief at the impending death of a fellow poet. The images in 'Apology' are worth examining because they so powerfully evoke the idea of an imaginative centre that is on the point of becoming invisible. We can explain that as a sign of Wordsworth's growing political conservatism, and yet even here the idea of a mutual relationship survives if only to be mourned.

The central image of the poem derives from reliefs on the walls of the temple at Persepolis, which show a procession of rulers paying homage to 'the Great King' (Cyrus), whose own effigy is absent from what remains of the ruins: handsome praise for Scott on his departure for Naples.

> No more: the end is sudden and abrupt,
> Abrupt – as without preconceived design
> Was the beginning; yet the several Lays
> Have moved in order, to each other bound
> By a continuous and acknowledged tie
> Though unapparent – like those shapes distinct
> That yet survive ensculptured on the walls
> Of palaces, or temples, 'mid the wreck
> Of famed Persepolis; each following each,
> As might beseem a stately embassy,
> In set array; these bearing in their hands
> Ensign of civil power, weapon of war,
> Or gift to be presented at the throne
> Of the Great King; and others, as they go
> In priestly vest, with holy offerings charged,
> Or leading victims drest for sacrifice.
> Nor will the Power we serve, that sacred Power,
> The Spirit of Humanity, disdain
> A ministration humble but sincere,
> That from a threshold loved by every Muse
> Its impulse took – that sorrow-stricken door,
> Whence, as a current from its fountain-head,
> Our thoughts have issued, and our feelings flowed,
> Receiving, willingly or not, fresh strength
> From kindred sources[.]

The frieze represents the poems collected in Wordsworth's volume, whose connection is 'unapparent' because a central, unifying figure is invisible. The idea of an absent centre then gives rise to another image, that of Scott's 'threshold', a source of power to the whole community of readers and writers. The compliment to Scott is double because he represents both that power and the power to organise and structure this particular volume of poems (which begins with two specifically about Scott, 'Yarrow Revisited' and the sonnet 'On the Departure of Sir Walter Scott from Abbotsford, for Naples').

Why use the Persepolis image? The reliefs express a hierarchy so rigid that we can hardly suppose Wordsworth was recommending it as a political model for his own time, for all his dislike of impending reform. Its appropriateness, surely, is that it is a ruin ('wreck'), a scene of truncation that nevertheless powerfully points to its own invisible completeness. The threshold image develops this paradox when, in a typical piece of syntactical sleight of hand, Wordsworth gives it both centrifugal and centripetal power. The poem itself is a 'ministration' that takes its 'impulse' from the threshold; Scott's threshold is a 'fountain-head', yet 'Our thoughts' have issued from it. If we dissolve the paradox and construe this as an elegant compliment (Scott's thoughts have become ours), we are left with a problem in the next lines, for our thoughts receive 'fresh strength / From kindred sources', and it is difficult to see where these are located. Further it is clear that 'we' ('the Power we serve . . . / The Spirit of Humanity') includes Scott. The point of all this is that here as elsewhere in the volume both the speaker and Scott are active and passive, writer and reader; but in this case Wordsworth is claiming Scott as a collaborator in a deeper sense, both with his own work and with the establishment of a community of readers that (for once) he sees as coterminous with the nation. There is no distinction, no sense of distance, between Scotland (land of Scott) and England, and the 'Apology' for the foregoing poems is in fact a palinode, erasing the sense of difference and continuity ('similitude in dissimilitude'?) that touring and visiting involve.

The two other poems about Scott in this volume are, in contrast, very much about cultural as well as geographical distance. The sonnet on Scott's departure, again using the image of Scott as 'potentate', explores the mythic power of early poets in both northern (Scottish) and southern legend and works hard to make connections between them; so 'Eildon's triple height' (recalling perhaps *Trimontium*, the name of the nearby Roman camp) is replaced by 'soft Parthenope' (i.e. Naples), so called after the siren Parthenope: Wordsworth would have found in his copy of Strabo a discussion whether the *sirenussae*, a three-pointed rock near Capri at the southern end of the bay of Naples, was named after the sirens (daughters of one of the Muses) who threw themselves in the sea after the wanderer Odysseus overcame their charms.[43] In this classical context the 'trouble' over Eildon may recall the rocks mourning the death of Orpheus (e.g. in Ovid's *Metamorphoses*, XI): certainly the whole fiction of the poem is that nature, transformed into 'Spirits of Power', laments Scott's departure.

Eildon has cultural associations of its own, not only with Scott (the Eildon Hills overlook Melrose and Abbotsford) but with the half-legendary figure of Thomas the Rhymer, a thirteenth-century poet whom Scott himself helped canonise as the earliest truly Scottish poet.[44] According to the ballad 'Thomas the Rhymer' the poet was abducted by the Queen of the Fairies and imprisoned for seven years in the Eildon Hills where he learned the gift of prophecy. He was allowed to return and astounded his companions with his gift, but, as Scott puts it, when 'a hart and a hind had left the neighbouring forest, and were composedly and slowly parading the streets of the village', he 'arose instantly and followed the animals to the forest, whence he was never seen to return'. There was a popular belief, however, that he would reappear. Clearly this is a legend that binds poetic inspiration to a particular place, and to Scott it is of national (i.e. Scottish) importance. The Queen of the Fairies combines the force of both muse and siren, and Thomas is the favoured poet, the originator of a national tradition, a Musaeus, an Orpheus. (Ossian is for the moment forgotten.)

If Scott is Orpheus, he is also Thomas; the 'wizard of the north' (who mythologised the Border country as particularly Scottish)[45] is also a siren of the south, 'waft[ed]' by 'winds of ocean' to Naples. Again, he is brother-poet, like Lycidas *wafted* towards resurrection. For all these allusions, the poem has an astonishing conviction that 'the whole world's good wishes' are with Scott, in spite of the separation of north and south. Moreover, there is a strong sense that Wordsworth has witnessed the *beginning* ('engender[ing]') of cultural power in the poetry of Scott. Fairies and muses are dissolved as 'Spirits of Power', and this phrase is further dissolved in the opening lines:

> A trouble, not of clouds, or weeping rain,
> Nor of the setting sun's pathetic light
> Engendered, hangs o'er Eildon's triple height[.]

The images suggest poetic power originates in nature, but the negatives deny it. The 'Spirits of Power' are both nature and not nature, and they lament the passing of a 'kindred Power': a phrase with indefinite associations in the final poem, 'Apology', as we have seen, allowing readers to colonise it with their own associations or, more conservatively, to choose their associations and consequently decide whether this is a lament or a celebration of (eternal?) rebirth.

For the point about Wordsworth's allusiveness in these poems is that the primary situation, Scott's translation from north to south, taken with the allusions, makes a combination of narrative and elegy that problematises origination and imitation. Basing poems on classical mythology and (northern) local legend, Wordsworth inevitably acknowledges himself a late-comer: meaning has already been made, the landscape textualised. At the same time legend validates imagination because it can be thought of as both communal and originary, the authorless 'expression' of place, and a poet engaging with local legend can represent himself as participating in an imaginative community of writers and readers, tellers and listeners. One advantage of doing so – balancing the 'disadvantage' (if it is one) of loss of independence – is that it provides ways of thinking about not only the reader–writer relationship (as I have suggested above)[46] but also the conditions of literary survival and change.

In the sonnet Scott is a late-comer *imagined as* an originator. His departure from Abbotsford (his death imminent)[47] is a deeply appropriate moment for this fiction because it is the point at which his textualisations become fixed and irrevocable. He will shortly have *gone before* (preceded and predeceased), his poems become part of the community of texts, if I can put it that way, that were once his inspiration and that surviving poets, Wordsworth among them, still have to negotiate with. This thinking profoundly links poetic fulfilment and personal extinction, a connection we can also find in Wordsworth's autobiographical explorations in *The Prelude*. As in Wordsworth's other late elegies on poets, such as 'Extempore Effusion of the Death of James Hogg' (1835), the speaker projects the event not just as bereavement but as an opportunity to question the survival of art, including his own. (Ossian, in some ways the obvious figure through which to explore northern cultural origins, is an exception which I shall discuss below.)

Returning to Scott, 'Yarrow Revisited' contrives to avoid the idea of extinction and makes a simpler defence of fiction generally:

> And what, for this frail world, were all
>   That mortals do or suffer,
> Did no responsive harp, no pen,
>   Memorial tribute offer?
> Yea, what were mighty Nature's self?
>   Her features, could they win us,
> Unhelped by the poetic voice
>   That hourly speaks within us?

> Nor deem that localised Romance
>   Plays false with our affections
> Unsanctifies our tears – made sport
>   For fanciful dejections:
> Ah, no! the visions of the past
>   Sustain the heart in feeling
> Life as she is – our changeful Life,
>   With friends and kindred dealing. (81–96)

As a tribute to Scott the poem properly emphasises '*localised*' romance and continually invokes the Yarrow. But Scott's function has been, the poem says, to turn the Yarrow into a metonym for 'a hundred streams', all now invested with 'the power of Yarrow'. This plays a part in an inevitable contrast between 'classic Fancy' and 'native Fancy', the Tiber doing duty as a metonym of classical culture. Interestingly, the cultural power of both the Tiber and the Yarrow is associated with a drowning, the Tiber being named after Tiberinus, king of Alba, who drowned in it, and the Yarrow being the river in which the corpse of the 'flower of Yarrow' was found ('Rare Willie drowned in Yarrow' [Childe, 215] is a related ballad).[48] There is a long distance between the king of Alba and Rare Willie, but it would be entirely characteristic of the poem to attempt to bridge it, yet with a sense – implied in the terms 'classic' and 'native' – that this is a new rivalry, the peripheral rivalling the central. Again, 'border', in the phrase 'Great Minstrel of the Border' reminds us of centres and peripheries. The poem engages with the new interest in non-classical mythology evident in the work of mythographers such as Edward Davies as well as with Scott's own more literalist antiquarianism.

The recognition that nature is always textualised ('Yea, what were mighty Nature's self?') may seem a retreat from what has been taken as a characteristically Wordsworthian (and Romantic) emphasis on the *individual* imagination and its dealings with 'nature', and I suspect this is one reason why the later poems about local legend are seldom much valued. But we should recognise them as serious explorations of the conditions under which fictional language becomes communal, a subject that I have argued was always of interest to Wordsworth, especially from 1807 onwards, and one which seems to me part of an essential and powerful dilemma in Romanticism: the cost of a Romantic construction of the self, of making the individual imagination the site of creativity in language, is loss of a means of theorising the communality of writing, whether in terms of literary tradition or, more important, in terms of relating the literary and the non-literary: a serious problem for an age so enamoured of the artless, the anonymous, and the local or regional as against the central. One of the sonnets in 'Yarrow Revisited', 'Fancy and Tradition', reflects the problem succinctly, with a typically slippery use of 'or':

> Thus everywhere to truth Tradition clings,
> Or Fancy localises Powers we love.

It is not entirely clear how the two lines are connected: is the second merely a reformulation of the first, or is it saying something quite different? For 'Fancy' and 'Tradition' are synonymous only if we redefine the former as communal, which the text seems to do by associating it with 'Powers *we* love'. (This is a long way from Coleridge's notion of fancy as essentially playful, idiosyncratic and uncreative.) Yet even that phrase has a logical ambiguity about it. Do we love them jointly or severally? And what is the relation of 'Powers' and 'truth'? It is easy to make a mare's nest of the lines with logic, but my point is that a touch of analysis shows how constructive, how determinative they are, and that one of their constructs is precisely a notion of communal fancy that links past and present, individual and communal, written and oral texts, the literary and the unliterary. If the Preface to *Lyrical Ballads* is something of a revolt against literariness, the later poems defend it as part of a continuum of language use. Scott is important in this exploration precisely because of his popular success; he is no longer the essentially lightweight competitor Wordsworth challenged in writing *The White Doe of Rylstone*, but a case study for the conditions of poetic success.

It would be wrong, however, to dwell entirely on those matters and exclude the elegiac tone that pervades all the Yarrow poems, not just 'Yarrow Revisited'. They are all conscious rewritings of the self[49] and therefore inevitably elegiac (as 'Tintern Abbey' is, too: Wordsworth's myth of the origination of the self in childhood makes all his poetic acts of self-reflection elegiac. *The Prelude* began with the question '*Was* it for this . . .?'); but 'Yarrow Visited' and 'Yarrow Revisited' explicitly link the sense of a personal past with the historical past. 'Our affections', 'our tears', 'our changeful Life': the terms grasp at cultural history as if it were simply like individual history. The time span in 'Yarrow Revisited' is both personal and cultural; but this tempting simplification is compromised by the problems of poetic communality I have discussed above. There is a tension between the two which is perhaps most apparent in the penultimate stanza:

> Bear witness, Ye, whose thoughts that day
> In Yarrow's groves were centred;
> Who through the silent portal arch
> Of mouldering Newark enter'd;
> And clomb the winding stair that once
> Too timidly was mounted
> By the 'last Minstrel' (not the last!)
> Ere he his Tale recounted.   (97–104)

The stanza recalls an episode in *The Lay of the Last Minstrel* and suggests on the surface a joke on the fact that the poem was the *first* of Scott's many romances. The joke depends on identifying Scott himself as the minstrel (Scott's habit of publishing anonymously shows his complicity). But there is the deeper suggestion of a new beginning in Naples: either way the lines play with beginnings and endings – writing and death – in a thoroughly Romantic way.

Why could not the Ossianic texts be used for an explanation of cultural origins? In the poem in which Wordsworth takes up the subject most extensively, 'Written in a Blank Leaf of Macpherson's Ossian' (1824), he is distracted by the problem of textual inauthenticity. He allows Ossian a status like that of Orpheus or Musaeus, not a line of whose poems, he reminds us, is extant, a legendary power to move 'the tender-hearted maid' and 'the rugged chief'. But Macpherson's bogus texts, as he saw them,[50] prevented Wordsworth from thinking of Ossian as a usable archetype of cultural transmission in which living writers join the dead. In any case the Ossianic texts had already been used culturally in a quite different way by earlier apologists enchanted by the late eighteenth-century (not Romantic) notion of Genius, as evidence of a time when the 'true Genius' was '[h]appily exempted from that tormenting ambition, and those vexatious desires, which trouble the current of modern life' and wandered 'with a serene, contented heart, through walks and groves consecrated to the Muses . . .'. I quote the view of William Duff in his *Essay on Original Genius* (1767) as representative.[51] Such a view of the bard is of little use to a writer who reflects the conditions of 'modern life'. If the terms of this debate seem oddly Victorian rather than Romantic (remembering Arnold's vexation at 'this strange disease of modern life'), we can reflect on how deeply Wordsworth and his contemporaries questioned naive views of origination, and how lasting their questions were.

Collaboration and patronage: Wordsworth and Beaumont

I have been using the word 'collaboration' in a sense both very broad and very specific, different from our dominant idea of collaboration, the idea of two writers contributing contemporaneously to a single text. Wordsworth and Coleridge did collaborate in this way over the first edition of *Lyrical Ballads*, and their writing for the next few years seems to have been conditioned and sometimes motivated by the opportunities and constraints of imagined conversation.[52] But I turn now to another kind of aesthetic relationship, that of poet and patron, Wordsworth and Sir George Beaumont. The subject is seldom thought of as central to Wordsworth's art, partly because Beaumont's influence was not strong before 1805, and partly, I suspect, because the concept of private patronage conflicts with simple (and unhelpful) notions of poetic integrity and genius. But Beaumont was very much part of Wordsworth's self-presentation, his self-definition, in the first collected edition of the poems in 1815. The edition is dedicated to Beaumont, and each volume has a frontispiece engraving of one of his pictures, 'Lucy Gray' in the first and 'Peele Castle' in the second. And 'Peele Castle' is *about* self-definition in a framework of friendship and complementary imaginative acts.

Sir George Beaumont is generally known for reasons other than his friendship with Wordsworth. He was a painter and collector of landscape paintings, and part of his collection, including a striking Canaletto, was bequeathed to the National Gallery. He befriended Constable as well as Wordsworth, and his friendships with artists seem to have mixed enthusiastic encouragement with well-conceived practical help. His first formal contact with Wordsworth in August 1803 was an offer of land at Applethwaite to provide a scene where Wordsworth and Coleridge (whom Beaumont had met earlier) could 'communicate [their] sensations to each other'. The act acknowledged their need of intellectual collaboration and of a scene, a landscape in which it could occur. Wordsworth's response to this and later gifts of land was pleasure mixed with embarrassment, and we can interpret the latter as embarrassment that the gifts were so particularly appropriate.[53] Beaumont invited Wordsworth to apply his *mind* to the field he first gave him:[54] a crucial challenge that implicitly asked how the landscape imagination could make itself content with a particular place. This is a remarkably tactful and appreciative response to 'Poems on the Naming of Places', but it is more than that: it is a challenge to Wordsworth to define and perhaps overcome the distinction between aesthetic and legal ownership,[55] and some of the poems about or to Beaumont involve just this issue, from 'Elegiac Stanzas' (i.e. 'Peele Castle' [1805]), in which Wordsworth re-imagines one of Beaumont's paintings, to 'Elegiac Musings' (1830), an elegy built on images of Beaumont's patronage.

The relationship offered specific challenges, not just the traditional advantages we imagine in private patronage. In later years Wordsworth, Beaumont and Lady Beaumont collaborated in landscaping the grounds of the Beaumonts' estate at Coleorton in Lincolnshire, and it can easily be thought that *actual* landscape gardening, an essentially eighteenth-century activity of the gentry and their contractors, ought to have been of less value to Wordsworth, the Romantic poet, than free, metaphysical shaping of 'Nature' on the page. All eight poems Wordsworth addressed to Beaumont, written between 1805 and 1830, are poems of praise and for that reason might seem forced growths, poems in which Wordsworth was not at liberty to say what he thought. But if we make that assumption it is on the spurious basis that the imagination is a scene of complete independence: part of the so-called Romantic ideology, but too restrictive to account for the realities of the relationship and, more important, for the opportunities it offers us to consider a broadening of Wordsworth's aesthetic. The assumption also implies a crude moral judgement. There is a false dichotomy between independence and patronage, and Wordsworth's life and work show it. If his writing is dominated, as I think it is, by imagined as well as actual relations with his readers, then the existence of a patron who was also a critical reader must be of positive interest.

Beaumont's and Scott's friendship with Wordsworth began in the same year, 1803, and each plays a large role in the way Wordsworth presented himself to the public in 1815. Scott was friend, competitor and, perhaps in both capacities, irritant: his romances of the marvellous had sold enormously well and created a new taste, but in *The White Doe* Wordsworth offered Scott's readers a more sustaining alternative. Wordsworth's relations with Beaumont were apparently quite different. As a painter, landowner and patron of art he was in no sense Wordsworth's competitor but potentially a collaborator. But there is a similarity between Scott and Beaumont because Wordsworth's poems about, or to, both ask us to imagine another readership or spectatorship as potentially Wordsworth's own. We read and are made to imagine other readers. In a broad sense collaboration is nothing more than conscious allusion to other poems or works of art: more narrowly it is a particular consciousness of bringing others' works into the realm of your own readership, however imagined, however inaccurately conceived. Wordsworth had an idea about Scott's readership, but he may have felt that collaboration with Beaumont should be contemplated (theorised) in a different way, involving different media and a conceptualised difference of social class. How does a man who spent so much time in 1798, 1800 and 1802 meditating the appearance of his own volumes of poetry cope with the interest and help of a man with a different aesthetic circle and taste?

'Peele Castle' is a poem about art that suffers from being read as a poem almost directly about life, the single, simple life of the poet, irrespective of the existence and the claims of others. It is said to acknowledge that responsiveness to life is morally superior to the practice of imaginative art, and the contemporaneous 'Ode to Duty' can corroborate this idea with a narrative in which imaginative freedom is given up in favour of moral discipline. The speaker in 'Peele Castle' once 'would have' made a painting of the castle reflecting a 'perfect' calm –

> I could have fancied that mighty Deep
> Was even the gentlest of all gentle things

– and thought it 'true'. The image is now dismissed as illusion ('Such, in the fond illusion of my heart, / Such Picture would I at that time have made') and replaced with another, in fact a verbal equivalent of Beaumont's pictorial image. A crucial point in this reading is the recurrence of the word 'dream', first in the famous lines

> The light that never was, on sea or land,
> The consecration, and the poet's dream;

and later in the penultimate stanza:

> Farewell, farewell the heart that lives alone,
> Housed in a dream, at distance from the Kind!
> Such happiness, wherever it be known,
> Is to be pitied; for 'tis surely blind.

It is easy to equate 'dream' with 'illusion' and being 'blind', and if we do so we may want to read the phrase 'the poet's dream' as suggesting that poetic imagination is always potentially illusory or blind. I've argued above that this idea must be part of our response to 'Resolution and Independence', but only a part.

Among many reasons for rejecting this reading there is the biographical fact that Wordsworth wrote after John's death that he 'never wrote a line without a thought of its giving him pleasure'.[56] It would be a poor epitaph to announce that you were about to give up writing or learn to despise imagination. Biography aside, it is a strange reading of an elegy (I have exaggerated it to prove the point) because elegiac writing so often thematises relations between the speaker and the dead and between the speaker and the resources of speech. It invokes literary tradition on the one hand and a notion of the personal, the individual, the original, on the other: these oppositions are strikingly present in pastoral elegies from Milton's 'Lycidas' to Yeats's 'Shepherd and Goatherd', and though Wordsworth's poem does not use pastoral conventions it needs to be read with this fact about elegies in mind.

The literary and artistic contexts of the poem are focused in images of aesthetic companionship with both John and Beaumont. 'The Kind' from which the speaker fears distance is embodied in this poem by those men, one a painter, the other a 'silent poet' as Wordsworth described him in the 'Poems on the Naming of Places', a silent collaborator who transfigured nature into landscape in the act of making a path, a focus, a scene.[57] But now John's death, a more radical absence than that envisaged three years earlier in 'When, to the attractions of the busy world', gives a broader context for associating different imaginative acts. The poem brings the two men together in potential friendship:

> Then Beaumont, Friend!, who would have been the Friend,
> If he had lived, of Him whom I deplore . . .

The event behind the poem is a literal shipwreck (corresponding to the danger of shipwreck portrayed in Beaumont's painting) in which

Wordsworth lost a brother who was not only a silent poet but also an actual patron. It had long been understood between John, William and Dorothy that his income from his eastern voyages would help to support them all.[58] So the two addressees, Beaumont and (silently) John have in common the power to command the speaker's imagination, as both artist and patron, as it turns to the future. But the power to command oddly coexists with feminine qualities in both figures. John is a '*silent* poet' in 'When, to the attractions of the busy world' (silent like Dorothy, except that she was not entirely silent in William's collections) and in 'Peele Castle' in the sense that it excludes any reference to him, even implicitly. In the two other extended poems on his death silence is a reported fact, a moral virtue, and a sign of essential truth. 'To a Daisy' is a fantasy about the moment of his death: as commander of a wrecked ship he gives a last order to his crew, and it is, oddly enough, 'Silence!'. In 'Elegiac Verses' Wordsworth reports a moment of silence before John's fatal voyage –

> Here did we stop; and here looked round
> While each into himself descends,
> For that last thought of parting Friends
> That is not to be found.
> Hidden was Grasmere's Vale from sight,
> Our home and his, his heart's delight,
> His quiet heart's selected home

– and speculates how the 'living John' becomes 'nothing but a name'. John is a figure both of power and reticence, his very reticence conferring power, as if he had an art beyond the range of Wordsworth's art. And yet this art has no definition, no cultural presence. John's silence is not a metaphysical (Beckettian) fact but a cultural one, not a matter of identity but of the conditions in which voice can become audible. Wordsworth's private comments on his brother are more explicit. He had 'a modesty [that] was equal to that of the purest Woman. In prudence, in meekness, in self-denial, in fortitude, in just desires, and elegant and refined enjoyments, with an entire simplicity of manners, life and habit, he was all that could be wished-for in a man . . .'.[59] The passage is full of negatives, but it does challenge us to consider the relations between 'Woman' and 'man'.

As for Beaumont, the 'Elegiac Musings', Wordsworth's most

important poem about him after 'Peele Castle', has a central image of
the dispersal of power. Patronage, easily thought of as a source of
power, becomes an enabling process so self-effacing as to be almost
invisible: certainly a mystery, in which actual absence (death) is both
a negation and a fulfilment of his power. Yeats's 'In Memory of Major
Robert Gregory' is a similar poem, a poem about the specific silences
of dead individuals and the deeper silence of an unimaginable
absence. In 'Elegiac Musings' Wordsworth celebrates Beaumont by
first recalling that he requested not to be celebrated in a monumental
epitaph. Beaumont chose for the inscription on his tombstone, 'Enter
not into judgment with thy servant, O Lord!', a potent gesture of self-
effacement that in its original context in Psalm 143 presents the
speaker as a kind of blank page awaiting the imprint of God ('Cause
me to hear . . . Deliver me . . . Teach me . . . Quicken me . . .
I am thy servant'). It precludes a laudatory epitaph of the kind
Wordsworth meditated in the first 'Essay upon Epitaphs', in which an
inscription is 'the joint offspring of the worth of the dead and the
affections of the living':[60] the survivor imagines the dead but, if he is
reflective, cannot do so without accepting that he must make public
his own affections, knowing they will be thought indulgent but
hoping they will be shared. The headnote, that is, gives a special force
to the common fiction of literary elegies that the writer has no
language equal to the merit of the dead: here it is a matter of the
subject's prohibition. That can generate its own kind of praise, praise
of modesty, and the poem is full of it, but we must not see this simply
as a *chosen* artistic constraint: it is a fact. The poem is a search for the
absent Beaumont but not in terms suggesting an intrinsic hidden self,
a single voice, rather a series of performances with specifically
imagined audiences:

> Yet *here* at least, though few have numbered days
> That shunned so modestly the light of praise,
> His graceful manners, and the temperate ray
> Of that arch fancy which would round him play,
> Brightening a converse never known to swerve
> From courtesy and delicate reserve;
> That sense, the bland philosophy of life,
> Which checked discussion ere it warmed to strife;
> Those rare accomplishments, and varied powers
> Might have their record among sylvan bowers.
> Oh, fled for ever! vanished like a blast

That shook the leaves in myriads as it passed; –
Gone from this world of earth, air, sea, and sky,
From all its spirit-moving imagery,
Intensely studied with a painter's eye,
A poet's heart; and, for congenial view,
Portrayed with happiest pencil, not untrue
To common recognitions while the line
Flowed in a course of sympathy divine; –
Oh! severed, too abruptly, from delights
That all the seasons shared with equal rights; –
Rapt in the grace of undismantled age,
From soul-felt music, and the treasured page
Lit by that evening lamp which loved to shed
Its mellow lustre round thy honoured head;
While Friends beheld thee give with eye, voice, mien,
More that theatric force to Shakespeare's scene. (7–33)

All seasons and all elements lack Beaumont's presence. But the more important claim of the poem is that he is recalled in conversation and theatrical performance. In a sense this undervalues Beaumont's painting because he is represented in terms of other arts. But the concept Beaumont is made to convey is of art that bridges any gap between connoisseurship and popularity ('for congenial view, / Portrayed with happiest pencil, not untrue') and that disperses itself among different particular media, that will be commemorated as 'genius, talent, skill' (l. 61). The phrase perhaps equates these qualities but more likely it does not. It spells out in a uniquely clear way a hierarchy of faculties or forces that we take as essentially Romantic: 'genius' is a spiritual quality, something given; 'skill' is merely learned, even mechanical; and 'talent' can be used belittlingly of the former or kindly of the latter. If I am right in suggesting the terms are not synonymous in the poem, then we can read the line in two ways, either as if Wordsworth was reluctant to define Beaumont's achievement or as if it embodied all three qualities.

Further, there is remarkable tact in the way Wordsworth imagines Beaumont's presence, beyond mere deference or cowardice. Beaumont is an actor and a figure of courtesy in Castiglione's sense, an inspirer and controller of subtle speech, a figure who exists in and is defined by influence rather than essence. There is no assumption that the poem will find Beaumont's 'intrinsic' self. In this way it respects the moral force of the headnote including the line quoted from Psalms and converts it, I think, into an aesthetic imperative. Like Yeats's

Robert Gregory, Wordsworth's Beaumont is evanescent, 'vanished like a blast / That shook the leaves in myriads as it passed': the image suggests someone ungraspable not just because of death but because his characteristic act is to disperse himself among others, invisibly.

It is a historical irony that the phrase 'the light that never was, on sea or land' has been used as shorthand for the imagination, first by Coleridge in *Biographia Literaria*, then by many writers including Hardy (in the Preface to *Late Lyrics and Earlier*). Wordsworth disowned the phrase in editions from 1832 until his death in 1850, substituting 'Of lustre, known to neither sea nor land':[61] the difference is that the former makes imagination the vehicle of primal light, prior to its earthly manifestations; the latter suggests an aberration from actuality. The former is a Romantic stereotype which the poem in fact questions by setting against it other images of light and, more important, by insisting that time changes meanings, that the apparent completeness and finality of a visual image is always an illusion. The latter formulation retreats entirely from questions and ambiguities. But Wordsworth's poems characteristically *use* ambiguities and attempt to control them; the 'light that never was' clearly got out of control, escaped from its context like other phrases for which Wordsworth has become famous ('the spontaneous overflow of powerful feeling'; 'emotion recollected in tranquillity'; 'I've measured it from side to side, / 'Tis three feet long and two feet wide'). It is a salutary example of the fact that no matter how deeply a writer thematises his relation with readers he is ultimately at their mercy. The process of assimilation in which a writer becomes accepted is, as Wordsworth acknowledged (if my argument in this book has been persuasive), both a glorification and an annihilation. That is a paradox that history resolves one way or another. Wordsworth kept the paradox alive as long as *he* was alive through incessant revisions and efforts to tighten the copyright laws, and attempted to prolong it by having *The Prelude* published after his death. But there is no copyright on taste.

Notes and references

1. Gill, *Wordsworth*, pp. 391–2.

2. See especially Clifford Siskin, *The Historicity of Romantic Discourse* (Oxford, OUP, 1988) and William H. Galperin, *Revision and Authority in Wordsworth* (Philadelphia, University of Pennsylvania Press, 1989).

3. See Frances Ferguson, *Wordsworth: Language as Counter-Spirit* (New Haven and London, Yale UP, 1977), ch. 2.

4. The familiar 1850 arrangement has 'Poems Written in Youth' for 'Juvenile Poems'; the juxtapositions are the same.

5. Volume design was not in itself a new matter for Wordsworth in 1809–15, but for earlier volumes, including *Lyrical Ballads* (1798), he did not use such idiosyncratic principles. Neil Freistat's *The Poem and the Book* (University of North Carolina Press, 1952, repr. 1985) is among the earliest investigations of the design of *Lyrical Ballads*, a subject which is treated in almost every recent edition.

6. F.D. Maurice, in a letter to Charles Kingsley, 1851 (quoted in *The Prelude*, ed. J. Wordsworth and others, p. 560).

7. Kenneth R. Johnston, *Wordsworth and 'The Recluse'* (New Haven and London, Yale UP, 1984), esp. ch. 10.

8. Coleridge contrasts a building like the Pantheon, where 'the whole [is in] *perceived* harmony with the parts that compose it', with a Christian church, in which 'the Whole, and that there is a Whole produced, is altogether a Feeling, in which all the thousand several impressions lose themselves in a universal Solvent' (*Lectures on Shakespeare, Milton*, etc, 1819; repr. in *Lectures 1808–1819 on Literature*, ed. R.A. Foakes [Princeton, N.J., Princeton UP, 1987], vol. 2, p. 400). Foakes suggests this distinction was based on F. Schlegel's paragraphs on Gothic architecture in *Geschichte der alten und neuen Literatur* (1815).

9. *Lectures 1808–1819*, II, p. 74; derived, according to R.A. Foakes, from F. Schlegel's *Geschichte*. Compare the notes taken by William Hammond: 'the massy architecture of the Goths, as wild and varied as the forest vegetation which it resembled' (*Lectures 1808–1819*, II, p. 79).

10. *Lectures 1808–1819*, II, p. 60. The quotation is from the notes taken by J.H. Green.

11. See above, Chapter 5.

12. 'The War of Languages' (1973), in *The Rustle of Language*, trans. R. Howard (Oxford, Blackwell, 1986).

13. Barthes is no exception to this: his brilliant (study of) autobiography, *Roland Barthes by Roland Barthes*, trans. R. Howard (New York, Hill and Wang, 1977), explores these issues. So does *The Lover's Discourse* in the guise of lexicon.

14. See Lucy Newlyn, *Coleridge, Wordsworth and the Language of Allusion* (Oxford, Clarendon, 1986); Edwin Stein, *Wordsworth's Art of Allusion* (University Park, Pennsylvania State UP, 1988).

15. Blake's experiments with book design and production are both more radical and more explicit, but that fact belongs to the history of art publishing more than to that of literary publication.

16. Christopher Ricks, *Keats and Embarrassment* (Oxford, Clarendon, 1974).

17. Cited in *OED*, s.v. 'provincialism'.

18. *BL*, II, p. 54.

19. Barrell, *Poetry, Language and Politics*, pp. 137–67, argues that there is a gendered hierarchy of concrete and abstract in 'Tintern Abbey'. I find that argument persuasive in the context of the myth of growth and maturity in that poem, but not in other contexts. 'The Idiot Boy' goes to the other extreme: concrete language is expressive even when it is irrationally constructed: 'The cocks did crow to-woo, to-woo, / And the sun did shine so cold.'

20. *PW*, III, p. 282; IV, pp. 197, 442.

21. *Biographia Literaria*, ch. 22; see also ch. 18.

22. Peter Murphy's chapter on Wordsworth in *Poetry as an Occupation and an Art in Britian 1760–1830* (Cambridge, CUP, 1993) has the most stimulating recent discussion of the Yarrow poems as responses to Scott and to the ballad revival generally. Broadly, he argues that in all the Yarrow poems, Wordsworth's and his predecessors', the Yarrow represents death, whether literal or metaphorical. But for reasons given below I do not think it is correct to speak of 'all the poems in the Yarrow family' (p. 210) as if they were essentially the same, nor do I think it obvious, as Murphy does (following the general opinion), that 'Yarrow Visited' is worse than 'Yarrow Unvisited' and 'Yarrow Revisited' is the worst of the lot.

23. Drayton, *Poly-Olbion*, 'The nine and twentieth Song', in *Works*, ed. J. William Hebel (Oxford UP, 1933), vol. 4, pp. 559ff. Drayton's poem is much concerned with English–Welsh rivalry, but the projected sections on Scotland were never completed and remained unpublished at his death. See Wyman H. Herendeen, *From Landscape to Literature: The River and the Myth of Geography* (Pittsburgh, PA, Duquesne University Press, 1986).

24. Stephen Gill, ' "Affinities Preserved": Poetic Self-Reference in Wordsworth', *Studies in Romanticism* 24 (1985), pp. 531–49.

25. The text corresponds to version O in Child's *English and Scottish Popular Ballads* (Boston and New York, Houghton Mifflin, 1898).

26. There is a black-letter version published by the Roxburgh Club as 'A Delectable new Ballad, Intituled *Leader Haughs and Yarrow. To Its own proper Tune.*' It is dated 1690? in the British Library Catalogue.

27. *Tea-Table Miscellany* (Dublin, 1729), pp. 50–1, 79. Scott, note to *Marmion*, Canto II, Introduction. Scott refers in this note to Wordsworth's 'Yarrow Unvisited'.

28. *The Lay of the Last Minstrel*, Canto 6 (*Poetical Works*, ed. J. Logie Robertson [Oxford, OUP, 1931], p. 48).

29. Robert Fergusson, *Scots Poems by Robert Fergusson Faithfully re-printed from THE WEEKLY MAGAZINE and the editions of 1773 and 1779* (Edinburgh, The Porpoise Press, 1925).

30. Published in Logan's *Poems* (1782), reprinted with variants in Anderson's *The Works of British Poets* (1795), XI, p. 1035.

31. *The Watchman*, ed. L. Patton (Princeton, N.J., Princeton UP, 1970), pp. 106–7. Patton suggests Coleridge found it in Anderson's *British Poets* (1795), XI, p. 1035 or *English Review*, xxv, April 1795. Anderson himself commented on the poem: 'Ovid, Propertius, and Tibullus, never composed a more affecting and impassioned elegy' (*British Poets*, XI, p. 1030).

32. Gill, p. 290.

33. Quoted from Percy's *Reliques of Ancient English Poetry*, ed. H.B. Wheatley (London, 1887), II, p. 365.

34. Dorothy is also 'erased' from 'Resolution and Independence': she was present when Wordsworth met the original Leech-gatherer. See Chapter 1 above.

35. See Harold Bloom, *The Anxiety of Influence* (Oxford, OUP, 1973).

36. See above, Chapter 1.

37. Child, number 214 E (the version printed in Scott's *Minstrelsy*).

38. The incident may have been taken from 'Annan Water' (Child, number 215, appendix).

39. Anderson, *British Poets*, XI, p. 1031.

40. Child, number 214 D.

41. *PW*, III, p. 410. Interestingly Wordsworth's poem contrasts these grandiose *official* acts of cultural definition with a reductive, popular act of naming, calling Edinburgh 'Wha wants me?' after the cry of the man who carried a bucket and cloak around the streets at night.

42. Gill, *Wordsworth*, p. 372.

43. Strabo, *Geography*, I, 2, 12–13, 17–18 (Loeb edn, pp. 81–3, 93–5).

44. Scott, *Minstrelsy*, IV, pp. 77ff.

45. See above, Chapter 2.

46. See above, Chapter 3.

47. See Wordsworth's note to *Yarrow Revisited and Other Poems*, PW, III, p. 525f. Though written before Scott's death (and sent to him), none of the three poems I'm discussing was published until after his death.

48. Wordsworth could have met the Tiber story in Ovid's *Fastii* or in a number of other classical sources.

49. As Gill argues in ' "Affinities Preserved" '.

50. 'The Phantom was begotten by the snug embrace of an impudent Highlander upon a cloud of tradition. . . . In nature every thing is distinct, yet nothing defined into absolute independent singleness. In Macpherson's work it is exactly the reverse; every thing (that is not stolen) is in this manner defined, insulated, dislocated, deadened, – yet nothing distinct' (Gill, pp. 654–5).

51. William Duff, *Essay on Original Genius* (1767), quoted in M. Gaull, *English Romanticism. The Human Context* (New York, Norton, 1988), p. 258.

52. The subject has been extensively studied. See, for example, William Heath, *Wordsworth and Coleridge: A Study of Their Literary Relations in 1801–1802* (Oxford, Clarendon, 1970) (still an indispensable work); Lucy Newlyn, *Coleridge, Wordsworth and the Language of Allusion* (Oxford, Clarendon, 1986); Paul Magnusson, *Coleridge and Wordsworth: A Lyrical Dialogue* (Princeton, Princeton UP, 1988); and Gene W. Ruoff, *Wordsworth and Coleridge: The Making of the Major Lyrics, 1802–1804* (London, Harvester, 1989).

53. Gill, *Wordsworth*, p. 219.

54. Moorman, I, pp. 586f.

55. I borrow the terms from Jonathan Bate's *Romantic Ecology: Wordsworth and the Environmental Tradition* (London, Routledge, 1991).

56. Letter to James Losh, 16.3.1805 (quoted by Gill, *Wordsworth*, p. 244).

57. See Chapter 2.

58. Gill, *Wordsworth*, p. 168.

59. Quoted in Gill, *Wordsworth*, p. 240.

60. PW, V, p. 452.

61. PW, IV, p. 259.

Bibliography

Aarslef, Hans, *The Study of Language in England 1780–1860* (Princeton, N.J., Princeton UP, 1967).

Abrams, M.H., *Natural Supernaturalism* (New York, Norton, 1971).

——*The Mirror and the Lamp* (New York, 1953).

Anderson, Benedict, *Imagined Communities: Reflections on the Origins and Spread of Nationalism* (London, Verso, 1983).

Anderson, Robert, *The Works of the British Poets* (Edinburgh, 1792–5).

Anderson, Robert (1770–1833), *Cumberland Ballads* (Carlisle, 1805).

——*Poems on Various Subjects* (Carlisle, 1798).

——*Poetical Works* (Carlisle, 1820).

Andersson, Lars, and Trudgill, Peter, *Bad Language* (London, Blackwell, 1990).

Armstrong, Isobel, *Language as Living Form in Nineteenth-Century Poetry* (Brighton, Harvester, 1982).

Arnold, Matthew, *Selected Poems and Prose*, ed. M. Allott (London, Dent, 1978).

Attridge, Derek, *Peculiar Language* (London, Methuen, 1988).

Barnard, F.M., *Herder's Social and Political Thought* (Oxford, Clarendon Press, 1965).

Baron, Michael, 'Speaking and Writing: Wordsworth's "Fit Audience" ', *English*, 32 (1983), pp. 217–50.

——'Yeats, Wordsworth, and the Communal Sense: the Case of "If I Were Four-and-Twenty" ', *Yeats Annual*, 5 (1987), pp. 62–82.

Barrell, John, *The Political Theory of Painting from Reynolds to Hazlitt* (New Haven and London, Yale UP, 1986).

——*Poetry, Language and Politics* (Manchester, Manchester UP, 1988).

——'Sir Joshua Reynolds and the Englishness of English Art', in Homi Bhabha (ed.), *Nation and Narration* (London, Routledge, 1990).

Barthes, Roland, 'The War of Languages' (1973), in *The Rustle of Language*, trans. R. Howard (Oxford, Blackwell, 1986).

——*A Lover's Discourse: Fragments*, trans. R. Howard (Harmondsworth, Penguin, 1990).

——*Roland Barthes by Roland Barthes*, trans. R. Howard (New York, Hill and Wang, 1977).

Bate, Jonathan, 'Wordsworth and the Naming of Places', *Essays in Criticism*, 39 (1989), pp. 196ff.

——*Romantic Ecology: Wordsworth and the Environmental Tradition* (London, Routledge, 1991).

Beattie, James, *The Poetical Works of James Beattie* (London, 1886).

Beer, John, *Wordsworth and the Human Heart* (Cambridge, CUP, 1978).

——*Wordsworth in Time* (London, Faber, 1978).

Belsey, Catherine, and Moore, Jane (ed.) *The Feminist Reader* (London, Macmillan, 1989).

Bewick, Thomas, *A Memoir of Thomas Bewick Written by Himself* (1862), ed. Ian Bain (London, OUP, 1975).

Bhabha, Homi (ed.), *Nation and Narration* (London, Routledge, 1990).

Bialostosky, Don H., *Making Tales: The Poetics of Wordsworth's Narrative Experiments* (Chicago, University of Chicago Press, 1984).

——*Wordsworth, Dialogics, and the Practice of Criticism* (Cambridge, CUP, 1992).

Bloom, H., *The Anxiety of Influence* (Oxford, OUP, 1973).

Brantley, Richard, *Wordsworth's 'Natural Methodism'* (New Haven, Yale UP, 1975).

Brennan, Timothy, 'The National Longing for Form', in Homi Bhabha (ed.), *Nation and Narration* (London, Routledge, 1990).

Brinkley, Richard, and Hanley, Keith (eds), *Romantic Revisions* (Cambridge, CUP, 1992).

Bromwich, David (ed.), *Romantic Critical Essays* (Cambridge, CUP, 1987).

——*A Choice of Inheritance: Self and Community from Edmund Burke to Robert Frost* (Cambridge, Mass., Harvard UP, 1989).

Bruner, Jerome, and Weisser, Susan, 'The invention of the self: autobiography and its forms', in David R. Olson and Nancy Torrance (eds), *Orality and Literacy* (Cambridge, CUP, 1991).

Burke, Edmund, *A Philosophical Enquiry into the Origin of Our Ideas of the Sublime and the Beautiful* (1757), ed. James T. Bolton (rev edn, Oxford, Basil Blackwell, 1987).

Burns, Robert, *Poems and Songs*, ed. James Kinsley (Oxford, OUP, 1969).

Butler, Marilyn, *Romantics, Rebels and Reactionaries* (Oxford, OUP, 1981).

——'The Orientalism of "The Giaour"', in Beatty, Bernard, and Newey, Vincent (eds), *Byron and the Limits of Fiction* (Liverpool, Liverpool UP, 1982).

——(ed.), *Burke, Paine, Godwin, and the Revolution Controversy* (Cambridge, CUP, 1984).

Chandler, James K., *Wordsworth's Second Nature: A Study of the Poetry and Politics* (Chicago, University of Chicago Press, 1984).

Child, Francis James, *English and Scottish Popular Ballads* (Boston and New York, Houghton Mifflin and Co., 1898).

Christensen, Jerome, *Coleridge's Blessed Machine of Language* (Ithaca, Cornell UP, 1981).

Clarke, Norma, *Ambitious Heights: writing; friendship; love: the Jewsbury Sisters, Felicia Hemans, and Jane Welsh Carlyle* (London, Routledge, 1990).

Coleridge, Hartley, *New Poems*, ed. E.L. Griggs (London, OUP, 1942).

Coleridge, S.T., *Biographia Literaria*, ed. James Engell and W. Jackson Bate (Princeton, N.J., Princeton UP, 1983).

——*Collected Letters*, ed. Earl Leslie Griggs (Oxford, Clarendon, 1956–9).

——*Lectures 1808–1819 on Literature*, ed. R.A. Foakes (Princeton, N.J., Princeton UP, 1987).

——*Notebooks*, ed. K. Coburn (London, Routledge and Kegan Paul, 1957–74).

——*The Watchman*, ed. L. Patton (Princeton, N.J., Princeton UP, 1970).

Crawford, Robert, *Devolving English Literature* (Oxford, Clarendon, 1992).

Crowley, Tony, *The Politics of Discourse* (London, Macmillan, 1989).

——'Bakhtin and the History of the Language', in Ken Hirschkop and David Shepherd (eds), *Bakhtin and Cultural Theory* (Manchester, Manchester UP, 1989).

Curry, Kenneth, *The Contributions of Robert Southey to the Morning Post* (Alabama, University of Alabama Press, 1984).

Curtis, J.R., *Wordsworth's Experiments with Tradition: the 'Lyric' Poems of 1802* (Ithaca, Cornell UP, 1971).

Davidoff, Leonore, and Hall, Catherine, *Family Fortunes* (London, Hutchinson, 1987).

Davies, Hugh Sykes, *Wordsworth and the Worth of Words* (Cambridge, CUP, 1987).

De Bolla, Peter, *The Discourse of the Sublime* (London, Routledge, 1989).

Dekker, George, *Coleridge and the Literature of Sensibility* (London, Vision Press, 1978).

De Man, Paul, *Blindness and Insight* (rev edn; London, Routledge, 1983).

——*The Rhetoric of Romanticism* (New York, Columbia UP, 1984).

De Quincey, Thomas, *Collected Writings*, ed. David Masson (new and enlarged edn; Edinburgh, Adam and Charles Black, 1890).

Devlin, D.D., *Wordsworth and the Poetry of Epitaphs* (London, Macmillan, 1980).

Drayton, Michael, *Works*, ed. J. William Hebel (Oxford, 1933).

Durrant, Geoffrey, 'Wordsworth's Metamorphoses', *English Studies in Africa*, 7 (1964), pp. 13ff.

Eliot, T.S., *Selected Prose of T.S. Eliot*, ed. F. Kermode (London, Faber, 1975).

Erdman, David V., 'Coleridge, Wordsworth and the Wedgwood Fund', *Bulletin of the New York Public Library*, 60 (1956), pp. 425–43, 487–507.

Essick, Robert N., *William Blake and the Language of Adam* (Oxford, Clarendon, 1989).

Ferguson, Frances, *Wordsworth: Language as Counter-Spirit* (New Haven and London, Yale UP, 1977).

Fergusson, Robert, *Scots Poems by Robert Fergusson Faithfully re-printed from THE WEEKLY MAGAZINE and the editions of 1773 and 1779* (Edinburgh, The Porpoise Press, 1925).

Ferry, David, *The Limits of Mortality: An Essay on Wordsworth's Major Poems* (Middletown, Ct, Wesleyan UP, 1959).

Fink, Z.S., 'Wordsworth and the Republican Tradition', *JEGP*, 47 (1948), pp. 107–26.

Foucault, Michel, *Language, Counter-Memory, Practice*, ed. Donald F. Bouchard (Oxford, Blackwell, 1977).

——'What is an Author?', repr in David Lodge (ed.), *Modern Criticism and Theory* (London, Longman, 1988).

France, Peter, *Politeness and its Discontents* (Cambridge, CUP, 1992).

Freistat, Neil, *The Poem and the Book* (University of North Carolina Press, 1952; repr 1985).

Fulford, T.J., and Paley, Morton (eds), *Coleridge's Visionary Languages* (Woodbridge, D.S. Brewer, 1993).

Galperin, William H., *Revision and Authority in Wordsworth* (Philadelphia, University of Pennsylvania Press, 1989).

Gaull, Marilyn, *English Romanticism. The Human Context* (New York and London, Norton, 1988).

Gill, Stephen, 'Wordsworth's Poems: The Question of Text', *RES NS*, 34 (1983), pp. 172–90.

——' "Affinities Preserved"; Poetic Self-Reference in Wordsworth', *Studies in Romanticism*, 24 (1985), pp. 531–49.

——*William Wordsworth, A Life* (Oxford, Clarendon, 1989).

——(ed.), *William Wordsworth* (Oxford, OUP, 1984).

Glen, Heather, *Vision and Disenchantment: Blake's 'Songs' and Wordsworth's 'Lyrical Ballads'* (Cambridge, CUP, 1983).

Gorak, Jan, *The Making of the Modern Canon* (London, Athlone Press, 1991).

Habermas, Jürgen, *The Theory of Communicative Action*, vol. 1, trans. Thomas McCarthy (London, Heinemann, 1984).

Hagstrum, Jean, *The Romantic Body* (Knoxville, University of Tennessee Press, 1985).

Hardy, Barbara, *Tellers and Listeners: The Narrative Imagination* (London, Athlone Press, 1975).

——*The Advantage of Lyric: An Essay on Feeling in Poetry* (London, Athlone Press, 1977).

Hartman, Geoffrey, *Wordsworth's Poetry 1787–1814* (1964; repr New Haven, Yale UP, 1971).

——*The Fate of Reading* (Chicago, University of Chicago Press, 1975).

——*Saving the Text* (Baltimore, Johns Hopkins UP, 1981).

Haydon, Benjamin Robert, *Correspondence and Table Talk*, ed. F.W. Haydon (London, 1876).

Heath, William, *Wordsworth and Coleridge: A Study of Their Literary Relations in 1801–1802* (Oxford, Clarendon, 1970).

Heffernan, James A.W., *Wordsworth's Theory of Poetry* (Ithaca and London, Cornell UP, 1969).

Herder, Johann Gottfried von, *Essay on the Origin of Language* (1772), trans. in John H. Moran and Alexander Gode (eds), *On the Origin of Language* (Chicago, University of Chicago Press, 1966; repr 1986).

Herendeen, Wyman H., *From Landscape to Literature: The River and the Myth of Geography* (Pittsburgh, PA, Duquesne University Press, 1986).

Herman, Judith, 'Wordsworth's Edition of 1815', *The Wordsworth Circle*, 9 (1978), pp. 82–7.

Hill, Alan G., 'Wordsworth and His American Friends', *Bulletin of Research in the Humanities*, 81 (1978), pp. 146–60.

Holmes, Richard, *Coleridge. Early Visions* (Harmondsworth, Penguin, 1990).

Holub, Robert C., *Jürgen Habermas, Critic in the Public Sphere* (London, Routledge, 1991).

Hutchinson, Sara, *Letters of Sara Hutchinson*, ed. K. Coburn (London, Routledge and Kegan Paul, 1954).

Jacobus, Mary, *Tradition and Experiment in Wordsworth's Lyrical Ballads 1798* (Oxford, Clarendon, 1976).

——*Romanticism, Writing, and Sexual Difference* (Oxford, Clarendon, 1989).

Johnson, Barbara, *A World of Difference* (Baltimore, Johns Hopkins UP, 1987).

Johnston, Kenneth R., *Wordsworth and 'The Recluse'* (New Haven and London, Yale UP, 1984).

Jones, John, *The Egotistical Sublime* (London, Methuen, 1954).

Keats, John, *Letters*, ed. M.B. Forman (third edn; Oxford, OUP, 1947).

Kelley, Theresa M., *Wordsworth's Revisionary Aesthetics* (Cambridge, CUP, 1988).

Kitson, Peter (ed.), *Romantic Criticism* (London, Batsford, 1989).

Klancher, J., *The Reading Audience of English Poetry* (Madison, Wis., University of Wisconsin Press, 1987).

Knight, Richard Payne, *The Landscape*, (second edn; London, 1795).

Lamb, Charles, *Letters of Charles Lamb* (London, Dent, 1909).

——*The Works in Prose and Verse of Charles and Mary Lamb*, ed. T. Hutchinson (London, OUP, 1908).

Landry, Donna, *The Muses of Resistance. Labouring-class Women's Poetry in Britain, 1739–1796* (Cambridge, CUP, 1990).

Leavis, F.R., *Revaluation* (London, Chatto and Windus, 1937).

Levin, Susan M., *Dorothy Wordsworth and Romanticism* (New Brunswick, Rutgers, 1987).

Levinson, Marjorie, *Keats's Life of Allegory: The Origins of a Style* (Oxford, Blackwell, 1988).

——*Wordsworth's Great Period Poems* (Cambridge, CUP, 1986).

Lipking, Lawrence, *Abandoned Women and the Poetic Tradition* (Chicago, University of Chicago Press, 1988).

Liu, Alan, *Wordsworth: The Sense of History* (Stanford, CA, Stanford University Press, 1989).

[Longman] *The Archives of the House of Longman* (Microfilm edn; Chadwyck-Healey, *c.* 1980).

Low, Donald A. (ed.), *Burns: The Critical Heritage* (London, Routledge and Kegan Paul, 1974).

McCarthy, T., *The Critical Theory of Jürgen Habermas* (London, Hutchinson, 1978).

MacCannell, Juliet Flower, *The Regime of the Brother. After the Patriarchy* (London, Routledge, 1991).

McGann, Jerome J., *The Romantic Ideology: A Critical Investigation* (Chicago, University of Chicago Press, 1983).

Magnusson, Paul, *Coleridge and Wordsworth: A Lyrical Dialogue* (Princeton, N.J., Princeton UP, 1988).

Mallett, Philip. (ed.), *Kipling Considered* (London, Macmillan, 1989).

Manning, Peter, 'Tales and Politics: *The Corsair*, Lara and *The White Doe of Rylstone*', in *Seventh International Byron Symposium: Byron's Poetry and Politics* (Salzburg: Studien zur Anglistik und Amerikanistik, Band 13, 1981).

Mayo, Robert, 'The Contemporaneity of *Lyrical Ballads*', *PMLA*, 69 (1954), pp. 486–522.

Mellor, Anne K (ed.), *Romanticism and Feminism* (Bloomington, Indiana UP, 1988).

——*Romanticism and Gender* (London, Routledge, 1993).

Moorman, Mary, *William Wordsworth, A Biography. The Early Years 1770-1803* (Oxford, Clarendon, 1957; rev. 1968).

——*The Later Years 1803–1850* (Oxford, Clarendon, 1965).

Morris, David B., 'Burns and Heteroglossia', *The Eighteenth Century: Theory and Interpretation*, 28 (1987) pp. 3–27.

Murphy, Peter, *Poetry as an Occupation and an Art in Britain 1760–1830* (Cambridge, CUP, 1993).

Newlyn, Lucy, *Coleridge, Wordsworth, and the Language of Allusion* (Oxford, Clarendon, 1986).

Nisbet, H.B., *Herder and Scientific Thought* (Cambridge, Modern Humanities Research Association, 1970).

Novalis (Friedrich von Hardenberg), *Werke*, ed. Uwe Lassen (Hamburg, Campe, 1966).

Olney, J., *Metaphors of Self: The Meaning of Autobiography* (Princeton, N.J., Princeton UP, 1972).

Ong, Walter J., *The Interface of the Word* (Ithaca and London, Cornell UP, 1977).

Owen, W.J.B., 'Costs, Sales and Profits of Longman's Editions of Wordsworth', *The Library*, NS 13 (1957).

——*Wordsworth as Critic* (London, Oxford UP, 1969).

Parrish, S.M., *The Art of the Lyrical Ballads* (Cambridge, Mass., Harvard UP, 1973).

Patterson, Annabel, *Pastoral and Ideology* (Oxford, Clarendon, 1988).

Peacock, Markham L., *The Critical Opinions of William Wordsworth* (Baltimore, Johns Hopkins UP, 1950).

Percy, Thomas, *Reliques of Ancient English Poetry*, ed. H.B. Wheatley (London, 1887).

Pinkerton, John *Select Scotish Ballads* (Edinburgh, 1783).

Pirie, David, *William Wordsworth, The Poetry of Grandeur and of Tenderness* (London, Methuen, 1982).

Pratt, Mary Louise, 'Linguistic Utopias', in Nigel Fabb, and others (eds), *The Linguistics of Writing* (Manchester, Manchester UP, 1987).

——*Imperial Eyes: Travel Writing and Transculturation* (London, Routledge, 1992).

Price, Uvedale, *Essays on the Picturesque* (London, 1810; repr London, Gregg International, 1971).

Priestley, Joseph, *A Course of Lectures on the Theory of Language, and Universal Grammar* (London, 1762).

Punter, David, *The Romantic Unconscious* (London, Harvester Wheatsheaf, 1989).

Ramsay, Allan, *Tea-Table Miscellany* (Dublin, 1729).

Reiman, Donald, 'The Poetry of Familiarity: Wordsworth, Dorothy and Mary Hutchinson', in D.H. Reiman, M.C. Jaye and B.T. Bennett (eds), *The Evidence of Imagination* (New York, New York UP, 1978).

Relph, Josiah, *A Miscellany of Poems* (Glasgow, 1747).

——*Poems* (Carlisle, J. Mitchell, 1798).

Repton, Humphry, *Sketches and Hints on Landscape Gardening* (London, 1794).

Reynolds, Joshua, *Discourses on Art*, ed. Robert W. Wark (New Haven, Yale UP, second edn, 1975).

Ricks, Christopher, 'A sinking inwards into ourselves from thought to thought', in *Harvard Studies in English*, 2 (1971), ed. R. Brouwer; repr in *The Force of Poetry* (Oxford, Clarendon, 1984).

——*Keats and Embarrassment* (Oxford, Clarendon, 1974).

Ritson, Joseph, *Ancient Songs and Ballads* (1790), ed. W.C. Hazlitt (London, 1877).

Roe, Nicholas, *Wordsworth and Coleridge, The Radical Years* (Oxford, Clarendon, 1988).

——'Pope, Politics and Wordsworth's *Prelude*', in David Fairer (ed.) *Pope. New Contexts* (London, Harvester Wheatsheaf, 1990).

Rogers, Pat, 'Boswell and the Scotticism', in Greg Clingham (ed.), *New Light on Boswell* (Cambridge, CUP, 1991).

Ross, Donald, Jr, 'Poems Bound Each to Each in the 1815 Edition', *The Wordsworth Circle*, 12 (1981), pp. 133–40.

Ross, Marlon, 'Naturalising Gender: Woman's place in Wordsworth's Ideological Landscape', *ELH*, 53 (1986), pp. 391–410.

Rousseau, Jean Jacques, *On the Origin of Languages*, trans. in John H. Moran and Alexander Gode (eds), *On the Origin of Language* (Chicago, University of Chicago Press, 1966; repr 1986).

Ruoff, Gene W., *Wordsworth and Coleridge: The Making of the Major Lyrics, 1802–1804* (London, Harvester Wheatsheaf, 1989).

Sanders, L. (ed.), *Selections from the Anti-Jacobin* (London, 1904).

Sanderson, Thomas, *A Companion to the Lakes in Lancashire, Westmoreland and Cumberland* (Carlisle, 1807).

Schneider, Ben Ross, *Wordsworth's Cambridge Education* (Cambridge, CUP, 1957).

Scott, Walter, *Minstrelsy of the Scottish Border*, ed. T.F. Henderson (Edinburgh, 1902).

——*Poetical Works*, ed. J. Logie Robertson (Oxford, OUP, 1931).

Shackford, Martha H., *Wordsworth's Interest in Painters and Pictures* (Wellesley, 1945).

Shaver, Chester, and Shaver, Alice, *Wordsworth's Library: A Catalogue* (New York and London, Garland, 1979).

Shelley, Percy Bysshe, *Shelley's Poetry and Prose*, ed. Donald H. Reiman and Sharon B. Powers (New York, Norton, 1977).

Shiach, Morag, *Discourse on Popular Culture* (Cambridge, Polity, 1989).

Simpson, David, *Wordsworth and the Figurings of the Real* (London, Macmillan, 1982).

——*Wordsworth's Historical Imagination: The Poetry of Displacement* (London, Methuen, 1987).

Siskin, Clifford, *The Historicity of Romantic Discourse* (Oxford, OUP, 1988).

Smith, Elsie, *An Estimate of William Wordsworth by his Contemporaries* (Oxford, Basil Blackwell, 1932).

Smith, Olivia, *The Politics of Language 1791–1819* (Oxford, Clarendon, 1984).

Spengemann, W., *The Forms of Autobiography* (New Haven, Yale UP, 1980).

Stam, James H., *Inquiries into the Origin of Language* (New York, Harper and Row, 1976).

Stein, Edwin, *Wordsworth's Art of Allusion* (University Park, Pennsylvania State UP, 1988).

Storey, Mark, *The Poetry of John Clare* (London, Macmillan, 1974).

Thomson, James, *The Complete Poetical Works of James Thomson*, ed. J. Logie Robertson (Oxford, OUP, 1908).

Todd, Janet (ed.), *A Dictionary of British and American Women Writers 1660–1800* (London, Methuen, 1987).

Volosinov, V.N., *Marxism and the Philosophy of Language* (1929, 1930), trans. L. Matejka and I.R. Titunik (New York, Seminar Press, 1973).

Ward, J.P., 'Wordsworth and the Sociological Idea', *Critical Quarterly*, 16 (1974), pp. 331–55.

——*Wordsworth's Language of Men* (Brighton, Harvester, 1984).

Weiskel, Thomas, *The Romantic Sublime* (Baltimore, Johns Hopkins UP, 1976).

Wimsatt, W.K., *The Verbal Icon* (Lexington, University of Kentucky Press, 1954).

Wollstonecraft, Mary, *Original Stories from real life*, second edn. 1796 (repr Oxford, Woodstock Books, 1990).

Wordsworth, Jonathan, 'The Five-Book Prelude of Early Spring 1804', *JEGP*, 76 (1977), pp. 1–25.

——*William Wordsworth: The Borders of Vision* (Oxford, OUP, 1982).

Wordsworth, William, *Home at Grasmere*, ed. Beth Darlington (Ithaca, Cornell UP; Hassocks, Harvester Press, 1977).

——*Lyrical Ballads*, ed. Michael Mason (London and New York, Longman, 1992).

——*Poetical Works*, ed. E. de Selincourt, second edn (5 vols, Oxford, Clarendon, 1949–54).

——*The White Doe of Rylstone*, ed. Kristine Dugas (Ithaca and London, Cornell UP, 1988).

——and Dorothy, *Letters of William and Dorothy Wordsworth*, ed. E. de Selincourt (Oxford, Clarendon); *The Early Years, 1787–1805*, rev. Chester L. Shaver (1967) [here, *Letters*, I]; *The Middle Years, 1806–1811*, rev. Mary Moorman (1969) [here, *Letters*, II]; *The Middle Years, 1812–1820*, rev. Mary Moorman and Alan G. Hill (1970) [here, *Letters*, III]; *The Later Years, 1821–1853*, rev. Alan G. Hill (4 volumes, 1978–88) [here, *Letters*, IV–VII].

Worthington, Jane, *Wordsworth's Reading of Roman Prose* (New Haven, Yale UP, 1946; repr 1970).

Wu, Duncan, *Wordsworth's Reading, 1770–1799* (Cambridge, CUP, 1993).

Index